GAYS and the LAW

Paul Crane

Pluto Press

First published in Great Britain by
Pluto Press Limited,
The Works,
105A Torriano Avenue,
London NW5 2RX

Copyright © Paul Crane

Text designed by Brent Curless
Cover designed by Michael Mayhew
Cover photograph by Laurie Sparham, Network

Photoset by Red Lion Setters,
22 Brownlow Mews,
London WC1

Printed in Great Britain by
St Edmundsbury Press Limited,
Bury St Edmunds,
Suffolk IP33 3TU
and bound by
W.H. Ware Limited,
Tweed Road,
Clevedon, Avon

British Library Cataloguing in Publication Data

Crane, Paul
    Gays and the law.
    1. Homosexuality – Law and legislation – Great
    Britain
    I. Title
    344.105'0253   KD7976.H/

ISBN 0-86104-386-3

Contents

Preface / ix

Introduction / 1

1. **The Criminal Law** / 8
   Lesbianism and the criminal law / 8
   Male homosexuality and the criminal law / 11
   'Cruising' / 15
   Affection in public / 17
   Love-making / 19
   Anal intercourse / 23
   Group sex / 25
   Introducing someone / 26
   Sex with the under 21s / 27
   Sex with someone who is 'severely
   subnormal' / 27
   Prostitution / 28
   Regulating the male gay world / 30
   Pubs, clubs and discos / 30
   Public toilets, parks and streets / 34
   Saunas / 35
   Gay communities / 35

2. **Police and Prisons** / 40
   Police attitudes / 40
   Police practice / 46
   Suspicion / 46
   Entrapment / 49
   Interrogation and detention / 51
   Police trawls / 53
   Summary of police powers in the UK / 55
   Prisons / 58
   Allocation to prisons and accommodation / 58
   Visits, correspondence, reading material / 59
   Surviving / 59
   Medical treatment / 60

3. **Young Gays** / 62
    The law / 64
    Prosecution policy / 65
    The myth of youth seduction / 68
    Working with young gays / 72

4. **Paedophilia** / 76
    Sentencing and judicial policy / 78
    Evidence of 'similar facts' / 81
    *Conspiracy to corrupt public morals and the
        Paedophile Information Exchange (PIE)* / 85

5. **Obscenity** / 87
    Pornography / 87
    Protection of Children Act 1978 / 89
    Censorship of the media / 92
    Newspapers / 92
    Contact advertisements / 94
    Theatre, cinema, broadcasting / 94

6. **Employment** / 99
    Protection from 'unfair dismissal' / 101
    Working with young people / 102
    The DES blacklist / 109
    Office, shop and industrial workers / 109
    The public sector / 110
    The private sector / 112
    'Getting it together' / 115
    Working with young people: personal
    experience / 115
    Trade unions / 118

7. **Lesbian and Gay Parents and Children** / 121
    Court attitudes / 122
    Custody disputes / 123
    Disputes following marital breakdown / 123
    Disputes with relatives / 128
    Disputes with local authorities / 128
    Issues at the hearings / 129
    The wishes of the children / 130
    The psychiatric issues / 131
    The welfare issues / 132

*Keeping out of court: advice about custody
    agreements* / 133
Why try to make an agreement? / 133
Reaching agreement / 134
When to make an agreement / 135
Types of custody and visiting arrangements / 135

8. **Housing and Living Together** / 139
    Housing / 140
    Private tenancies / 140
    Owner occupation / 141
    Public housing / 141
    Homelessness / 143
    Living together / 143
    Bereavement / 144
    Children / 145
    Break-up of relationships / 145
    Financial matters / 146

9. **Immigration** / 149
    Asylum / 150
    Marriage / 152

10. **The Gay Response** / 155
    The gay movement / 155
    Individual cases / 158
    Defence groups and getting support / 160
    Pressure groups / 160
    The media / 161
    Criminal cases / 161
    Civil cases / 173

11. **Conclusion: Towards Gay Rights?** / 175
    Limits of the law / 175
    The likelihood of law reform / 177
    Action needed to achieve reform / 181

    Appendices

I.   **The armed forces and merchant navy** / 184
II. **Transsexuals and transvestites** / 188
III. **Legal status of homosexuality** / 195

IV. Machinery of the law in the United
   Kingdom / 209
V. The gay movement / 214
VI. National gay rights organisations / 217

   Notes and references / 222
   Table of cases / 236
   Table of statutes / 238
   Index / 240

Preface

The subject matter of this book is potentially vast. Consequently I have had to choose those aspects which seemed the most pertinent from my particular standpoint. It has not been possible for me to treat the general law relating to Scotland and Northern Ireland, for example, as fully as that relating to England and Wales. I have included some material which others would no doubt have left out. Because they are often unreported elsewhere, employment cases heard at industrial tribunals have generally been fully noted. My views will not be shared by everyone who reads this book nor do I expect them to approve of my arguments or agree with my conclusions. But I do hope to persuade them to look at the evidence and to consider the subject seriously.

I am indebted to the people who spent time talking to me about their experiences with the law and others who have provided material and ideas. Generous encouragement, criticism and comments from those who read part or all of drafts of the manuscript was invaluable. Without the help of some of them (and they know who they are) I doubt if this book would have been finished. My thanks are due, in particular, to Barry Prothero, Andy Lipman, Peter Ashman, Adrian Fulford, Terry Munyard, Michael Kidron, Jane Hickman, Derek Ogg, Jeff Dudgeon, Gill Butler, David Barnard, David Burgess, Gabriel Burns, Julian Meldrum, Lisa Powell, Paul Olliver, Sadie Robarts, Sue Williscroft, Elaine Ginsburg, Andrew Friend, Tony Dowmunt, Sarah Maguire, Tony Halliday, Micky Burbridge, Tim Allen, Brian Green and Richard Kennedy. The errors that remain are my responsibility.

I am grateful for financial and other support received from the London groups of the Campaign for Homosexual Equality (and in particular for assistance from Paul Olliver and Brian Green), to the Scottish Homosexual Rights Group and to the Northern Ireland Gay Rights Association.

For permission to reprint variously published material I am obliged to John Warburton for an extract from *Open and Positive* published by the Gay Teachers Group, to Bob Cant for an edited extract from 'Living with Indecency' published by Gay Left, and to the Campaign for Homosexual Equality and the National Council for Civil Liberties for the use of items from their publications and materials. I would also like to acknowledge quotations from unpublished work by Dr Martin Dannecker and Matt Coles.

Apart from one major exception I have tried to state the law as it was on 1st May 1982. With regard to Northern Ireland, however, I have assumed that the existing law which prohibits even sexual relationships between men over 21 in private will be reformed by Homosexual Offences (Northern Ireland) Order 1982. This Order was laid before parliament on 14 July 1982 following an undertaking made by the Secretary of State for Northern Ireland that the law would be brought into line with the law in the rest of the United Kingdom so as to comply with the judgment of the European Court of Human Rights in the *Dudgeon* case. The government expect the Order to become law before the end of October 1982.

Introduction

'The liberation of homosexuals depends on changing basic repressions, particularly, the fear of the body, that seems to me a crucial prop for Western aggression and competitiveness. As feminists have insisted, liberation means more than winning civil rights. This is not in any way to denigrate those who fight, often very courageously, for gay rights whether through the electoral process, the courts or direct confrontation. But gays are being redefined (particularly in the USA) as yet another ethnic group – and as such we are being incorporated into an essentially stagnant system.'

Denis Altman[1]

This book is mostly about the legal position of gay men, not only because it is written by a gay man but also because it reflects the legal and social obsession with male homosexuality. Nevertheless, because gayness challenges conventional attitudes to gender and sexuality, it would be wrong to consider legal discrimination against gay men in isolation. So subjects have been included that to some may appear only indirectly connected. First, a number of issues affecting lesbian women are tackled where the law has made their sexual orientation an issue. Here the double standards of a male dominated legal system are highlighted. For example women are expected not only to repel unwanted sexual advances, but also not to place themselves in situations where men might be 'provoked' to make such an advance. Men on the other hand are given the fullest legal protection and the assistance of police surveillance against the most trivial sexual encounters from other men. Many fantasise about the risks of male homosexual 'predators' working with young people while treating the problem of sexual harassment of women at work as a joke. Lesbians are also discriminated against much more generally because they are women. This aspect of sexism and the law has been dealt with by other authors.[2]

Gays and the Law goes beyond mere description of the law. It discusses other issues in relation to gay sexuality and gender including contentious opinions on such subjects as pornography, paedophilia and transsexuality.

Many feminists would regard all pornography as concerned with perverted male sexuality. Though there are aspects of gay men's pornography that appear to be destructive, there has been a growing acceptance of it in a society where even casual expressions of homosexual intimacy are still hard to find. The chapter on paedophilia deals almost exclusively with man/boy love. Paedophilia has traditionally been used as a stick with which to beat all homosexuals. The law's reasoning reveals many false preconceptions about male homosexuality in general. Indeed, paedophilia has traditionally been seen as a 'cause' of homosexuality. An appendix on transsexuals considers the gender question in its most acute form and the law at its most clinically pedantic, intolerant of human variety. Whilst the challenge to conventional gender is less central in the gay movement than it used to be, it still remains the key division between conventional thinkers and radicals in sexual politics. Generally speaking I have not sought to represent the lesbian point of view: for this the reader must seek guidance elsewhere.[3] And for reasons of space I have not sought to represent the feminist viewpoint on subjects which are strictly outside the scope of this book, for example on heterosexual paedophilia.

A major feature of this book is its attempt to gather together all the laws affecting gay men and lesbian women in England and Wales, Scotland and Northern Ireland. Each of these three regions of the United Kingdom has a different legal system (see Appendix IV). Apart from the legal changes implemented as a result of the Irish civil war, the differences between the English and Northern Irish legal systems are not enormous. The differences are more marked when it comes to Scotland. The structure of the Scottish courts and their procedure, and traditional lawyers' subjects like land law are, for example, quite different. However, in other areas such as employment the law is virtually the same;[4] or as in the case of divorce and child custody law, there are differences on detailed points and not on the major principles.

In order not to lose sight of the general principles and arguments that commonly apply across the borders by including endless detail, I have simplified and sometimes deliberately avoided certain legal complexities and technical explanations, particularly where these are not central to the main themes of the book. The fullest discussion has been reserved for the law and practices directly related to homosexuality. This has led to an apparent unevenness in the treatment of various subjects. In part this reflects the fact that certain issues are raised more frequently in the courts, or that information is limited. It also reflects the fact that very different types of law are covered by the book. In areas like crime and immigration, the law is used directly by the state and enforced by the police or other officials. In civil law disputes like employment or child custody, the law is used (subject to a few exceptions) by individuals alone without direct state interference. This means that in civil law, court battles can sometimes be avoided by a negotiated settlement. This is usually done between the parties' lawyers.

I have not attempted to give practical advice on dealing with all the specific legal problems that are raised by the book. In most instances, reference has been made to appropriate legal advice services. The chapter on child custody is an exception to this, mainly because to omit some advice on the specific issue of negotiating custody agreements, which are quite common, would have given a lopsided impression of custody law in practice.

The law is very often ambiguous and deliberately vague so the authorities shall have the greatest discretion about how and when to use their powers. This is particularly true of many areas discussed in this book. The law is also imprecise for other reasons. Many new types of claim are brought by gay people, and debates on some of the issues are unformulated or in a state of flux.

Although discrimination and antipathy towards gays and lesbians are discussed in terms of the law, I do not want to suggest that these problems will end automatically once the law is changed. This will only come about when the notions of male supremacy that surround conventional heterosexuality are swept aside. In the meantime the need for a change in the social position of gays and lesbians cannot be reduced to the single issue of law reform. Such a position leads to the widespread misconception that the absence of discriminatory laws can be equated with positive acceptance and fundamental social change.

The law reflects and reinforces popular prejudices about male homosexuality and lesbianism, and attempts to place various limitations on the development of our lives as open gays. The law affects our sexual and emotional development, our relationships, our leisure, where we work, what we read, whether we can be parents and keep our children, the exercise of our civil rights, how far we can support and help ourselves. It is one source of the stigma that shapes the meaning of 'homosexual' in the public's mind, but as such the law has been and will continue to be affected by the presence of openly gay men and lesbians and the struggles around their cases.

The situation is complicated, because although the law has an overriding objective to control and regulate homosexual behaviour, social attitudes towards being gay or lesbian – and the lifestyles associated with that sexual orientation – are changing faster than at any time in the past.

There is much debate, for example, about the differences between gay men's and lesbian women's sexuality. Even the very category of 'homosexual' (and by implication its correlative 'heterosexual') is challenged. Many lesbians regard their sexual orientation, unlike most gay men, as a *rational* response to male supremacy. For many women who have discovered sexual desire for women in a feminist environment, lesbianism has had a very different meaning to conventionally defined homosexuality. Attraction to the same (or to the opposite sex) may be experienced by some people more as a question of choice than as a disposition fixed before the onset of puberty.

Positive self definition or identification, such as is implied by using the word 'gay' can be valuable as we grow as individuals or as a social or political movement. Such categorisation is not used to limit peoples' potential; it is an expression of it. Sexuality and personality are complex facets of human life which cannot really be summed up in a single word. However, there are undeniable social pressures everywhere to be something in particular. So people often get put into categories whether they like it or not.

It is more widely accepted now that 'homosexuality' is not a single unchanging way of being or activity; the forms of homosexual behaviour are as varied as those of heterosexual behaviour.[5] Nevertheless the terms gay and lesbian – which have been fought for by a political and social movement in many countries throughout the world for more than a decade – do express something important and real, not only about shared experiences of oppression and discrimination but also about human potential.[6]

Until recently discrimination and legal oppression against gays and lesbians went virtually unchallenged. However the revolution in attitudes among young people during the sixties and seventies and the impact of the gay and women's movements in particular have given people confidence and support in contesting discrimination through the courts and tribunals. Yet the struggle for gay rights through the British legal system has produced few positive gains. The law has continued to provide some of the main intellectual rationalisations for the suppression of male homosexuality and lesbianism. One of the purposes of this book is to examine both the current development of the law as a means of regulating homosexual behaviour and the attempts to secure gay rights through the law.[7]

In making this examination I believe that the law is neither the only nor even the main source of the oppression of gay people. Attitudes that lead to social discrimination, ostracism, violence, or even patronising tolerance do not rely on the courts for enforcement. The law is only one, and perhaps not even the most effective element in a number of anti-gay institutions. Among the most prominent of these are the media and the education system which help to define public attitudes, condemning or endorsing different kinds of behaviour.

Discriminatory laws give a very incomplete picture of the level of social tolerance for gays and lesbians. For example, only a small fraction of gay men actually come into contact with the police, but the state of public opinion reflected in the present criminal law has wider implications for all gays. Job discrimination is lawful, and it is publicly argued, particularly in relation to teaching, social services and occupations dealing with young people, that gays and lesbians should not be employed. Similarly access to public facilities may legally be denied to gay organisations and individuals.

Many people still hold misconceptions about what it means to be gay or lesbian, and use them to justify discrimination: the belief that homosexuals seduce young children (child 'molestation' is in fact overwhelmingly a practice of men against young girls); the belief that homosexuals are untrustworthy; the belief that homosexual men hate women, and that lesbians hate men. Those who discriminate against gays tend to share a number of assumptions. The most important of these is that something is wrong when a person diverges from the 'conventional' behaviour. Some express their attitude with open hostility: in jibes, insults or physical violence. More insidious is the disguised hostility of many who consider themselves enlightened and educated. This hostility is often concealed by shifting an irrational fear or prejudice to an intellectual level and presenting it as if it were rational. Perhaps the most usual expression of this is the relentless obsession with the question: how does someone become homosexual? This apparently valid inquiry is frequently the expression of hostilities or fears, presented as if they were part of a serious intellectual exploration. It is seldom also asked: how did a person become heterosexual? The origin of homosexuality only comes into question because it is considered a deviant course. It is assumed that the capacity to have children through sexual intercourse sets the standard in sexual conduct from which one should not deviate. Heterosexuality is thought to be in some profound sense the mainstream of thought and activity in the life of every individual and homosexuality is considered a sign of interference. Hence the obsessive hunt for the pebbles that diverted the stream.

It is generally understood that we all have the capacity to express emotional and sexual attraction, independently of the desire to reproduce, which is seldom the motive for any sexual activity. It has been argued[8] that satisfaction in life is more likely to be enjoyed by those who have children. These arguments ignore the different satisfactions of modern gay lifestyles. And if the arguments were consistent, judges would be called on not to rob lesbian mothers of their children and it would be argued that gay couples should be allowed to adopt children or to conceive by AID.

Like the law, the professions of medicine and psychiatry have been more obsessed with male than female homosexuality. Inquiries about the origins of homosexuality concern men more than lesbian women. Because men have special benefits in society, it is considered worse for a man to 'act like a woman' than vice versa. The traditional role behaviour of a man entitles him to prestige and power. The assumption is that everyone craves social advantages so that any man who gives them up must be crazy.

With the exception of most sexual offences, the law applies equally, at least in theory, to both women and men. However the law is mainly concerned with public behaviour and property and because far more women than men spend their lives in the domestic sphere, in practice the law has far less direct effect on women.

The law has not been widely invoked against lesbians; on the whole it pretends they do not exist. In contrast society perceives male homosexuality to be public, predatory and therefore in need of control. Hence the harsh criminal restraints. For hundreds of years homosexuality was unmentionable even in parliament and in the courts. Judges sentenced men to prison – and even to death – for acts considered to be so vile that they should not be talked about. Women have not been seen as needing to be restrained in the same way because their sexuality was in most circumstances thought not to exist in its own right. Although there have been no specific laws against lesbians, male society by granting 'social privileges and responsibilities' to women only if they married, has uniformly punished lesbians without having to acknowledge their existence. Broadly speaking, lesbians have not been oppressed *primarily* because of their lesbian identity but because of their femaleness. However where women do not conform to conventional roles and particularly as lesbians have refused to hide their lesbian identity, intervention by the law has been increasingly explicit. In particular this has happened in relation to disputes about the custody of children and employment. For many young lesbians who are open about their sexual orientation the possibility of care proceedings taken by a local authority remains a real threat.

Chapter One
The criminal law

Lesbianism and the criminal law

'Lesbianism has not been as legally punished as (male) homosexuality. However, it has been 'punished' by being completely legislated out of the realm of possibility for most women . . . Women are more totally repressed, both sexually and economically, and are more sexually timid (with either women or men) as well as more economically powerless than either homosexual or heterosexual men. In one sense it is more difficult for women to become and to survive as lesbians than it is for men to survive as homosexuals. For example, men either don't need – or don't think they need – women for economic survival. Most women need both and think they need men in order to survive economically as well as psychologically.'

Phyllis Chessler[1]

Lesbianism has never been specifically outlawed in the United Kingdom, although it is effectively illegal under British military law (See Appendix II). The English Criminal Law Revision Committee (CLRC) reaffirmed in 1980 that lesbian sexual acts should, in general, remain lawful. The existing law against 'indecent assaults' was thought to be sufficient.[2] By section 14 of the Sexual Offences Act 1956 it is an offence for a person (male or female) to make an 'indecent assault' on a woman. Section 14 (2) states: 'a girl under the age of 16 cannot in law give any consent which would prevent an act being an assault for the purposes of this section.' In other words any sexual activity, even for example kissing and mutual caressing between two people, one or both of whom is a girl under 16, constitutes indecent assault. In Northern Ireland the relevant age is 17.

The law of indecent assault was not designed for use against lesbians but for use against men. In 1921, the House of Lords rejected a Bill to criminalise lesbianism which would have introduced offences similar to those used against male homosexuality. These proposals never became law because, as one speaker said, this would have brought lesbianism 'to the notice of women who have never heard of it, never thought of it, never dreamed of it'.[3] A former Director of Public Prosecutions, Lord Desart, argued that to legislate against lesbians would only result in blackmail since no woman would openly admit to such a charge. It was also thought unnecessary to make lesbianism a crime.

The lack of criminal sanctions against lesbianism was partly a reflection of the attitude that women are generally passive and lack an assertive sexuality. Many feminists regard the absence of criminal sanctions as a reflection of the invisibility of women within both the legal system and the power structure generally.

Contemporary official attitudes towards lesbianism are evident in both the report of the English CLRC and the government's submission to the European Court of Human Rights in the *Dudgeon* case. (See pages 14 and 67.) The CLRC accepted advice from their policy advisory sub-committee and declined to create any new criminal laws against lesbianism.

'They have told us that the considerations which led them provisionally to recommend a minimum age of 18 for male homosexual conduct do not have the same force in the case of females. They say that homosexual relationships tend to arise later in life among women than among men, and that there is no comparable group of 16 to 18 year old girls whose sexual orientation has not yet become fixed and who are consequently in need of special protection. We are told too that adolescent girls do not seem especially attractive to older women in search of a partner of the same sex and there is not the same emphasis as in male homosexual culture on this age group.'[4]

In their submissions to the European Court, the government argued:

'The difference in treatment between the two forms of homosexuality reflects ... a genuine difference both in the nature and the scale of the social and moral problems presented by male and female homosexuality.'[5]

Another view is that it is women's sexuality, and not just attitudes to it, which is different. There is no lesbian sexual culture, for example, concerned with meeting for sex in public toilets, so a law against it would be irrelevant. The fact that lesbian sexuality/existence is very rarely expressed publicly partly accounts for the lack of concern by the criminal law in lesbianism.

Prosecutions concerning lesbian relationships are rare and on average fewer than ten women are convicted each year of indecently assaulting girls. The case reported below by the *Daily Mirror* is notable mainly for the absence of moral outrage usually vented by judges and the press when dealing with similar cases involving gay men. It also exemplifies the attitudes of the CLRC and the United Kingdom government noted above.

'At first, teacher Patricia Marshall offered a school girl sympathy and understanding. When the 15-year-old got depressed over her diabetes it was Patricia who could make her smile again. But then the friendship became something more . . . And it led 24-year-old Patricia to the dock at the Old Bailey yesterday.

The girl's father who at first welcomed the friendship, became suspicious about their growing closeness. His fears were confirmed the night be bored a hole through his bedroom floor into his daughter's room below. Through it, he saw them performing lesbian acts, the jury was told.

The relationship continued in secret after Patricia was banned from the house. And finally, in August last year, they vanished in a van. Police tracked them down in Aldershot a month later and Patricia was charged with indecent assault and abducting the girl. But this was not a case of a teacher corrupting a schoolgirl, the court heard yesterday.

Robin Gray, defending, said both had been taken by surprise by an infatuation they found impossible to resist. Timothy Davis, prosecuting, agreed that Patricia was not a seducer. The girl had clearly been a willing partner, and apparently could bend the older woman to her will, he said. Patricia – now seeking a sex-change operation – had even tried to cool things down, and had tried to persuade the girl to return home after they ran away, the jury heard.

Judge Neil McKinnon QC ordered the jury to return a not guilty verdict on the abduction charge. And putting Patricia on probation for two years, he said "This is not a case which calls for punishment. You have come to an awkward period in your life, but with the help you will get, I am sure you will come out all right".'[6]

Although few prosecutions are brought, the point is that lesbians *could* be prosecuted in certain circumstances. It is extremely rare for lesbian teenagers to get involved in criminal proceedings because of their sexual orientation. However their sexuality may be the reason for some form of intervention by the local authority social services department. Social workers acting for the authority have power to apply to the court to take someone under the age of 17 into care if it can be proved that the young person is 'exposed to moral danger'.[7] Moral danger covers a variety of 'sins', most commonly sexual. In addition, the authority must prove that the young person is in need of care and control which they are unlikely to receive unless the court makes the order. (See also pages 128-129 below.)

The remainder of this chapter concerns gay men and deals with the arsenal of criminal offences specifically aimed at male homosexuality, most of which are not relevant to lesbians.

Male homosexuality and the criminal law

'the unnatural and horrible offence of sodomy . . . if you have but a passing acquaintance with the Bible, you will know what happened to Sodom when Jehovah called forth fire and brimstone to punish the inhabitants for their unnatural practices. It has always been in this country, and in every civilised country, a serious offence to commit sodomy, which is punishable by life imprisonment. It is as serious as committing manslaughter or grievous bodily harm.'
High Court Judge, London 1974.[8]

'I thought men like that shot themselves.'
George V[9]

Until the mid-sixteenth century men who engaged in anal intercourse or fellatio were mainly dealt with by the church courts and not in the ordinary criminal courts. The earliest English legal textbook dealing with homosexual acts, the *Fleta* written in about 1300, states that 'those who have connection with Jews or Jewesses or are guilty of bestiality or sodomy shall be buried alive in the ground'. Around the same time, another English work spoke of the role of the clergy in identifying homosexuals for persecution: 'The inquiries of the Holy Church shall make their inquests of sorcerers, sodomites, renegades and misbelievers; and if they find any such, they shall deliver him to the king's court to be put to death.'[10]

Following the reformation of the church and the abolition of church courts, parliament passed a statute in 1533 making sodomy a felony for men which the criminal courts could punish by death.

Contemporary legal writers, like Lord Chief Justice Coke and Sir William Blackstone, continued to stress the religious origin of the law. Blackstone in his commentaries of 1797 said that sodomy was a crime which ' . . . the express law of God, determines to be capital. Of which we have a single instance . . . by the destruction of two cities by fire from heaven.' Over eighty men were executed for sodomy under English criminal and naval law between 1800 and 1835. Whilst on average during this period one man in thirty sentenced to death was actually executed, the majority of those convicted of sodomy were hanged. In 1806 there were more executions for sodomy than for murder. Later, between 1856 and 1859, 54 men were sentenced to death for sodomy. But it appears that none of these executions was carried out. In the final year of this period, more men were sentenced to death for consenting sexual acts with men than for killing them.[11]

The death penalty for sodomy was abolished in 1861 in England and Ireland and in 1889 in Scotland. However the latter part of the nineteenth century witnessed both a widening of the criminal law and a development of clinical notions about homosexuality. Male homosexuals began to be defined as sick rather than simply wicked.[12]

In 1885, the government accepted a private amendment to a more general Act of Parliament – the Criminal Law Amendment Act. This extended the law far beyond the prohibition of anal intercourse to include all male homosexual sexual activity whether it took place in private or in public. Thirteen years later the Vagrancy Act, which prohibited soliciting for 'immoral purposes' and prostitution, soon was used by the police against homosexual men.

Homosexual sexual activity has existed in all types of society and social classes, surviving rabid persecution. Society, however, has varied widely in its attitudes to male homosexuality, its meaning and how those who engaged in homosexual activity thought of themselves. Jeffrey Weeks attributes the development of harsher legal penalties in the latter nineteenth century to, among other things, social changes in the family brought on by massive industrialisation and urbanisation. 'Social roles became more clearly defined, and as sexuality was more closely harnessed ideologically to the reproduction of the population so the social condemnation of homosexuality increased.'[13]

In 1954 the Home Office in Britain set up a committee chaired by Sir John Wolfenden to examine the criminal law relating to homosexual offences and prostitution. The Committee broadly concluded that adult male homosexual relationships in private should no longer be criminal. Apart from that 'We do not think it would be expedient at the present time to reduce in any way the penalties attaching to homosexual importuning. It is important that the limited modifications of the law which we propose should not be interpreted as an indication that the law can be indifferent to other forms of homosexual behaviour or as a general licence to adult homosexuals to behave as they please.'[14]

It took ten years for the committee's reform proposals, which had been made in 1957, to be implemented in 1967. By then it was generally accepted that total prohibition of male homosexuality was largely unenforceable. This tended, it was said, to bring the law itself into disrepute. Throughout the parliamentary debates it was emphasised that reform legislation did not seek to change social attitudes and prejudices against homosexuals or homosexual love-making. It was seen as a measure of charity to victims of an unpleasant disability. As the Home Secretary, Roy Jenkins, put it: 'The question was whether on top of their disability one should subject homosexuals to the rigour of the criminal law.' Others were concerned that homosexuals should be encouraged to seek 'help'. 'We do not condone homosexual practices nor regard them as in any way less sinful but in supporting the Bill we are concerned mainly for the reformation and recovery, if it can be, of those who have become victims of homosexual practices,' (the Bishop of London); 'It is not before time the law looked as though it was in the process of being changed – not in order that society would accept the homosexual, but so that the homosexual would be able to come to terms with himself.' (Lord Byers)[15]

The Sexual Offences Act 1967 – and the subsequent legislation for Scotland and Northern Ireland – failed to strike at the roots of discrimination and prejudice. In fact it helped to legitimise that prejudice within the law. In simple terms, the reform Acts in the United Kingdom have shifted the focus of the law firstly towards sexual behaviour in 'public places' and secondly towards relationships between adults and young people. The definition of 'public places' was made unusually wide to include public lavatories and any place where a third person might merely be present. Youths were defined as any man below the age of 21: a clear condemnation of homosexuality since the same youth from the age of 16 could lawfully have sex with a woman. In general terms, the law conceded that if two 'adult' men wanted to go to bed in their own home then that alone should not be a crime any more. These measures did not reflect an acceptance of homosexuality, rather the method and extent of control was refined.

For most law reformers the main concern was to ensure that lawful homosexual sexual conduct could take place only in absolute privacy. This concern led to the compartmentalising of sexual encounters in a completely unrealistic way. 'Soliciting or importuning' remained a criminal offence. The words 'soliciting or importuning' are used to describe any form of sexual invitation and transform behaviour which is acceptable in heterosexual men into a crime when it is between gay men. The reform of the law makes it possible for adult gay men to have sex in private, but continues to make it difficult for them to meet one another lawfully. While appearing to liberalise the legal treatment of gayness these changes in the law in fact provided the means for tougher regulation of homosexuality. While it had been extremely difficult to detect 'crimes' committed by consenting adults in private, it is much easier to bring prosecutions for 'soliciting' and so-called 'gross indecency' in 'public'. 'Gross indecency' is generally used in the law to describe any homosexual love-making except anal intercourse. The 1967 Act *raised* the maximum penalty for 'gross indecency' where one of the men involved is under 21 from two years' imprisonment to five years. Previously cases were only tried before a judge and jury; the Act now gives the option of having the case quickly disposed of by the magistrates' court. The police have resolutely exploited these new avenues and convictions for 'homosexual offences' have quadrupled in England and Wales since 1967.[16]

From the outset even the chief architect of the 1967 reforms, Lord Arran, was throwing down humiliating and provocative challenges: 'Any form of ostentatious behaviour now or in the future, or any form of public flaunting, would be utterly distasteful and would, I believe, make the sponsors of the Bill regret that they had done what they had done. Homosexuals must continue to remember that while there may be nothing bad in being homosexual, there is certainly nothing good.'[17]

In 1981, the European Court of Human Rights ruled that the United Kingdom had failed to justify the maintenance of Victorian legislation in Northern Ireland which had the general effect of making private consenting homosexual relations between men into criminal offences.

' . . . the moral attitudes towards male homosexuality in
Northern Ireland and the concern that any relaxation in the

law would tend to erode existing moral standards cannot . . . warrant interfering with the applicant's private life to such an extent. "Decriminalisation" does not imply approval, and a fear that some sectors of the population might draw misguided conclusions in this respect from reform of the legislation does not afford a good ground for maintaining it in force with all its unjustifiable features.'[18]

The decision compelled an otherwise reluctant government to introduce legislation – the Homosexual Offences (Northern Ireland) Order 1982 – which brings Northern Irish law into line with the rest of the United Kingdom. These minimal reforms have yet to be extended to the Channel Islands, the Isle of Man and to those serving in the merchant navy and armed forces (see Appendix I).

In the light of subsequent developments the defects of the 1967 Act are now apparent. At best the legal position of gay men's sexual relationships or contacts is uncertain and unclear in many circumstances. At worst the Act has become an effective tool for prosecutions and large numbers of gay men of all ages remain 'sexual outlaws'.

'Cruising'

In certain circumstances, even chatting up between gay men – 'cruising' – can be a crime. The Sexual Offences Act 1956 section 32 which applies to England and Wales, provides that it is unlawful *'for a man persistently to solicit or importune another man in a public place for immoral purposes'*. In *Dale* v *Smith* (1967)[19] it was held that the use of the word 'hello' by Mr Dale to a teenager in Bradford railway station was an act of importuning because the same word had been used by him to another youth on the previous evening and had been followed by a clear act of importuning, namely asking if he wanted to look at sexy photos. Leading on from this case, the following points emerge. *'Solicit or Importune'*, since they are not defined by the statute, can be used by prosecutors to describe anything commonly understood as chatting-up or making a pass – literally any physical gesture or words, depending on the context. Two separate acts of importuning made within the period specified in the police charge are sufficient to make the importuning 'persistent'. In *Dale* v *Smith*, the court accepted that *'persistently'* meant a degree of repetition of 'either more than one invitation to one person or a series of invitations to different people'. In *'a public place*' means anywhere other than a private home or hotel room; for example, private members' clubs, discos, pubs, streets, parks, public toilets are all 'public places' in law if not in common sense.

The courts have decided that the term '*immoral purposes*' refers to any homosexual sex including love-making in private between men of 21 or older (which in itself of course is no longer a criminal offence). However it still remains for a jury in each particular case to decide whether immoral purposes refers to all homosexual sex. In *R* v *Graham Ford* (1978)[20] Mr Ford has been standing outside a public toilet in Bournemouth 'persistently' suggesting to another man, who was in fact a policeman in plain clothes, that he should go back with him to his flat for 'homosexual purposes'. Both were over 21 and it was accepted that the sexual conduct would have taken place in private. The Court of Appeal held that the trial judge was right to rule that what had happened could amount to an offence and then left it to the jury to decide whether the conduct involved 'immoral purposes'. Lord Chief Justice Widgery tersely remarked ' . . . they clearly took the view that it did involve immoral purposes and so do we'.

The present Lord Chief Justice, Lord Lane, re-affirmed this approach in *R* v *Grey* (1981).[21] The Court of Appeal refused to quash Mr Grey's conviction although the trial judge had made a material irregularity and misdirected the jury by deciding that all homosexual activities amounted to 'immoral purposes' as a matter of law. Lord Lane conceded that 'in the field of contemporary morals judges might not be the best fitted to assess the attitudes of the mass of right thinking members of society'. Nevertheless the court concluded that since the jury had rejected Mr Grey's evidence that he had not intended to have sex with the man he met, they would have convicted him anyway. Despite the outcome of this particular case, there remains an important point to deploy in all such trials: that it is for the jury to decide whether certain activity amounts to 'immoral purposes'.

In soliciting cases the only prosecution witnesses are invariably the police themselves. Usually it is they who have been allegedly solicited or importuned. Not only is it unnecessary in law for the police to bring to court any evidence that a member of the public was actually offended, but it is also unnecessary for them to show that anyone – other than the police that is – actually saw and was affected in any way by the alleged soliciting.[22] Convictions are comparatively easy to get in the magistrates' court since police evidence is infrequently disbelieved. It is all too easy for evidence to be fabricated. Conviction rates in the higher courts tend to be lower where jurors have had to watch the limp-wristed contortions of a police officer in the witness box attempting to demonstrate the alleged demeanour of the defendant.

The maximum sentence that a crown court judge can give is two years' imprisonment and/or a fine (there is no fixed limit); the maximum sentence in a magistrates' court is six months' imprisonment and/or a fine of £1000.[23] The usual sentence for a first offender is a fine plus the payment of police prosecution costs.

In *Scotland*, any homosexual conduct in public, including cruising, can be interpreted by the courts as the common law offence of '*shameless indecency*'.[24] There is no statutory maximum sentence but again a fine would be expected. Prosecutions for this kind of 'indecency' would normally be dealt with in the lower courts i.e. at district court level.

In *Northern Ireland*, homosexual soliciting is still prohibited by the Vagrancy Act 1898 section 1(1).[25]

The English Court of Appeal has ruled that the crime of soliciting is specifically a homosexual offence and that the Sexual Offences Act cannot generally be used against straight men who make passes or 'kerb crawl' adult women.[26] However, it is an offence for a man to solicit a young girl (certainly a girl aged 14 or under) for sex.[27] In Birmingham the police have arrested kerb crawlers in a notorious 'red light' district and have asked magistrates to 'bind them over to keep the peace' rather than bring criminal charges. This happened after the police had received complaints from local residents.[28] The only other comparable offence is that of soliciting by a 'common prostitute' for the purpose of prostitution.[29]

To sum up: the law on soliciting discriminates against gay men and against all women. In practice the law is used against gay men. It fails to protect women from intimidating advances of heterosexual male predators. The police very rarely entrap them, but they are a menace to many women.

Affection in public

In *England and Wales, Scotland, Northern Ireland*: as with heterosexuals, the police can arrest homosexuals on minor charges if they find objectionable any particular display of affection in public. In practice the police find gays and lesbians kissing, holding hands or hugging a lot more objectionable than couples of opposite sexes behaving in the same way. Chief among such charges is insulting behaviour likely to cause a '*breach of the peace*'. This is a very common catch-all charge in Scotland for behaviour that the police do not like. The Burgh Police (Scotland) Act 1892 and the other local Scottish statutes create a large number of offences related to breach of the peace. These involve using insulting words or behaviour, behaving in an indecent manner, committing a nuisance and jostling or annoying others. In Scotland affection in public between gays and lesbians could also be prosecuted as 'shamelessly indecent' conduct. 'Breach of the peace' also exists as a common law charge in the rest of the United Kingdom; in practice the police will use either the Public Order Act 1936 section 5 or a local Act of Parliament (such as the Metropolitan Police Act 1839 section 54(13)).

Under the Public Order Act, (which applies throughout the United Kingdom) the police have to show some evidence that a member of the public may have been offended and that a breach of the peace is '*likely* to have been occasioned' before a conviction can be secured. It is not sufficient if only the defendant and police officers were present.[30] They must at least say that a member of the public could have been − but this is not usually difficult. This is the most likely charge for heterosexual consenting sexual acts in public places: a rarity since the police do not go looking for 'courting couples'.

There is no legal definition of 'insulting behaviour'. It is entirely a question of fact to be decided by the particular magistrates.[31] The supposed rationale is that it is an insult to behave towards someone as if they were gay. Since this is an insult it is argued that it would be likely to have a violent reaction. Although many people have pleaded guilty to this charge, cases have been won where they have been properly defended.

In London, two men who had been demonstrating against the screening of the film *Cruising* (about murders within the New York gay subculture) were arrested for kissing in the street. The stipendiary magistrate at Bow Street Court dismissed the charge of insulting behaviour likely to cause a breach of the peace and observed: 'I have no doubt one man did take exception to it. I dare say, I would, but the test is "was it insulting?". It is a very grey area of law, but I can't say that this was insulting behaviour.' Costs were not awarded to the acquitted defendants on the grounds that they had 'brought the prosecution on themselves'.[32]

In Leeds Central railway station two lesbians were detained for half an hour by transport police after they had some parting kisses before one took a train to Bradford. Although they were not charged and were released after questioning the women were threatened with a charge of breach of the peace. The officer made an announcement over the loudspeaker system apologising for the 'incident' that had occurred in the station entrance hall, and for any offence it had caused passengers.[33]

There is also a whole host of local council and railway by-laws and park regulations covering a variety of minor 'infringements'. These are not often used, since the police will not normally have the power to arrest for a by-law infringement (this will not necessarily deter them from doing so). In any event, normal procedure would be to take a suspect's name and address; later a summons would be served through the post ordering the person to appear in court to answer the charge. Getting into an argument with the police could lead to an arrest and subsequent charging with either obstruction of the police in the course of their duty or obstruction of the highway.[34]

Love-making

A major difficulty faced by gay activists concerned with law reform has been to shift the centre of discussion from such concepts as 'disgusting and sad behaviour', 'corrupting practices' and so on, to the question of why so many heterosexuals react with such strong revulsion to gay sexuality. Some gay people share heterosexual society's views and indeed some gay organisations have been embarrassed in their defence of gay male sexual activity, even to the extent of claiming that anal intercourse occurs only among a small minority of gay men. Similar difficulties have arisen around men's sexual activity behind the closed doors of toilet cubicles: many gay activists have found 'cottaging' so embarrassing that they have been unable to present cogent arguments against current legal attitudes and sanctions.

The criminal charges most frequently brought arise from having some sort of sexual encounter in public lavatories. Casual sex in toilets – 'cottaging' – developed because of the social rejection of homosexuality, a rejection which although weaker than say twenty years ago nevertheless remains. Before the war anonymous sex in public lavatories had been one of the few comparatively safe ways of meeting men and having sex; gay clubs and pubs were often raided by the police and there was a greater risk of being black-mailed if one was seen at these venues. Outside the big cities, there is a real lack of social facilities to meet other gay men. Even within them these facilities are aimed mostly at the youthful and attrac-tive who have money to spend. For many there is no alternative to cottaging. Of course not all men who cottage identify as gay (many are married); and not all of them are secret about their gayness.

A great many police hours are spent 'supervising' public lava-tories. Enforcement can depend on the moral fanaticism of par-ticular chief constables or on the inclinations of individual police officers who have lavatories on their beats. (See also page 40 below.) Constables have discretion as to how much time they spend on any part of their beat. It is sometimes said by the police that the level of activity is a response to complaints from the public. In fact if they wanted to stop people giving offence to the public, rather than shunt them through the courts, they could simply warn (or 'caution') them as the police do with traffic offenders.

'Gross indecency'

All forms of gay love-making, with the exception of anal inter-course, can in certain circumstances, be prosecuted as crimes of 'gross indecency'.

> 'It is an offence for a man to commit an act of gross inde-cency with another man, whether in public or private, or to be a party to the commission by a man of an act of gross inde-cency with another man, or to procure the commission by a man of an act of gross indecency with another man.' (Sexual Offences Act 1956 section 13)

Virtually the same wording is used in *Northern Ireland* by the Criminal Law Amendment Act 1885 section 11; and also in *Scotland* under the Sexual Offences (Scotland) Act 1976 section 7. Consenting men aged 21 or over having sex in 'private' are removed from this prohibition by virtue of the Sexual Offences Act 1967 section 1, the Criminal Justice (Scotland) Act 1980 section 80, and Homosexual Offences (Northern Ireland) Order 1982 section 3:

> '. . . a homosexual act in private shall not be an offence pro-vided that the parties consent thereto and have attained the age of twenty-one years.

(2) An act which would otherwise be treated for the purposes
of this Act as being done in private shall not be so treated if
done – (a) when more than two persons take part or are present; or (b) in a lavatory to which the public have or are permitted to have access, whether on payment or otherwise.'

Generally, what kind of sexual activity amounts to 'gross indecency' is a question of fact to be decided by the magistrates or the
jury hearing the particular case. The term has usually been
thought comprehensive enough to include all forms of homosexual
sex, excluding anal intercourse.

It is also a question of fact for a jury to decide whether sex has
taken place *'in private'*. In *R* v *Reakes* (1974)[35] the English Court of
Appeal approved one judge's definition of the word 'private': 'You
look at all the surrounding circumstances, the time of night, the
nature of the place including such matters as lighting and you consider further the likelihood of a third person coming upon the
scene.' In this case, the alleged act took place in an enclosed unlit
private yard at 1 a.m. There was a gate from a public road into a
yard where there was a lavatory used by customers of two neighbouring restaurants and employees of a taxi business. Someone
had come into the yard shortly after sex had taken place. The jury
decided that the act had not taken place 'in private'. The conviction was upheld.

In *R* v *Preece* (1970)[36] the English Court of Appeal decided that
in order to prove gross indecency *'with another man'*, the prosecution must show that the indecent act was 'directed towards another
man who willingly participated and co-operated in the indecent
exhibition'. Proof of actual physical contact is unnecessary. In this
case two men were convicted on evidence that they had been masturbating in adjacent toilet cubicles and could see one another
through a hole in the wall.

By comparison, if one of the men implicated states that he would
not and did not consent to a sexual act, then the other could be
properly convicted only of an attempt to commit an act of gross
indecency.[37]

In *Scotland* the maximum penalty for gross indecency is two
years' imprisonment. In *England, Wales and Northern Ireland* for
sex with a man under 21, the maximum sentence is five years in
prison; for sex with a man 21 or over, two years. It is impossible to
generalise about the average sentence in practice. However, barely
one per cent of men convicted of 'public' homosexual sex are given

prison sentences. Such sentences are normally less than six months, very rarely nine months and never the maximum of two years. The English Court of Appeal has stated that a sentence of immediate imprisonment for an offence of this sort committed by men of previous good character is 'inappropriate and excessive'. In *R* v *Clayton* (1981)[38] Mr Clayton was alleged to have been masturbated by another man in an alleyway during the early hours of one morning. Having been convicted by a jury of gross indecency, the crown court judge sentenced him to four months imprisonment. The Court of Appeal quashed this sentence and substituted a fine of £50. Home Office research shows that in cases involving a man over 21 and a man under 21, about four per cent were sent to prison. In practice, the longest sentence was two years rather than the five years' permitted maximum.[39]

Outraging public decency

In an attempt to overcome the technical problem posed by the ruling in *R* v *Preece* which requires an act of 'gross indecency' to be directed towards a 'willing participant', so that solitary masturbation as such is not 'gross indecency', the English police have attempted to resuscitate the common law offence of '*outraging public decency*'. Traditionally this has included 'all open lewdness, grossly scandalous behaviour, and whatever openly outrages decency or is offensive and disgusting'. The indictments for such charges all refer to 'the great disgust and annoyance of divers of Her Majesty's subjects within whose purview such act was committed'.[40] This means that at the very least it must be proved that the act complained of was committed in public and that more than one person was able to see it. In *R* v *Mayling* (1964) the court weakened any burden of proof on the police; disgust and annoyance may be inferred and the evidence of one police officer is sufficient. 'If the jury were so satisfied the offence was proved . . . it was not necessary for the prosecution to go further to prove actual disgust and annoyance on the part of any observer . . . In our view there is no justification for holding that a police constable on duty cannot be disgusted or annoyed . . .'.[41]

Breach of the peace

The courts have decided that where there are allegations of 'indecent behaviour of a homosexual nature' in most cases it would be wrong to prosecute under section 5 of the Public Order Act 1936 (as amended). In *Norman* v *Parkin* (1982)[42] the English Divisional

Court ruled that where a man is alone in the urinals except for a plainclothes policeman and behaves in a way which amounts to importuning (for example masturbating) he should not be charged with insulting behaviour likely to cause a breach of the peace. The court thought that such behaviour might be regarded as insulting by the 'average heterosexual'. However since neither the man nor the officer was likely to cause a breach of the peace, and no third party was likely to have seen the incident, the court could not be sure that a breach of the peace was likely.

This ruling effectively called a halt to the use of a public order provision which was never designed to deal with these kind of cases. Its use by police prosecutors had been attractive presumably because the charge could only be dealt with by magistrates, unlike charges of importuning and gross indecency where an accused person could opt for trial by jury.

Anal intercourse

Not only has there been a long history of legal sanctions against male homosexuality in general, but the law enshrines a particularly strong revulsion against anal intercourse. The language used in the law itself and by judges reflects this particular disgust. Such phrases as 'immoral acts', 'unnatural offences', 'abominable crimes', 'corrupting practices' and the words 'buggery' and 'sodomy', are themselves heavily loaded with virulent connotations in the legal context. During the parliamentary debate on homosexual law reform in 1967, one Conservative MP observed that the more he saw of the Bill's progress the more he wondered whether its promoters really knew what the act of homosexuality entailed. 'If it were not that there were young people in the public gallery, it might be useful to explain it' he said, 'but that one offence is so utterly disgusting and degrading that I don't wish to give the details of it in public here or anywhere else, but let nobody be in any doubt of the disgusting nature of that offence.'[43]

Various psychological explanations have been suggested to account for the intensity of the reaction to anal intercourse from many heterosexuals.[44] These explanations aside, it is clear that the current position of homosexual men within the criminal law and in the courts is determined by ancient religious influence, ignorance and fear.

It is not an offence to have anal sex in 'private' (as defined above) providing both partners are willing and are 21 or over.[45] If these conditions are not satisfied, then it is an offence and once penetration of the anus by the penis is proved, both partners, if consenting and over 14-years-old, are equally guilty. An act which comes close to the completed offence may still be prosecuted as attempted buggery.

In *England and Wales* anal intercourse is listed as the 'unnatural offence of buggery' under section 12 of the Sexual Offences Act 1956 and also applies to anal sex with women and animals. This is similar to the law in *Northern Ireland* which still uses the original Victorian statute describing anal sex as the 'abominable crime of buggery': section 61 of the Offences Against the Person Act 1861. In *Scotland* 'unnatural carnal connection between adult male persons' is described as 'sodomy'.[46] It is a statutory offence that does not apply to anal intercourse with consenting adult women, which is quite lawful.

Most prosecutions have concerned cases where one of the partners was under 21. Particularly where corroborative evidence is needed, the police will remove many personal items – lubricants, clothing, sheets, magazines among other things, and endeavour to obtain a confession from the older of the partners. At the police station medical evidence may be taken.[47] This may include requesting an anal examination and clipping tufts of pubic hair for comparison with hairs found elsewhere. (See page 63 below.)

The maximum prison sentences that can be imposed by a crown court judge reflect the assumption that the experience of anal sex is physically as well as psychologically damaging. (See also pages 79-89 below.) The statutory tariff is: (i) where the case involves a boy under 16: life imprisonment; (ii) where the case involves someone who is 16 or over but who has not consented: ten years; (iii) where the case involves someone between 16 and 21 who has consented: five years (if the convicted man is over 21) or two years (if the convicted man is under 21); (iv) where the case involves someone over 21 who consents but took place other than in a private place: two years.[48]

In theory for example this means that an 18-year-old who has anal sex with a 15-year-old is liable to life imprisonment. In practice, most men 21 or over convicted of consenting buggery with men of the same age or older are very rarely imprisoned. More than half of the defendants convicted of anal intercourse with men aged 16 to 20 are imprisoned; the great majority of convictions relating to those aged 14 or younger result in prison sentences.[49] (See chapter 4.)

Consenting buggery between men and women in England, Wales and Northern Ireland is still technically an offence regardless of the partner's age. In practice this provision is a dead letter. Very few men are prosecuted for heterosexual buggery, consensual or non-consensual. Most convictions involve anal intercourse with girls under 16 or in the case of rape. The Criminal Law Revision Committee recommended in 1980 that consensual anal intercourse should no longer be an offence where the woman has reached a specific age – either 16 or 18.[50]

Group sex

If more than two men make love together or at least one other is present while a couple make love, at home or in any other place, they have committed a crime. A case heard at the Cardiff crown court in 1982[51] is an example of the use of this provision. Three accused men had sex together at the house where one of them lived. The lovemaking was filmed on video. Later police officers called at the house and during a search discovered the video cassette. The threesome was admitted and the video was subsequently used in evidence against them. All three were fined after they pleaded guilty to mutual acts of buggery and gross indecency. This is not the case for men and women, who are free to engage in any number of sexual permutations without running foul of the law.

The homosexual law reform Bill for Scotland passed by the House of Commons would have brought the law on gay sex into line with that for heterosexuals. This sensible amendment was defeated in the House of Lords. Ironically, a contributing factor to this defeat appears to have been a sensational front page story in *Gay News* which was foolishly headlined: 'Gays Protest as MPs Pass Orgy Law'.[52]

The Criminal Law Revision Committee returned in 1980 to 'a matter that troubled parliament in 1967, namely the character of some clubs catering for homosexuals and the need for regulation of their activities'. Although 'indecencies in the presence of others do not take place on their premises' there was apparently no certainty as to 'what might happen in these clubs if section 1(2)(a) [quoted on page 21 above] were repealed without any replacement, so that homosexual acts in the presence of others became allowable'. The Committee recommended that the right to privacy did not require that conduct in clubs should be unregulated and accordingly 'the law should continue to prohibit homosexual acts in the presence of others in clubs as well as in public in the ordinary sense of the word'.[53]

Introducing someone

Procuring

It is an offence for a man, under some circumstances, to introduce even gay friends to one another – to 'procure' (or attempt to procure) or, less archaically than in legal English, 'bring about' an act of gross indecency or buggery with another man.[54] For example, to put two men in the same bedroom, knowing that they are both gay and would have sex together could be quite enough to bring a charge of procuring. The introduction does not have to be for any payment in order to be criminal. An extraordinary use of this offence was the private prosecution brought against the director of the stage play *The Romans in Britain*. It had been alleged that he procured an act of gross indecency between two actors who simulated a rape-like sequence of anal sex. (See pages 94-95 below.)

The law on procuring is in an absurd mess. As a result of a curious legislative oversight, for example, it is not an offence for a woman to procure an act of gross indecency for a man. The law originally made it an offence for a man to procure an act of gross indecency (section 13 of the 1956 Act). However it was then made lawful to commit an act of gross indecency in certain circumstances (section 1 of the 1967 Act) and to procure for oneself an act of gross indecency (section 4(3) of the 1967 Act). What appears to remain unlawful is to procure (a) acts of gross indecency between two others even where the act is itself lawful or (b) acts of buggery between two people other than the procurer (section 4(1) of the 1967 Act). It seems uncertain whether or not it is lawful for someone to procure an act of buggery between himself and the person he has procured. It is also possible to be charged with *attempting* to procure. In these circumstances the police do not have to prove that a specific invitation was made to participate in sexual activity. It would be enough to prove in the light of the surrounding circumstances that a man's actions or conversation conveyed a wish that sex should take place.[55] By comparison with this bizarre spider's web, 'procuring' between adult men and women is not an offence unless the woman is a prostitute or is under 21, or where her consent (if any) is not genuine i.e. where threats or false pretences have been used or she is mentally ill.[56]

Incitement
It is an offence to 'incite' (or attempt to do so) that is, influence or try to influence another person to have homosexual sex, where the complete act would be criminal.[57]

Sex with the under 21s

A man aged under 24 may be acquitted of having unlawful sexual intercourse with a consenting girl under 16 if he can satisfy the court that he believed her to be at least 16. Apart from Scottish law, there is no equivalent provision for a man charged with consensual buggery (or any other homosexual offence) with a man under the age of 21.

A boy under 16 is treated by the law as being incapable of consenting to sex.[58] Consent is therefore not a defence for an older person who may be charged with 'indecent assault', a crime punishable with a maximum of ten years' imprisonment. (See also chapter 3.)

Sex with someone who is 'severely subnormal'

A man who is suffering from severe subnormality within the meaning of the Mental Health Acts in England, Scotland or Northern Ireland cannot in law give any consent to homosexual sex. However, any man who is charged with an offence is not guilty if 'he did not know and had no reason to suspect that man to be suffering from severe subnormality'.[59] 'Severe subnormality' means

'a state of arrested or incomplete development of mind which includes subnormality of intelligence and is of such a nature or degree that the patient is incapable of leading an independent life or guarding himself against serious exploitation or will be so incapable when of an age to do so.'[60]

Men on the staff of mental hospitals, or who have responsibility for mental patients, are in a special category under the Sexual Offences Act 1967 (and under the statutes for Scotland and

Northern Ireland). Homosexual sex in private between such employees and patients even when they are over 21 is still criminal.[61]

Prostitution

A man cannot be a 'common prostitute' and so cannot be charged with loitering or soliciting in a public place for the purpose of prostitution. The police can bring this charge only against women under section 1 of the Street Offences Act 1959. There is no legal category of being a homosexual prostitute. In practice most 'rent boys' would be charged with persistently soliciting or importuning in a public place for immoral purposes. (See pages 15-17 above.) In addition, of course, any man under 21 cannot lawfully have homosexual sex even in private and with a man over 21. It is not relevant to the question of guilt or innocence that someone wanted to pay or be paid for sex; though this may well affect the sentence. For straight men however, not only is there no offence of soliciting a woman but also there is no offence of 'accepting an unlawful solicitation'.[62]

It is too easy to regard prostitutes with distaste. But one should not be patronising and, without suggesting that every man who is 'for rent' feels the same, it is worth taking seriously the views of a successful male ex-prostitute. John Rechy expresses the confidence − and alienation − of a successful male 'hustler':

'There is a terrific, terrible excitement in getting paid by another man for sex. A great psychological release, a feeling that this is where real sexual power lies − not only to be desired by one's own sex but to be paid for being desired, and if one chooses that strict role, not to reciprocate in those encounters; a feeling of emotional detachment as freedom − these are some of the lures; lures implicitly acknowledged as desirable by the very special place the male hustler occupies in the gay world, entirely different from that of the female prostitute in the straight. Even when he is disdained by those who would never pay for sex, he is still an object of admiration to most, at times an object of jealousy. To "look like a hustler" in gay jargon is to look very, very good.'[63]

Of course, very few prostitutes become successful authors and some end up on the proverbial scrap-heap of life, as Rechy freely admits himself.

Prostitution is particularly objectionable and exploitative when it involves the young who are economically disadvantaged. In 1981, five men were jailed for sexual offences arising from the scandal at the Kincora boys home in Belfast. The house father, a para-military Protestant fanatic, was sentenced to four years' imprisonment. Following public disquiet about more allegations, the government announced that the matter would be the subject of a judicial public inquiry after further police investigations had been completed. It is no coincidence that in a part of the United Kingdom where it is possible to whip up moral fervour about sodomy (see page 139 below) and where the law is at its most oppressive, the exploitation of young people by men claiming to be guardians of moral and political order was concealed for more than twenty years.[64]

Any organisation of male prostitution is dealt with under the Sexual Offences Act 1967 in *England and Wales*,[65] or in *Scotland* under the Criminal Justice (Scotland) Act 1980.[66] Both statutes penalise pimps who 'procure others to commit homosexual acts'; make it an offence to live wholly or partly on the earnings of male prostitution; and make it an offence to be involved in the running of a brothel.

It seems fairly safe to guess that the prostitution of men exists on nothing like the organised scale of the prostitution of women in British cities. From time to time cases of organised prostitution have come to light involving teenage boys. In England the most recent major example of this was the Playland vice trial in 1975. In this case four defendants were sentenced to between two-and-a-half and six-and-a-half years' imprisonment on various charges involving conspiracy to procure homosexual acts. The prosecution's case had been that young, friendless and penniless runaways from local authority homes were attracted to the Playland Arcade in Piccadilly and became easy prey for men who offered them money, meals and shelter.

How do young men become prostitutes? Criminologist D.J. West comments:

'The myth that youths are seduced into prostitution by the importunate advances of older men receives no confirmation from any observer. Nearly always boys come to the game ready primed by their more sophisticated peers with information about where to go and what to do.'[67]

Whilst this is not perhaps the place to explore the reasons for and the nature of gay prostitution, it is possible to ask more fruitful questions than simply how can the police more effectively stop men from corrupting boys? What, perhaps, is the connection between prostitution and the unemployment and homelessness of young men? Or, what is the connection between seeking affection from adults, including taking money, and family rejection of the young gay son? What are the effects of the appalling lack of social facilities for teenagers who identify themselves as gay? Is there not a connection between the repression of their own homosexuality by married men and the use of male prostitutes?

Regulating the male gay world

'There's nothing greater in terms of our life on earth than an enduring relationship, if it's truly loving. But we are brainwashed into accepting the standards of the heterosexual majority, and we need to keep reminding ourselves that we needn't, shouldn't conform to straight standards, that long lasting love isn't incompatible with promiscuity, that love can enter into one-night-stands too. Such love could be higher in its nature than domestic love because it verges on that thing we all talk about so much but rarely meet – love of mankind.'

Christopher Isherwood[68]

Gay men have a distinctive social and sexual culture. The male gay world has developed both because and in spite of the law. Most large British cities contain a number of pubs, bars, clubs, discos, saunas, parks, streets and public toilets where homosexual men can make contact and in some instances have sex. Even small towns are likely to have a park or a public toilet known to gays, and probably to the police, as a meeting place. These meeting places provide the opportunity for many individuals to discover their homosexual desires and the existence of a world in which they can be satisfied. This section concerns the practices used by the police to regulate and control the male gay world.

Pubs, clubs and discos

These make up the gay 'commercial scene', a 1970s growth industry. Most are privately owned businesses.[69] Some are companies with diverse business interests, some of the owners are straight, some are large corporations such as leisure combines. Not surprisingly London offers the most choice, but there are well developed businesses in most large British cities.

In the 1950s, the police used the anti-soliciting law to justify raids on gay clubs and pubs. Referring to this period, Peter Wildeblood wrote:

'The proprietors of the clubs were not taking any chances. There was always the possibility of a raid. The police did not interfere very much with the clubs. The public houses which had become recognised as meeting places for homosexuals were less discreet and a good deal more dangerous. With one or two inexplicable exceptions, they were always being raided, and "warned" by the police.'[70]

Almost inevitably the mushrooming of gay discos in the seventies led some police forces to attempt to seriously disrupt or at least inhibit new-found gay freedom. In 1974 the licensee and manager of the Father Redcap pub in Camberwell, South London were each fined £100 for permitting and abetting in running a '*disorderly house*' after the police had moved in to stop gay discos.[71] By 1978 the Manchester police were threatening to prosecute the owner of Napoleon's club for permitting gay dancing, contrary, they claimed to the city's by-laws which prohibited 'licentious dancing'. Angry gays demonstrated and leafleted the city; the police never pressed any charges.[72] The by-law was not renewed under the new Manchester Corporation Act.

At the Old Bailey in January 1981, Judge Leonard QC speculated 'under my reading of the law as it presently stands the proprietor of a gay bar who openly advertises it as such or even who does nothing about homosexuals meeting there possibly for sexual purposes could be acting unlawfully'.[73] He went on to suggest that two co-proprietors of a gay pub could be indicted on a charge of conspiring to corrupt public morals. Although it was mere conjecture, this comment serves to underline the uncertain legal position of such gay social facilities. (See also pages 73-75 below.)

Individual officers still operate both inside and outside gay clubs and pubs. Some of these will be from the licensing squad. All clubs are routinely checked by plain-clothes officers for possible breaches of the club's licence (e.g. after-hours drinking, drinking without buying a meal, membership restrictions not being enforced, under-age drinking, criminal activities like gambling). Information from the licensing squad may lead to a raid or to an objection to the renewal of a club's licence. The police effectively have free rein to enter premises to check on compliance with licensing conditions. They are not required to obtain prior permission from a magistrate in the form of a warrant.[74] Early in 1980 for example, some six London West End gay clubs were raided by the police in what appeared to be a simultaneous exercise.[75]

Obviously such raids are bad for business from the management's point of view, particularly if they smack of harassment, as seemed evident from some owners' comments. Such raids are also the opportunity for harassment of gay customers.

Following a police raid on the Catacomb's disco-coffee bar in Earl's Court, London in March 1978:

> 'customers were stopped from leaving. They were made to form orderly queues to give their names to police officers. They were asked for their addresses too, and some were asked other questions – how many drinks have you bought, how much did you pay to get in? A member of *Gay News*' staff was even asked how tall he was. After answering the questions, each person was given a white slip printed "Metropolitan Police". This slip had to be handed to an officer on the door before that individual was allowed to leave the premises.'[76]

In September 1980, 40 officers raided a gay club in Northampton; according to an eye-witness:

> 'they took the names of all 300 members present and forced them to pose for mug-shots for police files. Those who refused to have photos taken had their heads held while it was done. They were warned that if they didn't co-operate they would be arrested and charged with breach of the peace.'[77]

In both cases, complaints were made on behalf of customers by the National Council for Civil Liberties that the police conduct was unlawful. The police response was that such methods are 'normal procedure'. Even if this police comment were true it could not excuse their conduct. Moreover the implications of being caught up in a licensing raid on a gay club are different to being caught in raids on other clubs. Information thereby obtained may be used in unrelated inquiries based on police stereotypes.

In Brighton, members of the Curtain and Palace clubs have been threatened with charges of aiding and abetting the licensee in breach of the licensing laws.[78]

After the club or pub has closed for the evening, foot or car patrols may operate to move and harass or arrest gays who are waiting around. Various charges come up time and time again – obstruction of the highway, being drunk and disorderly, soliciting. In this respect, police behaviour towards gay men who use the Coleherne pub in Earl's Court, London has been a continuing source of resentment and friction for many years. There were violent clashes in June 1976 when the police piled into customers who were congregating on a hot summer night after closing time.

> 'People wander up and down Wharfdale Street looking for a partner and this problem has been made worse by police action that has closed down local gay clubs. But the police do not see it that way. They assert that the local residents are complaining about crowds of gays spilling onto the street in front of the Coleherne itself. This has led to the police clearing the pavement with threats of arrest for causing obstruction and, on occasion, police officers physically shoving customers back into the pub bar . . . this sort of action appears never to be taken against the patrons of non-gay pubs nearby . . . And the police do not care for the niceties while they are clearing the pavement outside The Coleherne, say customers. 'Queer' and 'poof' are the standard forms of address used by the police. One customer told *Gay News* he was ordered by a police officer to clear the way 'for decent people' . . . The situation has been made worse by allegations that plain clothes police officers are acting as agents provocateurs in that area to arrest gay men for importuning. According to a spokesperson for the patrons, "The problem is that a lot of the people who use the Coleherne have not come out as gay. That is why they do not protest and that is why they so often plead guilty at magistrates' courts to avoid publicity.'[79]

In December 1980, Huddersfield police raided the local gay club and arrested over twenty people. Allegations were made that sexual activity took place in a backyard. A number of charges were prepared, including one under the Vagrancy Act 1824 of 'loitering in the yard for an unlawful purpose'. Following nationally supported protests from the local gay community, most of the criminal charges brought by the police were withdrawn.

Public toilets, parks and streets

All cities in Britain have their 'beats', areas of streets, or parks where some gay men 'cruise' one another. More often than not there is a certain tension about the experience not only because of 'queer bashers', but also because of fear of the police. The most notorious areas in the public's mind are toilets. The police get to know which toilets are meeting places for gay men. Sometimes they turn a blind eye; sometimes they will embark on blitzes; rarely will there be continual surveillance. Because of the ease of detection, most convictions of gay men for public indecency offences arise out of 'cottaging'.

The view that most people have about cottaging is informed, not surprisingly, by apologetic speeches of mitigation reported in the papers. ' . . . It happened whilst under the influence of drink . . . ', 'he didn't know what came over him . . . ' and so on. In fact, toilets do provide men – some who identify as gay, some who do not – with a chance for sexual fulfilment not otherwise available for one reason or another; for many it is the only form of sexual fulfilment or, if they are married, the only chance of sexual expression with other men. Because cottaging has developed as an institution, some gay men enjoy it for itself, some also for the threat of danger and tension.

When merely walking in a park with arms linked gay men have been stopped, questioned and searched. The sexual activities of men and women go relatively unnoticed. The various parks known as meeting places for gay men are patrolled by the police on foot or in cars. As Brian Deer writing in the *New Statesman* commented:

'Police behaviour towards gays often suggests a strange sense of priorities in the enforcement of the law. In south London, the few dozen gay men who turn up after dark at a hidden cruising spot among the trees on Clapham Common have been forced to flee several times nightly in recent weeks as police cars drive among the bushes – often at dangerously high speeds. Officers questioned on the Common about the need for this kind of patrolling claim variously that they are investigating an attack and that complaints have been received from the public. But one gay man who was attacked on the Common recently had cause to doubt their peace-keeping role. After staggering on to the road in front of a police car he was himself arrested.'[80]

It has been argued successfully before magistrates in at least one unreported case that a park can be treated as a private place when the person apprehended was so off the beaten track that no one (other than detectives) could come across him. (See also page 21 above.)

Saunas

In many cities of the United States, Canada, Australia, and Western Europe there are large sauna baths exclusively for gay men. They are money-making enterprises; an entrance fee is paid to get a warm, reasonably comfortable environment in which to have sex with other men. In the main, they are unmolested by the police, even though in many states they could be closed and the owners and customers prosecuted for breaches of local public indecency laws – which did happen in Toronto during 1979.

In England and Wales, small sauna baths do exist for gay men, sometimes in hotels. They are furtive, often watched by the police and periodically raided and closed. Managing a place where people can freely have sex where there is no question of prostitution appears to amount to the offence of '*keeping a disorderly house*'. In law, a 'disorderly house' is 'one which is not regulated by the restraints of morality and which is so conducted as to violate law and good order'.[81] It is an extremely vague offence. There must be an element of 'open house' but it does not need to be open to the public at large.

In 1979, a jury at the Manchester crown court convicted the proprietor of the city's Unit One Sauna Club (who was an ex-police officer) of this offence. The police alleged they kept watch for twelve days and saw men 'performing homosexual acts in the sauna and its rest rooms.' One of the proprietors admitted to the police that sex took place but claimed this was done 'in private'. 'They are all members', he said, 'and to become a member you have to be gay, so nobody in there can be offended by what goes on.'[82]

Since neither a club nor its rooms or cubicles are 'private' places any participants could be charged with sexual offences.

Gay communities

The effect of widescale police inquiries in a city or a specific area can be the blatant intimidation of a local gay community. Because the police frequently use diaries and address books to provide leads to people for questioning, distrust is created within the gay community, and networks of friends are destroyed. Such methods of inquiry alienate the gay community from the police in particular. The police themselves have remarked on this fear and distrust when they have been investigating murders, for example, and find they cannot get help from the gay community. Surveillance of clubs and discos by police discourages people who have not come out from using available social facilities thereby increasing their social isolation. One of the most notorious recent examples of such inquiries was the police exercise in Cornwall during 1977 when dozens of men were arrested and questioned. Here is an acount of what happened, taken from the Campaign for Homosexual Equality's evidence to the Royal Commission on Criminal Procedure.[83]

'In early January 1977, Z, a packing clerk aged 19, was questioned by his stepfather about the way in which he spent his evenings. Z confessed that he used to pick up men in public lavatories for sex. His stepfather took him to the local police station where, under interrogation, he admitted that he had had sexual relations with nearly 100 men. He supplied the names and addresses of several of these, together with details of his sexual activity with them. The police arrested these men and under questioning further suspected offences came to light and more people were arrested or taken in for questioning. All this took place within a few days of the police questioning of Z. In all some 68 men were charged with various homosexual offences. The papers in the cases of 28 were sent to the DPP, who authorised prosecution in the cases of 16. Most were charged with 10 or more offences. At their trial, 14 pleaded guilty and were fined or given suspended sentences. Two pleaded not guilty and were acquitted on the direction of the judge.

The police called on T, a clerk with the Inland Revenue aged 50, at about 9 p.m. on the evening of 3 January 1977 and asked to speak privately with him. They told him that Z had made a statement that T had had sex with Z some months previously in a cemetery. T admitted this, was arrested and taken to the local police station where he was told he would be kept in the cells for the night and interviewed in the morning. At about 11 a.m. the next day T was taken to his home by the two arresting officers who asked if they could look around his bedroom and if he would provide them with a photograph of two friends whom they had learned had stayed with T nine months previously. They seized some girlie magazines and took T back to the station and put him in the cells. About an hour later he was told that he had to make a statement about his sexual relations with Z and his two friends, which he did. After a further hour he was photographed, fingerprinted and then given police bail. He was driven home at about 4 p.m. on 4 January 1977. T had no complaints about the police behaviour, which he described as respectful and courteous throughout. At his trial, T pleaded guilty to two charges involving Z and his two friends.

At about 5.15 p.m. on Sunday 9 January 1977, two policemen called at the home of Q, a labourer aged 25, and asked to speak to him privately (he lived with his parents). They asked him to accompany them to the police station, but because he had been suffering from bronchitis for a week he refused. The police insisted so he agreed to go with them. His father appeared at the door and on asking why his son was being taken away was told that he was being arrested and charged with buggery. He was kept in the cells overnight and the following morning was interviewed by two policemen. He was told that X, a postman aged 41, had made a statement that he and Q had had sex some twelve times, twice in a car. Q agreed that this was so. He was given the names of eight other men and agreed that he had had sex with them. He mentioned during this interview that he was the local agent for selling *Gay News*, the newspaper for homosexuals. All this information was taken down in the form of a statement. He was then photographed and fingerprinted and returned to the cells where he remained until the following day, Tuesday, 11 January. On the Tuesday morning he was taken with two other men to the police station in a neighbouring town and was medically examined by the county police doctor. Q was then returned to his local police station, charged with gross indecency, and given police bail. At 4 p.m. on Tuesday he was taken back to his home by two policemen who then searched his bedroom, without asking his father's permission to enter the house or his permission to search his room. The police seized all his copies of *Gay News*, some personal gay magazines as well as his card index of customers and personal address book.

Q complained that he was subjected to foul language during police questioning and that despite suffering from bronchitis he was kept in a cell with a wet floor and not allowed to keep his

shoes. At his trial Q pleaded guilty to charges of having had sex
in the car (as not being 'in private') and not guilty to other
charges, on which the judge directed the jury to acquit him.

At approximately 7.30 p.m. on Monday 10 January 1977 two
policemen called at the home of R, a social worker aged 29, who
told him he was being arrested on suspicion of having committed gross indecency and buggery. He was taken to the local
police station where he was interviewed. He was told that Y had
alleged that Y and R had had sex on the night of Y's 21st birthday party, which took place two days before his actual birthday,
and on one other occasion. R denied this and was told that a
night in the cells might make him change his mind. The following morning he was photographed and fingerprinted and again
interviewed. He repeatedly denied the allegations and was then
released on police bail. He complained that he was called a
'filthy degenerate' and 'pouf' several times by the interviewing
officers and that he was constantly asked to supply other names.
All charges against R were eventually dropped.

At about 2 p.m. on 10 January 1977 two policemen called at
the home of Y, a chef at the local police station aged 21. He was
asked to accompany the officers to the local police station but
was given no reason for this. On the way he was officially cautioned. He was interviewed at the station and told that his fian-
cée would be involved if he did not co-operate. After the
interview he was returned to his cell and he asked if his parents
could bring in some warm clothing, chocolate and cigarettes,
and this was agreed to. His parents arrived at 10.30 p.m. and
were told they would not be permitted to see him. Y's father
refused to leave unless he was allowed to see his son and about
half an hour later this was permitted. Y was kept in the cell
overnight and the following morning was photographed, fingerprinted and charged. Later that morning he was taken with Q
and another man to be medically examined by the county police
doctor. He complained about having his anus examined and was
told that everyone else enjoyed it and asked for more. He was
returned to his local police station, given bail and taken home,
where he was told to tell his parents to permit the officers to
search his bedroom or he would not be permitted bail (according to the bail form Y was to be released on bail some 15
minutes after he arrived home). He agreed to this and the
officers searched his room and seized some gay magazines. Y was
charged with two offences of gross indecency with R but at his

trial the judge ordered the jury to acquit him. After the case Y was dismissed from his job but sued the police authorities for unfair dismissal and was awarded £1600 in compensation.' (See page 45 below.)

Chapter Two
Police and prisons

'While the Federation accepts that private homosexual conduct between consenting males over the age of 21 ought not to be a criminal offence it deplores the way official thinking on this subject appears to be surrendering to the pressure groups who try to persuade society that homosexual conduct is perfectly normal.'

Police Federation press statement 10 April 1981

'In selecting cases for hormone treatment the genuineness of the individual's request is only one of several problems. I have one man who had a long list of convictions for larceny, in addition to being an incorrigible masturbator of small boys. This case taught me that it always pays to study depositions and other documents in the prison records. It turned out that all this man's breaking and entering was that of boys' schools and all his larcenies were boys' bicycles, boys' clothes and property. In due course I ascertained that his primary object in seeking the company of small boys was not overtly sexual, but the small boys interpreted this interest by an adult as sexual and behaved accordingly. The subject I really believe indulged in mutual masturbation merely to oblige his friends. Had one given this man hormone implants the treatment would probably have been useless as he would still seek the company of boys even if impotent, and, because of his record, would almost certainly be convicted of acts of indecency.'

Visiting psychotherapist, Dartmoor Prison[1]

The first part of this chapter covers police attitudes towards homosexuality and their practice in dealing with suspects. The following part on prisons is concerned mainly with conditions for inmates convicted of having sex with boys and the controversial subject of hormone treatment.

Police attitudes

From the chief constable down to the ordinary constable on the beat, the police have wide discretion as to how and when the law is enforced.[2] They are not responsible to any outside authority for their policing and in practice are not effectively accountable to the courts. In dealing with suspects, the police can determine how vigorously and in what ways detective work should be carried out, how diligently attackers of gay people will be pursued and so on.

It is almost inevitable that men in an organisation run on semi-military lines will have anti-gay attitudes. By definition most will see themselves as 'real men' as opposed to 'queers'. Homophobia* in the police force is necessarily intensified by virtue of their job because gay men are for them a category of criminal suspect. It is their duty to enforce the criminal law, which itself discriminates against homosexuals. Coupled with that, crimes of public indecency are easy to find, easy to deal with (no physical resistance, no lack of co-operation at the police station), easy to prove and can be dealt with in the lower courts.

The Police Federation, which represents officers up to the rank of inspector in England and Wales, has vigorously attacked the suggestion that the minimum age for lawful gay relationships between men should be reduced to 18. In addition, reported cases and police publications provide insight into otherwise undisclosed attitudes.

The views expressed in published police training manuals give a hint of the official police mind. It seems that the use of stereotypes plays an exaggeratedly important part in detecting homosexual criminal suspects. Black people will recognise in this criticism a problem they themselves experience with white police officers who use racist stereotypes.

The following appeared in the 1980 edition of a training manual for Scottish police:

'It is a sad reflection on modern society that there are still to be found in our midst persons who are so lewdly disposed that they will stoop to the most revolting and almost unbelievable acts of indecency. The terms 'sodomy', 'indecent exposure', 'lewd and libidinous practice' and 'gross indecency' etc., which are used in law give but little indication of the nature of these offences; the manner in which they are usually committed, and the evils they are liable to bring in their train. It is perhaps no exaggeration to say that many innocent children

---

*Homophobia describes the irrational fear and loathing of homosexuals by hetero-sexuals, or, in the case of homosexuals, self-hatred. See: G. Weinberg, *Society and the Healthy Homosexual*, New York, Anchor Books 1973

fall victims of the foul activities of moral degenerates to the detriment of mind and health of body . . . Consequently, no effort is ever spared by the Police to suppress this insidious form of evil whenever and wherever it may occur.

Apart from actually detecting an act of indecency, the constable will play his part best by giving special attention to those parts of his beat, such as public parks and secluded public lavatories, which lend themselves to the activities of the morally degenerate. The movements of persons of manifestly lewd disposition should always be closely watched as many and varied are the artifices employed by these persons to achieve their evil objects.'[3]

English police have been advised in more specific terms to watch for:

'The "athlete" dressed in a tracksuit, running about residential streets, either at dusk or in the early morning. While one must not become morbidly suspicious, experience does indicate that there seems to be a correlation between such persons and homosexual nuisances. I know a man, respectably dressed in middle-class clothes, who was recently driving to residential areas, with a tracksuit over his clothes, and then running around looking for youngsters to molest. He then took off his tracksuit, put it in the boot of his car and, totally different now from any description remembered or circulated, left the scene safe from interrogation.'

Officers are also advised to:

'Watch for the possession of 'These are your rights' cards or pamphlets by loiterers generally. While this may be slightly suspicious, there is real reservation. Obviously, they will be carried by persons who consider it at least possible that they will break the law and be interrogated by police. Thus they are carried by male homosexuals, by industrial and other agitators, by "Angry Brigade" inadequates and similar amateur criminals, but rarely by shrewd and hardheaded professional thieves. The latter have no need for academic discussion of legal niceties – they know from bitter experience how to behave in custody. Anyway, possession of such written matter often means subsequent false complaint against you. Be circumspect with intellectual malcontents; they can be bitchy and small minded in these complaints.'[4]

These attitudes are amplified in documented cases about the way the police have handled crimes committed against gay people.[5] All of the following reports are taken from *Attacks on Gay People* compiled by Julian Meldrum which covers instances reported by the press between 1977 and 1980.[6] They illustrate why many gay people are wary of going to the police, and the viciousness and callousness shown by individual officers. Women who complain of sexual attacks from men have faced similar difficulties when requesting the police to investigate. Thames Valley detectives, for example, were strongly criticised for their bullying interrogation of a rape victim, shown on BBC television.

Individual officers not caring, or sympathising with 'queer bashers'.

Nottingham: 'Late in 1977, two gay women were surrounded by ten youths as they were leaving a lesbian conference. They were shoved and abused, and an attempt was made to overturn their car. The police arrived having been called thirty minutes before the attack, as there was a disturbance, in fact saw the assailants jeering, but did not pursue them. The women were advised not to make a written complaint.'

Chester: 'Five gay people, men and women, were set upon by a group of young men outside a gay club. They started with verbal abuse to which one of the gay men reacted verbally; his glasses were removed, though later recovered. There was a further argument and then a fight which began with an attack on a gay woman. The victims were kicked and their clothing was damaged; the first gay man to get involved was kicked in the throat and has had recurrent speech difficulties as a result. All five victims went to the police station and spent three hours there, although no statement was taken and none were contacted about the enquiries 'the police alleged they would make'. Our informant, one of the five, objected to being called 'queer' by the police and is indignant that he was accused of being anti-police, as he insists he was polite and helpful to them.'

Darlington: 'Residents of a quiet avenue have run a sustained campaign to get rid of a local public lavatory after finding themselves living in fear of 'queer-bashing' gangs. In November 1978 two youths were fined a total of £120 after a man was attacked in the street. Matters came to a head in May, after two separate incidents in which residents were confronted by victims of the gangs. One young man 'begged on his knees on a doorstep to be let in, as thugs clubbed him', blood was streaming from a head-wound he suffered during the attack. Local police say they have had "countless incidents" reported to them and that many more have not been reported at all. At one time there were two gangs operating, armed with sticks, bottles and even knives; one gang aged between 18 and 30, the other between 12 and 16. Low-key police surveillance seems to have been ineffective in stopping the menace, which continued over a period of months. The Council voted against demolition, apparently in the belief that the problem would simply move on (which is not necessarily true) and in support of a police view that 'queer-bashing' can best be controlled by keeping up the level of indecency convictions against gay men.'

Individual officers may be bashers themselves.

Camberwell, South London: 'Two police constables were convicted of assaulting two gay men. When off-duty and at a party, the policemen had between them kicked one man in the face and hit the other over the head with a glass. RM received a six month suspended sentence and was fined £250. JH was given 18 months, also suspended, and fined £25.'

Belfast: 'The Secretary of the Northern Ireland Gay Rights Association, KM, was assaulted by police officers while demonstrating outside a newsagent's shop in protest at its refusal to stock *Gay News*. KM was dragged into the back of the police landrover, hit twice in the face and left blood-spattered and bleeding from the nose.'

Helping the police with enquiries may lead to prosecution.

Earl's Court, London: 'A 30-year-old man picked up a 19-year-old 'rent boy' (according to the man) on Earl's Court station, only to find that after they reached the man's flat and had sex the younger man produced a shotgun and held his partner terrified for three quarters of an hour. The victim escaped through the bathroom window and called the police, who arrested both men and charged them with gross indecency, to which they later pleaded guilty. The 19-year-old was also charged with firearms offences and put on probation for three years; his victim was given a 12 month suspended sentence.'

Unsavoury/vicious methods of law enforcement used by individual officers.

Merseyside: 'Three plain-clothes policemen in a car drew up and stopped a gay man near to a well-known "cottage", where many men had been arrested. He was asked for his name and address, which he gave. He claims that the policemen then punched him and knocked him down twice, before they charged him with being drunk and disorderly to forestall any complaint. (He says he had three pints of beer that evening and has never been drunk and disorderly in his life.) In court the man pleaded guilty to being d. and d. having been advised he had no defence that could stand against the word of the policemen. He was then (for the first time) charged with having interfered with the arrest of others (he insists there were no 'others' present) and with having used abusive language against the police. He pleaded not guilty to these charges but was convicted; he was fined £25 with £4 costs and bound over for the sum of £100 for 12 months.

In West London a 28-year-old wearing a gay badge claims he was first subjected to verbal abuse (called a "pouf", a "queer" and so on) and then pushed around by a policeman at a police station. When he tried to defend himself he was allegedly kicked and punched by three policemen. He was fined £4 for being drunk and disorderly (he denies this absolutely). There was no independent witness, so any complaint would have been unlikely to succeed even if fully justified.'

Finally, the case of a police canteen chef illustrates the extraordinary lengths to which individual officers will go to justify their prejudice.

Mr Bell (referred to as Y on page 39) was employed as a chef in a police station canteen. As part of a large-scale police enquiry about gay men in the Redruth area Mr Bell was interviewed and gave statements about the gay relationships he had had before getting the job as chef. The charges brought against him were eventually dismissed at Bodmin Crown Court where the trial judge directed that the jury acquit him. After the acquittal, a superintendant at the police station was deputed to find out what the canteen users thought about Mr Bell's continued employment there. The officers showed Mr Bell's original statement concerning his relationships to about a third of the police and civilian users and took fourteen statements about their reactions. Four statements contained virtually the same words: 'I have nothing against him but what was described in the statements concerning him [I found] to be revolting. I would therefore not be able to eat food prepared by him.' All the police officers interviewed also said they would stop using the canteen.

This led to Mr Bell's dismissal and an internal appeal against dismissal was unsuccessful. The tribunal ruled that the dismissal was unfair. 'Having received these statements and not having showed them to Mr Bell, it was in our view unfair to act on them without any further investigation . . . [The statements of] objection must appear rather unreasonable and we do not consider it fair for an employer to accept such objections against a fellow employee without any attempt to get the employees together to find out how serious the objection is, and without endeavouring to solve the problem by consultation and communication, before taking the drastic step of dismissing the employee.'[7]

Police practice

The legal police powers to stop, search, detain, question and prosecute people with offences are different in England and Wales, Scotland and Northern Ireland. It is expected that there will be a major reform of English police powers in 1983. This section includes an outline of the most relevant police powers to bear in mind. It is important to keep a sense of proportion about how useful such legal knowledge can be. The police will always want to keep the initiative. So, for example, they will not be prepared to discuss their legal powers in the street.

The prime aim of this section is to provide an idea of what decisions must be made in an encounter with the police in the context of the decisions that the police are themselves making. The decisions made by someone suspected by the police will obviously depend on the particular circumstances. The most likely would be: being the object of some vague suspicion of the 'I-don't-like-your-looks' variety or a particular suspicion of 'public' homosexual sexual activity; being suspected of sex with someone under 21; being a suspect or witness in connection with a police enquiry.

Suspicion

The police are taught to be suspicious of people and activities that most individuals would not give a second glance. This means that anyone who appears to be out of the ordinary has a fairly high chance of being picked on.

Should someone stopped by the police (1) co-operate fully; answer all the usual questions: name, address, date of birth, where they have come from and where they are going? agree to allow them to look through pockets and anything being carried? (2) refuse to answer any questions and refuse to be searched without a convincing legal justification? (3) draw the line somewhere between these two points? Subject to the exceptions noted on page 55 below both approaches (1) and (2) would, strictly speaking, be lawful. It does not seem useful to give hard and fast advice in these circumstances. The following statement given to the NCCL by a gay woman illustrates the difficulty of attempting to cope reasonably with an awkward police officer.

'It was between 3 and 3.15 p.m. I had just stepped off the tube and was making my way towards Waterloo main line station. Halfway up a flight of steps I noticed a policeman and policewoman walking very close alongside me. At first I thought nothing of it until he grabbed hold of my arm and escorted me the rest of the way up the stairs. When we got to the top he pushed me against the wall. She stood to my right, he to the left.

"Where are you going?" he asked.

"Waterloo main line station," I replied, not understanding why I'd been pulled up.

"You're going the wrong way aren't you?" he said.

"I'm sorry. I must have taken a wrong turning," I replied. Then he asked for my ticket, which I showed him, but he wasn't satisfied with that.

"Are you homosexual?" he asked.

I realised almost immediately he wasn't concerned about where I was going or my ticket but about my appearance. I started to feel a little irritated about this and I didn't think it was any of his business. But I replied all the same.

"Yes. I am homosexual. Are you heterosexual?" I fired back, thinking if he feels he's the right to ask me if I'm gay, I've the right to ask if he's "straight". That was it. No sooner did I confirm his suspicions then he started getting more carried away. He grabbed hold of my arm squeezing it very hard which hurt, and I asked him to let go.

"I won't let go until you co-operate."

"But I haven't done anything. I think you're just picking on me for being gay."

I felt it was time to defend myself as best as I could. He squeezed my arm again and said through gritted teeth, "We've dealt with your sort before. We're going to the station to ask you a few questions."

"But I haven't done anything but lose my way and it's not fair you picking on me like that."

He got annoyed and said angrily: "If you don't shut up and play the game my way you'll end up a lot worse off than you are."

So with still a hold on my arm they both escorted me to the office on a platform on the main line station and put me in a room. The WPC came in and asked me my name and address. I gave only my name and age, as I didn't have a permanent address. I didn't want to give my friends' address as I didn't want them to get involved. Then she asked me again if I was homosexual to which I said "yes" and I was becoming more upset as they seemed to be asking more questions about me being gay than anything else.

Another PC came in and asked the same question with "Do you take drugs?" thrown in. When I said "No" he said: "Take your shirt off. Let's have a look at your arms."

I refused as he stood there grinning with door ajar and PCs floating about all over the place. To me it didn't seem very professional. After I refused he asked again:

"Are you gay?"

So I said "Yes" for the umpteenth time, and he smiled and said:

"Are you boy or girl?" So I said "Girl" and he walked away locking the door behind him.

Then the WPC came in and told me to turf my pockets out so I did so and the PC that took me in came in and searched me. He saw my darts set on the bench and said "I'll have those" and off he went.

I was locked in again and sat there until 4.15 p.m. and every now and then a PC kept peering through the glass window and grinning at his mates. I found their attitude very humiliating and insulting.

The WPC came in again and asked me for my name, age and address again and said: "You're homosexual, aren't you?"

I said: "Yes, and I'm going to meet my girlfriend at 4.30 and I shall be late and she'll worry. I've done no harm, and you all know that. You're just having a go at me about my homosexuality more than anything else."

She told me they were waiting for a phone call from records and if that was clear they'd let me go. Shortly after I was released but without my darts.'

Entrapment

In a very high proportion of cases, accused men claim to be the victims of fabricated evidence or entrapment by a police decoy – an *agent provocateur*. Gays do not want to have sexual relations in front of unsuspecting members of the public. This is why the police go to such extraordinary lengths to hide themselves in order to spy and entice.

In public toilets, the police will hide in the attendant's room, looking through two way mirrors, peeping over the top of windows concealed by blankets or some other vantage point such as a broom cupboard, or perhaps outside looking through a grille, waiting for a suitable moment to catch an unsuspecting man or number of men. Since the crime has no victim, the only witnesses are officers, and the temptation on their part to lie or embellish the evidence can prove irresistible. Therefore in the preparation of such cases it is essential to take a physical check on the accuracy of all police claims that particular areas could be seen from their observation point. Scale plans and photographs are very helpful. Despite substantial criticism of this kind from defences, magistrates will *still* convict. Jurors will also do so, but less frequently. Thorough cross-examination of the officers is crucial. In some cases, barristers have thought it necessary to produce photographs of distinct-looking erect penises which obviously do not tally with the police account.[8]

Occasionally, in order to save time, a plain-clothes officer will openly hang around the toilet to encourage a sexual advance from a gay man. There have been well documented cases of these kinds of police practice.[9] Officers have been reported to smile at men, look about and even masturbate. The use of *agents provocateurs* in these circumstances has been effectively condoned by chief constables. The Home Office has issued guidance to police chiefs on the subject of entrapment but this is mainly concerned with drawing the line between acceptable co-operation with suspects and unacceptable provocation of serious criminal offences.[10]

In any event it is not a defence to a charge that the crime was actively instigated by the police or a police undercover agent. The House of Lords has said that a judge 'had no discretion to exclude evidence obtained by entrapment'. The courts have no responsibility for 'passing a necessarily subjective judgment on the ethics of the police or prosecution'.[11] Entrapment can be used as mitigation (see page 168) where the defendant was not the 'prime mover' and might not have done anything if he had not been tempted. However, the courts do give the police plenty of elbow room when dealing with consensual offences like cottaging which, they say, cannot be detected without some 'testing of suspects'.[12] There appears to be no Scottish case law on the subject of entrapment.

Here is a typical account of police entrapment and its consequences:

'I parked my car in an adjoining street and walked over to the side of the road. The "cottage" in question is on an island and I had to wait for a minute or so while the traffic cleared. I saw no one else go down ahead of me – if they did it was entirely coincidental.

I went down the cottage which has six stalls and there were two people already standing there some distance apart. I stood at the stall nearest the stairs next to one of the men. The man furthest away left after about a minute. The person next to me was gay but I wasn't interested and no attempts at picking up were made.

After about two minutes, a tall, good-looking man came down and stood furthest away from me at the left. We looked across at each other and I gained the impression he was gay too. After a further minute or so, I left and walked half way up the stairs but, sad to say, I returned and stood next to this man. After about a minute a further man came down and stood at the stall next but one to my right. The man I was standing next to continued to look at me and he then turned half right towards me and stepped back a pace. He had a semi-erection and I grabbed his cock forthwith whereupon he allowed me to hold on for a good five seconds before grabbing my arm and saying "police". He and the other man who had just come down bustled me up the stairs at the top of which we were joined by a third policeman. I asked them to release my arms as I had no intention of running away and we walked up the road to an unmarked car. As we walked, I was cautioned and I replied that I had nothing to say.

I was then driven to the police station during which journey I was asked my name and address which I gave. I was asked what my job was and I refused to answer at which they got "heavy" and made threats about "it will be worse for you if you don't co-operate" etc.

At the police station I was formally charged and I asked to be allowed to telephone a friend who would stand bail. They did not allow me to telephone personally but phoned themselves to find my friend out. I was stripped of belongings and locked up in a cell after agreeing to be fingerprinted.

After about ten minutes they contacted my friend and after a further thirty minutes, he arrived, stood bail and I was released.

I saw my solicitor the following day and we resolved to elect for trial at the magistrates' court the following week.

I wanted to elect for trial because of the nature of the arrest and also to see what written evidence the police would present. The police were clearly using *agent provocateur* tactics.

The evidence eventually arrived and, after much heart searching, I resolved to plead guilty because of a previous conviction for a similar offence (actually just visiting a cottage too many times) and because I had, in fact, grabbed the officer's cock. Also a barrister had expressed doubt as to whether the *agent provocateur* evidence would be strong enough for an acquittal.'[13]

Interrogation and detention

The police will try to get a suspect to talk and will ask questions about the offence and the circumstances of the suspect's private life. Anything that is said or written down could be used (subject to certain qualifications discussed below) in evidence in subsequent court proceedings. Usually the police will write down what they are going to say the suspect said *after* the interview. It is therefore in the interests of a suspected person to say as little as possible.

Serious and prolonged interrogation is very difficult to resist. A survey published in 1980 conducted for the Royal Commission on Criminal Procedure in England and Wales showed that over a six-month period at Brighton police station only one suspect managed to remain silent while being held. The survey also suggested that the police distinguished between 'sex offenders' and 'hardened criminals' in the belief that since 'sex offenders' were likely to have only limited experience of the police they were more susceptible to interrogation technique.[14]

Detailed police interrogation takes place mainly in connection with 'age of consent' cases. The Home Office's Administrative Directions to the Police provide that anyone below the age of 17 should be interviewed only in the presence of a parent or guardian, or failing them, an independent person of the same sex as the young person.[15] In notable cases young people have retracted their evidence in court, claiming that they were pressured by the police to make allegations. Roger Moody's book *Indecent Assault*[16] describes not only the treatment of the young people involved in his case, but also the nightmare which men accused of these offences can expect. The book gives a particularly good account of the experience of interrogation over a prolonged period. Long periods of questioning punctuated with short and irregular intervals of rest, threats, the hard and soft treatment and more sophisticated methods of persuasion are some of the techniques used to gain confessions. Interrogations are less important in cases involving public indecency where the police themselves may claim to be eye-witnesses.

People detained at police stations are not obliged by law to 'help with enquiries', nor to give answers to police questions, nor do they have to make written statements. In practice the police will rarely release an unidentified suspect; so it is often best for a detained person to give his/her name and address, whilst refusing to answer all other questions until they have consulted a solicitor at the station.

Any confession made by a suspect must be shown to a court to have been given voluntarily and in the absence of oppression.[17] This means that a confession must not be extracted as a result of any promise or threat being made or in unreasonably stressful circumstances. Involuntary admissions of guilt will be excluded in court proceedings. In addition, the courts in England, Wales and Northern Ireland have discretion to exclude statements obtained by the police if the so-called Judges' Rules[18] have been broken (for Scotland see page 171). These Rules state among other things that suspects should be 'cautioned', that is, told that they do not have to answer questions. This must be done twice – when the police suspect that a person has committed a particular crime and later when the police have sufficient evidence to bring a charge.

As soon as the police have sufficient evidence that a person has committed an offence s/he must be charged. The need for 'sufficient' evidence must be interpreted reasonably by the police, unduly high standards should not be used nor is it permitted to delay the charge simply because this would make it difficult to inquire into other suspected offences.[19] Only in exceptional cases is questioning permitted after a person has been charged (for example, to clear up an ambiguity in a previous statement) and a third caution must be given in these instances. Disregard of this rule is taken very seriously by the courts.

Although the law is not precise about the reasons the police may use to deny a solicitor access to his/her client, it is reasonably clear that the police do not have an automatic veto. So, for example, it would be wrong for the police to refuse simply because a solicitor might advise a client to say nothing.[20] According to the Court of Appeal the police should justify their refusal to the solicitor in question.[21] The police would be acting properly, it is said, if they refused access where a solicitor could not come to the station promptly and as a result an interrogation would be delayed unreasonably.

The law provides that the police must notify the detention of a suspect to someone reasonably named by the suspected person. However, this may be delayed as long as it is necessary 'in the interests of the investigation or prevention of crime or the apprehension of offenders'.[22] Someone in this situation should ask to notify a local law centre (many have 24-hour telephone numbers) or a solicitor, or a friend who can get one, or Gay Switchboard (also a 24-hour telephone number).

A good defence requires a clear and sure account of events; after the trauma of the experience much can be forgotten very quickly. Cases can be seriously damaged because the defendants had unclear and confused recollections of events by the time they appeared in court. To overcome this, a full and detailed account of the events, both before and after the arrest, should be written down as soon as possible.

Police trawls

Since 1976, there have been major police inquiries concerned with the gay communities in Belfast, Bradford, Cornwall, Leicester, Rotherham, Leamington Spa, Glasgow, Northampton, Hull and Huddersfield. Literally thousands of gay men have been interviewed in what became in each town a fairly systematic investigation of the male homosexual community. Such trawls most frequently develop in the course of murder enquiries where there has been a gay element. Sometimes the gay connection is extremely tenuous and sometimes the investigations are not tied to murder inquiries at all. In Huddersfield the police began a wide inquiry around the sex lives of two young men and a number of arrests were made.

Whether a trawl is linked to a murder inquiry or not, the police procedure is to interview a couple of gay men and to take from them the names and addresses of friends and acquaintances and any other information they can get about them. When the police say they are investigating a murder and the information will be useful in finding the killer, people questioned are invariably anxious to help and will talk freely and indiscreetly about their own and their friends' private lives. Even people who are wary of the police say that in these circumstances they have been seized by the irrational fear that the police may seriously suspect them of murder and they have co-operated in the full knowledge of the other charges they may lay themselves open to. Typically, interviewees have been encouraged or pressured to reveal the names and addresses of gay friends and acquaintances, required to sign statements acknowledging their homosexuality and giving extensive details of their personal history.

According to one man interviewed during the course of a murder inquiry in Northampton:

'I was visited by two detectives who said they had got my name from a gay in Northampton who gave them a total of seventy names. In addition to the usual questions – where was I at the time of the murder and could I prove that I was at home – they asked me about other gays in the area. I refused to give them any names. They also asked me about paedophilia, people attracted to children. But what concerned me was the number of detailed questions they asked me about myself. I could not see that they were in any way relevant, particularly as there is no evidence that this was a homosexual murder. They said they had so far interviewed 200 gays in the area.'[23]

Such inquiries would not get off the ground if the gay men interviewed by the police did not freely and indiscriminately provide irrelevant information about their friends and acquaintances. People who believe that they have information relevant to a murder should most certainly give it to the police, but under the present law any information could be used against gay men for unrelated 'crimes'. The safest way to pass information to the police is to use Gay Legal Advice (GLAD) to act as intermediaries. This step protects both the informer and innocent parties and would not jeopardise a police enquiry.[24]

It is not known how much of the information collected in the course of trawls is put on a police computer or in what circumstances, but it is almost certainly retained on file. At the present time, the police can refuse to return witness statements to the people who have made them, and when the statements relate only to the person's private life and are not relevant to any criminal proceedings. Additionally, the Home Office policy is to retain information relating to charges brought under certain sections of the Sexual Offences Act, even when the case results in acquittal.[25]

Summary of police powers in the United Kingdom

England and Wales

Powers to stop and question. It is not an offence for someone to refuse to give his or her name and address or an explanation of what they are doing. It *is* an offence however for motorists and cyclists to refuse to give their particulars.

A person suspected of certain offences (e.g. possession of drugs; possession of firearms; possession of stolen goods – in certain cities only) who refuses to give his or her name and address can be lawfully detained at the police station until those particulars are verified.

Powers to detain at the police station and question. The police can detain for questioning in a police station or any other place anyone they have 'arrested' i.e. held because they believe that person has committed, is committing or might commit an offence punishable with imprisonment. Unlike Scots law, there is no formal power to detain for questioning on the basis of vague suspicion.

There is no effective time limit imposed on the police. Within 24 hours anyone taken to a police station should, unless the offence is a 'serious' one, be released on bail or brought before a magistrates' court.[26] There is no clear objective definition of what is or is not a serious offence.

The police can search as well as question the arrested person. Fingerprints may be taken by force only if an order is made by a magistrate (they must be destroyed following an acquittal). Otherwise fingerprints and photographs may lawfully be taken only with the consent of the arrested person.

Body samples may be taken, and medical examinations may be lawfully conducted only with the consent of the arrested person.

Obligations. The police are required to tell people they have arrested: the reason for the arrest; that they need not answer any questions; and that someone may be notified in due course of their arrest.

A record has to be kept: of the time the arrested person was given this information; the time when they asked for someone to be notified of the detention; the time the request was complied with.

These powers and obligations are due to be changed by the government in the 1982-83 parliamentary session.

Scotland

Powers to stop and question. Where a police officer has 'reasonable grounds to suspect that an offence has been or is being committed' s/he can require a suspect to give his or her name and address and ask for an explanation of the circumstances giving rise to suspicion. The suspect can be detained long enough to verify the name and address given where this can be done quickly (e.g. by radio) and to note any explanation given. There is a similar power to require a potential witness to give his or her name and address.

These powers can be used at the scene of a suspected crime, in a public place or any other place where the police officer is entitled to be. The officer is required to inform the suspects or potential witnesses of the general nature of the offence which s/he thinks is being or has been committed; to warn them that it is an offence (punishable by a fine of £200 in the case of a suspect, or £50 in the case of a witness) for either failing to give their name and address or, without a reasonable excuse, stay with the constable when asked to do so.

Powers to detain at the police station and question. The police can detain for questioning in a police station or any other place anyone they have 'reasonable grounds to suspect' has committed or is committing an offence punishable with imprisonment. The detention can be up to six hours after the suspect is first stopped; it must end earlier if there are no longer grounds for suspicion or if the suspect is arrested.

The police can question the suspect, search him/her and take his/her fingerprints (which must be destroyed following any decision not to initiate criminal proceedings or on a finding without guilt). The police can use 'reasonable force' to ensure that a person comes to the station and submits to searching or fingerprinting.

Obligations. The police are required: to tell the detained person the nature of the suspected offence; the reason for being detained; and that any questions, other than those asking for name and address, need not be answered.

A record has to be kept: of the place of detention; the general nature of the suspected offence; the times of arrival of detained persons and their departure or arrest; the time they were informed of their rights and the identity of the police officer giving the information; the time when the detained person asked for a solicitor or friend to be notified of the detention and the time the request was complied with.

Northern Ireland

In addition to having powers similar to those given to the police in England and Wales, the Royal Ulster Constabulary (and soldiers on duty) have special powers under the Northern Ireland (Emergency Provisions) Act 1973. However these special powers should not be used in ordinary criminal matters.

Powers to stop and question. It is a crime for someone to refuse or fail to answer to the best of their knowledge questions about their identity and movements, anything they know about recent explosions, any incident endangering life or any person killed in an incident or explosion.

Powers to detain at the police station. People arrested as suspected terrorists may be detained for up to 72 hours; they must also submit to being photographed and having palm and fingerprints taken, even before being charged.

Those arrested for any other reason (except under the Prevention of Terrorism Act) must be charged with a criminal offence and brought before a magistrate within 48 hours, or released. The police do not have the right to photograph or fingerprint without consent before charging.

Obligations. In cases where people are detained other than under the Prevention of Terrorism Act and the Emergency Provisions Act, suspects in Northern Ireland have the same rights under the Judges' Rules as in England and Wales. 'Terrorist' suspects are entitled to have access to a solicitor in a police station after the first 48 hours' detention and subsequently at 48-hour intervals.

Prisons

This section deals mostly with prison issues affecting homosexual paedophiles because they are the most likely to be imprisoned if convicted of a sexual offence. The law relating to paedophilia is explained in chapter 4. Homosexual men are of course among the general prison population sentenced for non-sexual offences. This section does not attempt to cover this group but discusses only particular issues relating to men imprisoned for homosexual sexual offences. General questions concerning, for example, categorisation, conditions on remand and after conviction, access to lawyers and disciplinary procedures that could affect gays imprisoned for offences unconnected with sexual orientation have been dealt with in other books.[27] The following points are concerned with prison life after conviction.

Allocation to prisons and accommodation

Every prisoner goes to a closed local prison on conviction to be assessed for security category and allocation to a prison. The factors that influence which prison this is and whether he will later be sent elsewhere are: length of sentence, previous criminal record (if any), security rating, the nature of the offence, work skills, whether married and if so how stable the marriage is.

The Prison Department divides all sentences broadly into three categories: short term (up to 18 months), medium term (18 months to four years) and long term (over four years). Each region has one or two prisons for long term prisoners. While long term prisoners will almost certainly be transferred from the prison they are first sent to on conviction, this is less certain for short and medium term prisoners. Prisoners are more likely to be transferred after assessment to a closed training prison if they have some sort of trade or skill and/or are married and are first timers. In addition, those who have a low security rating may be transferred eventually to an open prison.

Sex offenders and those with records of violence are very rarely allocated to an open prison at any time during their sentence. The reason given by the Home Office for this is that since homosexual offenders are subject to ridicule from other inmates, they would be at risk in an open prison where there are fewer staff to provide protection.

Under Prison Rule 43,[28] a prisoner can apply to the governor to remain in his cell for self-protection. Most paedophile offenders have this imposed on them from the outset because of inmate hostility. Usually this means being locked in the cell for 23 hours out of 24. Such prisoners usually get their food last; access to the prison library is restricted and visits are supervised by warders.

Each region in England now has one prison with a special accommodation section for Rule 43 prisoners. In these units prisoners can work in limited association with similar inmates. Prison Department publications suggest that there is a waiting list for transfer to these centres so it is very unlikely that anyone newly convicted could expect immediate allocation there.

Visits, correspondence, reading material

Keeping in touch with the outside world can be difficult for an isolated gay prisoner. Inmates may correspond[29] with people they did not know before being imprisoned and with organisations (such as Friend and CHE). All correspondence is censored, which inhibits any intimacy in letters. Records are kept of visits and correspondents. All convicted prisoners are allowed one visit a month under the Prison Rules. Many prisons allow visits more frequently than this – usually increasing them to once a fortnight – but this never becomes an official entitlement. The Rules also permit two letters to be sent every week.

Governors have complete discretion to refuse any literature sent in. In prisons where there is dormitory accommodation, governors have used the excuse that others might be offended to justify refusing *Gay News* and Jeffrey Weeks' book *Coming Out*.

Surviving

For most prisoners, the importance of having a friend inside and of not losing touch with the outside world are vital. The fact is that there is often solidarity between some prisoners and low grade staff against the governors and certain other inmates e.g. sex offenders. Gay and paedophile prisoners are abused and have been assaulted.

In 1980 the Criminal Injuries Compensation Board apparently made its first award to a paedophile inmate attacked in prison. Vincent Johanssen was viciously assaulted shortly before he was due to be released. His eyes were very badly hurt. Normally the Board will not make awards to prisoners because one of the factors they take into account is the good character of the applicant. In this case a substantial award was in fact made, which was reduced by one third, presumably because Vincent Johanssen was a prisoner at the time.

Medical treatment

Because of the secrecy that surrounds the whole prison system it is often many years before the general public hears of new developments. Long prison sentences handed down by the courts and a comparatively high rate of second and subsequent convictions have encouraged some doctors in the prison medical service to develop courses of hormone treatment for paedophile prisoners. This type of medical treatment – by implantation and administration of drugs – has been going on since at least 1961. The object is to remove all sexual desire – not just in relation to boys. In this sexless state, a 'liberated' inmate may feel he has a better chance of being released on parole. This treatment, which has unpleasant physical and psychological side effects, is still in an experimental stage.

Courts may make Hospital Orders when sentencing a convicted offender.[30] Such orders are potentially without any time limit and some paedophile offenders are likely to remain in a secure hospital for a great deal longer than they would have stayed in an ordinary prison.

In deciding to make such an order, the judge must be satisfied that there is sufficient medical and general evidence; a patient cannot later be transferred to prison if it turns out to have been a mistake. In particular, evidence must be obtained from two doctors, one of whom must be a specialist, that the person is suffering from 'mental illness, psychopathic disorder, subnormality or severe subnormality' and that the disorder is 'of a nature or degree which warrants the patient's detention in hospital for medical treatment'.

As to general evidence, the court must be of the opinion, bearing in mind such things as the nature of the conviction, the character and previous criminal record of the person and other available sentencing options, that the most suitable sentence is a Hospital Order. Thus, men who have had previous convictions for paedophile offences are likely candidates for Hospital Orders.

The Home Secretary has power to direct the transfer from prison to a secure hospital of sentenced prisoners who are 'suffering from mental illness, psychopathic disorder, subnormality or severe subnormality'.[31]

In 1972, Ben Wilson was sentenced to life imprisonment for indecent assault and buggery with boys. It was his fifth conviction. He had previously received prison sentences of four, five and six years. The judge passed the maximum sentence of life imprisonment on the grounds that he would receive treatment and in fact might be released sooner than if sent to prison for a definite term of years. There arose a stark contradiction between sentencing policy and the attitudes of the prison medical service who are wary of prescribing hormone therapy to prisoners who may only want it in order to get out of prison more quickly. Since starting his sentence, Ben Wilson has received three hormone implants resulting in the development of breasts, which have been surgically removed. Despite the judge's clear intention, he has served far longer than he would have done on a definite prison term. In addition, it appears that hormone implants are not likely to be effective and may have seriously endangered his health.

It has been reported that London prisons have only now abandoned the use of implanted female hormones in the treatment of sex offenders because of side-effects and because 'they are not 100 per cent effective'.[32]

Chapter Three
Young gays

'Now I feel "Thank God I'm Gay". The only thing that makes me depressed sometimes is other people's attitudes to homosexuality.'
Martin, aged 17, from *I Know What I Am* Joint Council for Gay Teenagers.[1]

Teenagers who realise that they are gay have a particularly difficult time coming out, at least to themselves, often with virtually no support from parents, relations, friends or others at school or work. The law in itself is usually not the major worry. Parental control and other people's hostile reactions are greater problems.

This chapter is mainly about young gay men. In relation to them the law often simply buttresses negative attitudes and behaviour. The result is that teenage boys may be inhibited about being open about their sexual orientation; their lovers, particularly if they are older, are quickly labelled by others as criminal molesters. In addition there is a massive amount of heterosexual propaganda aimed at young people – in advertising, entertainment, the media, the church, schools and so on. On the one hand this encourages anti-homosexual behaviour, while on the other hand it contributes to undermining the self-respect of gay teenagers.

Parents of young gays are armed with legal sactions that other teenagers do not experience. Even though the police may not eventually prosecute they will often investigate when a complaint has been made by parents. This may be coupled with pressures to seek psychiatric advice or even get married to 'cure' homosexuality. Even though prosecutions are not frequent, this does not mean that the police do not give young gays a hard time. The police do detain young people simply to question them about their sex lives.

For example, Richard, aged 19, left home to work in London. After a while he met Mike, aged 23. They began a relationship and eventually lived together. When Richard told his parents, they did everything they could to persuade their son to leave Mike. Sometime later, Richard was telephoned by a police inspector and was asked to come to the station. He was told by the officer that he had talked to Richard's parents, but now wanted to hear his story. His mother had thought Richard might be taking drugs as well as 'indulging in homosexuality'. After brief questioning about drug-taking and his relationship, the inspector left the room in order to 'take further advice'. On his return he asked Richard if he would consent to a physical examination. The officer said that he was concerned that if Richard was having sex and was a 'passive' partner he would also be guilty. Richard refused to have the examination and denied he was having sex. The officer then said that since Richard was saying he was not committing any offence and would not have a physical examination there was no evidence one way or the other to suggest an offence had been committed. Having gone through this form, Richard was then taken to see his parents who were waiting in the police station. His parents told him that they had informed the police only because 'we love you'.

A particularly disturbing example of police treatment occurred at the beginning of 1980 when a number of young gay men were arrested in Huddersfield. Take the case of one of those men aged 19. He was arrested at work one morning at about 11 o'clock. Three officers then took him home, removed bed linen, lubricants, diary and address book and then drove him to the police station for questioning. He was not released until 2 p.m. the following day having been held for about 27 hours. During this period he was questioned about all his sexual relationships. He alleged that the police tried to get him to say that he had had sex with people he had not. He was told to strip. Swabs were taken from his anus and penis, a blood sample was taken, a tuft of his pubic hair was clipped and he was given a rectal examination by a police doctor.

Most gay men do not have this kind of experience, but because of the unrealistically high minimum age for lawful homosexual relationships, the police are encouraged to conduct these kind of investigations. For those men it does happen to, the experience is appalling. How do men subjected to such treatment feel about themselves, their place in society, their homosexuality? The irony is that this law, that supposedly protects the young and vulnerable, is the very instrument of their degradation.

The main issue is not that large numbers of young gays are actually hauled through the courts, but that there is a belief that there is a risk of enforcement and a police duty to inquire. The law does not produce vast conviction rates; it simply increases the stress and worry for young people who realise that they are gay. It adversely affects self-image and self-respect.

The law

Oppression by the law is often overlooked in discussions about sex among young people. Youths are presented as victims, falling prey to corruption. This is a false picture. 'It is a saddening and disturbing experience for judges to find, as many have, that the wicked seducer was an adolescent boy,' commented Lord Justice Lawton in *R* v *Willis* (1975).[2]

To change attitudes towards young homosexuals and their own view of themselves, requires changes in the law and educational curricula to which there is considerable resistance. At best changes are suggested on the grounds that if charges cannot be brought against them for committing an offence adolescents will more readily seek advice to change their condition. In this way the law gives the lead to educational authorities, teachers and teachers' unions to deny young gays their right to self-expression under the guise of protecting them.

In *England and Wales* the Sexual Offences Act 1967 provides that 'homosexual acts' between two consenting men in private are criminal offences if one of the partners is below the age of 21. This means that any young man under 21 who wants a homosexual relationship, himself commits a criminal offence, as well as his lover. The police can prosecute independently in most cases involving adults accused of homosexual offences. However in cases involving someone under 21, the police must obtain authorisation from the Director of Public Prosecutions. Court cases arising out of the relationships of young gay men are comparatively unusual.

The law presumes that boys are incapable of penetrative sexual intercourse until they are 14.[3] Theoretically this means that boys aged over 14 can commit the offence of buggery. There is no technical reason however why a boy under 14 but older than 10 years could not be guilty of an act of indecent assault or gross indecency.

'Indecent assault' relates to sexual activity with anyone below the age of 16 (who by law cannot give consent)[4] or anyone above that age who does not give consent. The fact that someone below 16 actually wanted to have sex does not prevent the activity from being an 'assault' on that person. Kissing and mutual fondling would be sufficient to found a charge of indecent assault. Usually to constitute an 'indecent assault' the other person's action must be overtly sexual, generally a positive physical act involving touching, or a threat to touch.

If an older person asks, for example, to be touched on his penis and the younger person does so, the older person may be guilty of gross indecency. Additionally, 'an act of gross indecency with or towards a child under 14 or encouraging a child under that age to do such an act with him' is a special offence under the Indecency with Children Act 1960. The maximum punishment is two years' imprisonment.

The police can stop anyone under the age of 17 in the streets and detain that person at a police station if they think a young person is 'exposed to moral danger'.[5] Either the local authority social services department or the police can later apply to a court to keep a young person in a 'place of safety' (e.g. a community home) for up to 28 days. In very serious cases, the local authority may apply to have a young person taken into care. (See page 11 above and pages 128-129 below.)

In *Scotland*, the provisions of the Criminal Justice (Scotland) Act 1980 are similar to those of the Sexual Offences Act 1967. The major difference is that Scottish law provides for the defence of mistake as to age, but only if the defendant is himself below the age of 24, had no previous charges for similar offences and reasonably believed the person was 21 or older. Under the age of 21, 'gross indecency' between men remains an offence under the Sexual Offences (Scotland) Act 1976 section 7. It is a crime at common law to 'indulge in indecent practices' towards children under the age of 14 ('lewd, indecent and libidinous practices and behaviour') with or without their consent. This could include performing sexual acts in the presence of a child. The police cannot independently prosecute: this must be done by the Procurator Fiscal's Department.

In *Northern Ireland*, the provisions of the Homosexual Offences (Northern Ireland) Order 1982 are the same as those of the Sexual Offences Act 1967. Unlike Scottish law, there is no defence of mistake about a partner's age. Police prosecutions involving men under 21 would be referred to the Director of Public Prosecutions in Belfast for further action.

Prosecution policy

In *England and Wales* without the permission of the Director of Public Prosecutions (DPP) no prosecution can proceed in any case where one or both of the accused men are under 21.[6] In his evidence to the Royal Commission on Criminal Procedure, the DPP said with regard to sexual offences:

> 'My decisions are often strongly influenced by the relative ages of the offender and the 'victim'. If there is no element of corruption by the former and the latter was a fully consenting party . . . I do not normally prosecute a man of 22 for a homosexual offence against a man of 19 although if, for instance, the elder went into a public toilet intent on finding a partner and the younger was or might become a male prostitute, I would probably decide to prosecute both.'[7]

The DPP is not, of course, bound by his own guidelines. So any men under 21 and their partners cannot be certain about the legal consequences of their relationship.

Even in those cases in which the DPP decides not to press charges, his decision can take a long time. For the people accused, there are anxious months of worry and uncertainty, sometimes with serious consequences. Although decided before the present DPP came into office, a case handled by the National Council for Civil Liberties in 1971 illustrates the point. A man aged 20 was living with a 28-year-old man when they were both arrested. The DPP took ten months to make a decision. The 28-year-old man was an epileptic whose condition had improved over the previous years, but his fits became so much worse during the period of waiting that he was unable to continue working. Eventually, the DPP said that he would not prosecute and agreed that the two men could continue to live together provided they both signed an undertaking not to have sex for the couple of months that remained before the younger partner's 21st birthday. As Gay Activists' Alliance said in their report to the Royal Commission on Criminal Procedure:

> 'Masquerading as magnanimous liberalism, the discretionary power operates in such a way that anxiety and stress is caused for the accused people, punishing them without trial in the very process of absolving them from prosecution . . . the DPP's discretion allows the state both to keep the criminal law as it is and to pretend that it is not there. In the present system, the undesirable procedure is necessary to support and to implement an unjust and discriminatory law.'[8]

In *Scotland* prosecutions are brought, not by the police but by a separate government agency called the Procurator Fiscal's Department. This is under the direction of the Chief Scottish Law Officer, the Lord Advocate. Prior to the Criminal Justice (Scotland) Act 1980, the Lord Advocates for some years had a policy of not prosecuting cases of homosexual sex between consenting adults in private, even though these were criminal; though because of the requirement of third party corroboration (see page 172 below) convictions were not particularly easy to obtain. Since the 1980 Act no statement has been made with regard to prosecution policy for young men under 21.

In *Northern Ireland*, prior to the decision of the European Court of Human Rights in the *Dudgeon* case, the Attorney General in London and the Director of Public Prosecutions in Belfast had specifically reserved the right to bring prosecutions in any circumstances. In 1979, the Attorney General's Office stated:

'Prosecution policy is the responsibility of the Attorney General. In view of the Secretary of State's announcement on 2 July [1979] that for the present the government proposes to take no further action in relation to the draft Homosexual Offences Order, it will be for the Attorney General and the Director of Public Prosecutions for Northern Ireland to consider each case on its merits as and when it arises'.

As Lord Gifford observed in the *Dudgeon* case when addressing the European Court of Human Rights in April 1981:

' . . . this is in no way a policy not to prosecute in any particular case. It leaves with the prosecuting authority a completely open discretion. It lays down no guidelines as to what will or what will not be the subject of prosecution, and it leaves the applicant in a position which the Court must find quite unacceptable in that he must consider what relations of a personal nature he might be permitted to make on the basis of whether officers of the state feel that they have merits or that they do not have merits. It is one of the worst examples, perhaps, of the arbitrariness that can result when a law is sometimes enforced and sometimes not enforced and left to a general discretion.'[9]

The European Court accepted this argument and ruled that total prohibition of male homosexual relations in private was a breach of the European Convention of Human Rights.

During the period 1972 to 1980 there were 62 recorded prosecutions for homosexual offences in Northern Ireland. Most of these concerned men who had sex with someone below the age of 18.

However in June 1976, two men were tried in Coleraine for 'gross indecency' on the basis of homosexual sex occurring in the home of one of them. One man aged 20 was sentenced to one year's probation coupled with an order to receive psychiatric treatment. His lover, aged 24, was sentenced to a suspended sentence of six months' imprisonment. The judge said that he was sure that both deserved to go to prison: 'the penalty for this sort of offence used to be death,' he is reported to have commented.[10] Following the enactment of the Homosexual Offences (Northern Ireland) Order 1982, the DPP retains control of proceedings in cases involving men under the age of 21.

The myth of youth seduction

It is often argued that the different legal treatment of gay teenage boys on the one hand (who cannot have sex lawfully until well out of their teens) and heterosexual teenage boys and women on the other (who may have sex lawfully at 16 in England, Wales and Scotland or 17 in Northern Ireland) does not conflict with the principle that everyone should be equal before the law. This is because, it is claimed, male homosexuality shows specific characteristics that justify 'special treatment' in the criminal law. Simply, there is a higher 'social danger' from male homosexuals.

> 'Many young people aged 16 are still at school or have just
> started work, some of the latter are lodging in all-male hostels
> in their town of work. They are all to some extent at risk of
> seduction by homosexuals, especially those in authority over
> them. Some boys may be confused about their sexuality and a
> boy who is so confused is particularly open to exploitation.
> The majority of us do not think that it is a sufficient answer
> to say that a 16-year-old boy is strong enough to repulse any
> unwanted homosexual advances; the fact that the boy con-
> sents to homosexual advances does not mean that he is
> unlikely to be harmed'.
>
> Policy Advisory Committee on Sexual Offences.[11]

Central to these arguments is the idea of the 'seduction of juve-niles by male homosexuals', that is, the old assumption that the origins of homosexuality must be attributed, either generally or in specific cases, to seduction during childhood or adolescence by adult homosexuals. Based on this assumption, the argument is taken cautiously further by some (such as the Policy Advisory Committee) that early homosexual experiences can lead to undesirable 'crises of maturation', and that these crises should be prevented by all legal and social means. The Policy Advisory Committee which reported in 1979 commissioned no research and ignored the most authoritative body to give evidence on the crucial issues. The Royal College of Psychiatrists stated that there was no substantial objection to an equal age of consent of 16 for both heterosexual and homosexual sexual relations.

A more rigorous approach has been taken in some other European countries. In Holland the Speijer Committee (1969) took evidence from, amongst others, all Dutch professors of psychiatric disciplines, psychopathology and social medicine. The Committee also heard oral evidence and consulted a lengthy bibliography. None of this has ever been done in Britain. The overwhelming evidence from the Dutch professors was to the effect that from the age of 16 (i.e. the heterosexual age of consent) no young person needs protection by law from homosexual activity. In Switzerland, the Shulz Committee (1981), also including psychiatrists and professors of medicine, as well as a large number of lawyers, reached the same conclusion but went further and proposed an age of consent of 14 for both heterosexual and homosexual relations. In the 1970s these two bodies, and their counterparts in Sweden and Denmark, adopted a more thorough approach to the available expert evidence than has ever been done in the United Kingdom.

In West Germany, a non-governmental study of nearly eight hundred homosexual men was conducted by Reiche and Dannecker of Frankfurt University between 1970 and 1974. It remains the most comprehensive work ever undertaken in Europe. It repudiates the theory of adolescent seduction into homosexuality. Again no similar large-scale study has been undertaken in Britain.

The argument however, is not for more research to be conducted in this country.[12] Gays in Britain are not innately different from gays in Europe. The demand should be for the existing work to become more widely understood in schools and among the general public at large. To this end, I think it is worth quoting Dr Martin Dannecker's own summary of the propositions derived from his research which show that there is no evidence to support the so-called seduction theory.[13]

'... there is no such thing as seduction into homosexuality. Nobody becomes a homosexual through homosexual experiences during youth ...

Even in those cases where homosexual contact is established between a juvenile and an older homosexual, this does not lead to homosexual fixation. This is, among other things, impossible, as homosexuality represents a psychological disposition acquired in early childhood. This disposition forces such individuals for internal reasons to behave as homosexuals. This disposition first becomes evident with changes during puberty in the organisation of sexuality. It means that these individuals sense in themselves the desire for homosexual contacts, or to put it more generally, are attracted sexually towards men. This desire grows more and more conscious as development proceeds. However, realisation of such desire is often difficult, not because the individuals are in any way uncertain about their homosexuality, but because social discrimination and the anxiety caused by it make the manifestation of a homosexual disposition more difficult. However, social discrimination cannot do any more than postpone the realisation of homosexual desires.

This is well evidenced empirically. Often young homosexuals try to negate their homosexual desires, and take up heterosexual contacts, or else live in abstinence, except for masturbation. This, however, is possible only for a short time, and sooner or later their homosexuality will break through. This process has to be imagined as an autonomous one; there is no need of a seducer, and certainly not of a male homosexual one. The development of homosexuality during puberty, adolescence or later of an individual with a homosexual disposition proceeds in a way analogous to the development of heterosexuality, except for the consequences of social discrimination. One's sexual practice starts at a point of time that is determined individually.

. . . the research of American sexologist Dr Alfred Kinsey in the late 1940s had shown that almost 40 per cent of the total American male population have 'at least some homosexual experiences up to orgasm, between puberty and old age'. The overwhelming majority of these homosexual experiences occurred during puberty and adolescence. Nevertheless, according to Kinsey's data, only 4 per cent of the total American population were exclusively homosexual. These results showed beyond doubt that early homosexual experiences are in no way likely to seduce anybody into homosexuality if the necessary psychological preconditions are lacking. And even

where these contacts do take place with a juvenile of a homosexual disposition, they do not lead to homosexual fixation,
but only release the fixation that has existed from early childhood.

A further nonsensical part of the seduction theory must be
mentioned. It imagines on one side an adult, self-confident
homosexual (the seducer), and on the other side a juvenile
(the seduced). This assumption is wrong. In our empirical
study of 789 homosexuals (*The Ordinary Homosexual* 1974),
we could show that about 30 per cent of these subjects had
their first homosexual experience before the age of 18, and
that they involved a partner who himself was not older than
18 years. Only 34 per cent of our subjects had their first
homosexual experience before the age of 18 with a partner
who was aged 18 or older. Apart from the fact that there is no
such thing as seduction into homosexuality, it is also clear
that another common supposition is wrong; the supposition
that normally the first homosexual experience would take
place between an older man, supposed to be homosexual, and
a juvenile. Rather, the facts are that especially when the first
homosexual contacts are made at a relatively young age, the
partners are in the majority of cases approximately the same
age. The experiences are gathered in the context of homosexual experience during puberty which also apply to a large
number of heterosexual men. The initial thesis that the
genesis of homosexuality can be attributed to seduction by
homosexual adults is, therefore, empirically wrong. Moreover,
the thesis is nonsensical as, given that there *was* such a thing
as seduction into homosexuality, it would be impossible to
identify homosexuals, as they would not show any specific
characteristics. Whether somebody is homosexual depends on
whether he experiences homosexual contacts as satisfying, and
this, in turn, depends on whether he is of a homosexual disposition. Under these conditions, of course, all homosexual
contacts are experienced as satisfying, whether they involve an
adult homosexual or a peer who may not even be homosexual.

A further point interpreted as pertaining to the 'social
danger' of male homosexuality was that of male homosexuals'
promiscuity. Indeed, it can be said that sexual promiscuity
among homosexual men exceeds that among homosexual
women. 'Social danger' however, cannot be taken to follow
from this fact, as this promiscuity has its place within the

homosexual category itself, i.e. homosexual men change their partners more frequently than homosexual women do. But naturally, homosexuality is not propagated through this, and nobody is endangered by it. As nobody can be seduced into homosexuality, promiscuity among homosexual men does not pose a threat to juveniles.'

Working with young gays

'The problem is as much how to deal with the attitudes and behaviour of heterosexual people, young and old, towards homosexuality as it is how to deal with young gay people themselves. The law at present operates as an obstacle in the way of tackling this situation. On one side of the coin schools, youth services and so on feel inhibited in dealing openly and helpfully with homosexuality in their curricula and programmes; while on the other side young gay people who need positive acceptance of their personal identities if they are to fully realise their part in society, both in work and leisure, are denied any relevant sex education and suffer the ignorance of others, and agencies or individuals who would help them are constantly at risk.'

Joint Council for Gay Teenagers[14]

It is still only a fortunate minority of gay teenagers, who have contacted gay help services, who are able to grow up without first going through a long period of isolation and self-rejection. The situation is beginning to change, however, for those living in the larger cities, particularly London, where there is a growing number of organisations, groups and venues for younger people.

Because of the widespread prejudice about the seduction of gay adolescents youth organisers are frequently wary of working with young homosexuals (or others confused about their sexuality) for fear of their legal position. These fears may be quite specific – fear of being accused of some sort of sexual advance, procuring a sexual encounter, or aiding and abetting, or even the more general accusation of encouraging homosexuality among young people which the authorities may consider to be 'corrupting public morals'.[15] As a result youth agencies have at times found themselves subject to pressures from higher authorities when promoting discussion on the subject. Especially since the trial of members of the Paedophile Information Exchange (PIE) (see pages 85-86 below) fear of conspiracy charges has become a reason for refusing to deal with some problems specific to gays.

Such legal difficulties have arisen over a proposal to set up a hostel for gay teenagers. The project would have provided a supportive environment for those who had lost their accommodation and become homeless – as a result, for example, of declaring their sexuality. From the legal point of view the proposal was overloaded with uncertainties. The obstacles were so great that it seemed impossible to establish a reasonably humane regime for the hostel.

The law is also an important factor inhibiting schools from making radical innovations in sex education. The needs and emotions of gay and lesbian pupils are excluded. This silence is directly harmful since it reinforces not only any guilt or fears about discussing homosexuality but also the hostility and prejudices of pupils who identify as heterosexual. It is now recognised that girls and black students need positive images if they are to achieve their fullest potential in school; it is no different for gay students. At present the curriculum, like all other areas of school life, denies the existence of positive gay women and men.

For a gay or lesbian teacher silence must often be the norm because of fear of losing one's job on the one hand and the lack of support by teachers' unions in cases of discrimination on the other. Industrial tribunals often appear to accept assumptions made by some employers that gay employees have little to offer but the risk of sexual harassment of younger people. (See chapter 6 below.)

There is little doubt that much essential work is inhibited by the existence of the vague crime of conspiracy to corrupt public morals. In 1973, the House of Lords specifically identified the 'encouragement of homosexuality' as the sort of thing that 'reasonable' jurors should consider a 'corrupt practice'. It is possible that the jury of the 1980s (as compared with one of the early 1970s) is likely to be more apathetic about adult homosexuality; this is less likely to be the case with teenage homosexuality.

A prosecution of conspiracy to corrupt public morals is a political decision taken at the highest level. An expensive trial of this kind is meant to be a show trial to affirm the boundaries of public morals. In taking such a decision, any Director of Public Prosecutions would want to feel fairly certain that the tide of public opinion was running clearly against what the defendants were doing.

The leading case on conspiracy to corrupt public morals is *Knuller* v *Director of Public Prosecutions* (1973).[16] In the course of upholding the conviction of the publishers of an underground paper (*International Times*), which carried fairly explicit gay contact advertisements, Lord Reid said:

'I find nothing in the Act [the Sexual Offences Act 1967] to indicate that parliament thought or intended to lay down that indulgence in these practices is not corrupting. I read the Act as saying that even though it may be corrupting if people chose to corrupt themselves in this way that is their affair and the law will not interfere. But no licence is given to others to encourage the practice. It must be left to each jury to decide in the circumstances of each case whether people were likely to be corrupted. In this case the jury were properly directed and it is impossible to say that they reached a wrong conclusion'.

During this period, marking a formal state reaction to certain fringe elements in the youth liberation movement, the same charge was brought against the publishers of another underground paper *Oz*. In *R* v *Anderson*[17] the editors of the paper published a special 'School Kids' issue aimed at and written by teenagers. Prosecuting counsel greatly emphasised that the cover had girls in 'lesbian poses', that there were cartoons and articles on explicit heterosexual sex, one advocating 'fucking in the streets', and that there were gay and other personal advertisements. The jury found the editor and two others guilty of publishing obscene articles and of sending such articles through the post, but acquitted them of the charge of conspiring to corrupt public morals. Nevertheless, the verdict was seen as victory for moral order. The *Daily Telegraph* commented:

'It is particularly disturbing when these people turn their attention towards young children. Innocence is a great protector. They go out to break it and remove the protection. Most children are unaware of sadism and homosexuality until they are told. Telling them lurid details must risk corrupting them.'[18]

The point remains that although such a charge might never be used against gay help services, it remains (like the 1967 Act itself) as an excuse for others to put a brake on the activities and proposals of more radical elements in the gay movement.

It is worth noting that the English Law Commission, in their report on conspiracy and criminal law reform, felt that the offence of conspiracy to corrupt public morals was particularly undesirable because it was so uncertain. The Commission recommended that the courts should no longer be the 'residual guardians of public morality' and that this offence should be abolished.[19] Instead specific 'immoral and anti-social' conduct should be prohibited by specific legislation. This recommendation has yet to be implemented.

If it is accepted that there is a need for a minimum age for lawful sexual relationships, then this age should not discriminate between men and women, heterosexuals and homosexuals. The reasons seriously put forward for discrimination are based on demonstrably erroneous views or prejudices. Pseudo-democratic arguments that legislation must not outstrip the development of public opinion on this issue are sometimes posed. These arguments are unconvincing since they are very frequently ignored when it suits those who use them.

Chapter Four
Paedophilia

'Judges and magistrates, who often share with common criminals an extreme dislike of child molestation, seem to fear that it may do lasting harm to the victim, perhaps by imbuing a girl with an aversion to men, or a boy with an unhealthy liking for them.'

Professor Glanville Williams[1]

Paedophilia is the term used to describe sexual love of children and is used to refer to adults who are sexually aroused by pre-pubertal boys or girls. The term has become more widely used following the publicity attracted by the campaigning activities of the Paedophile Information Exchange (PIE) in the late 1970s.

Paedophilia is perhaps the most threatening of the sexual categories[2] and the law is used relentlessly against paedophiles. Some of the principles developed in cases involving men and boys have been used more generally in cases concerning male homosexuality. This chapter considers the legal implications of man/boy love. Heterosexual paedophilia is not within the scope of this book even though most paedophile convictions concern cases of female children. In England and Wales about 75 per cent of men convicted of sexual offences with children under ten years old are heterosexual.[3] Like most criminal statistics, it is likely that this figure may be understated since a great many cases never come to light, even when other members of the family and social workers know about the relationship.

The overwhelming majority of self-identified paedophiles are men. This may be because the expression of sensual feelings towards children by women receives social approval as a necessary part of child-rearing. And for women this may provide sufficient fulfilment of their feelings towards children. On the other hand, women do identify a distinction between motherly love and sexual feelings and this should not be diminished. Many feminists regard paedophilia, certainly heterosexual paedophilia, as a dubious exercise of power by the strong over the weak. Although all adults have economic, physical and psychological power over children and young people, it is argued that this is one of the ways men choose to use and abuse this power.

Men who have found that their sexual desire is exclusively confined to children have to endure long periods of abstinence to avoid breaking the criminal law and long-term imprisonment. Men convicted of sexual attacks on children or consenting sexual relations with children are punished very severely in the United Kingdom, particularly if the partner is a girl under 12 or a boy under 14. If certified mentally unfit, paedophiles may be detained in a prison mental hospital for an unspecified number of years and may be given medical treatment to divert or eliminate all sexual drive. (See pages 60-61 above.)

The severity of sentences given to homosexual paedophiles is justified by seeing the crime of paedophilia as the 'corruption' of boys. This argument is rarely used in cases involving girls. Studies have failed to find any evidence (see page 69 above) that casual homosexual contacts with adults are liable to cause homosexual orientation in later years. Yet a senior English Appeal Court judge, Lord Justice Lawton, has said:

> 'One of the difficulties which judges have in sentencing
> offenders of this type is their own reactions of revulsion to
> what the accused has been proved to have done. Right-thinking
> members of the public have the same reactions and expect the
> judges in their sentences to reflect public abhorrence of the
> graver kinds of criminal homosexual acts. There is a widely
> held opinion that homosexual offences involving boys lead to
> the corruption of the boys and cause them severe emotional
> damage. Judges of experience are often of this opinion
> because when considering homosexual offences they are fre-
> quently told in pleas of mitigation that the accused was made
> an homosexual as a result of being involved when a boy in
> homosexual acts by a man.'[4]

The word 'corrupt' is used because it is not generally recognised that a boy could ever spontaneously want to have a sexual experience and therefore have taken the initiative. This popular idea of 'corruption' sees such a relationship as entirely devised for the pleasure of an adult. Boys are thought not to have sexual and emotional feelings. In one study, two-thirds of the children had been sufficiently willing partners to co-operate in sexual experiences more than once with more than one man. Children who have participated in sex have frequently persuaded their friends to do likewise.[5]

Even when it is recognised that a boy is not 'corrupted' by

homosexual experience it is argued that he will be caused psychological or emotional damage. It is certainly credible that boys can suffer mental disturbance from a man's advances especially if they have already been inoculated with a horror of sex by their parents. An hysterical parental reaction is very likely to cause severe distress, as are the effects of criminal proceedings, giving evidence in court and the turmoil of having someone who is perhaps a loved one sent to prison.

Sentencing and judicial policy

There is a great difference in the maximum sentences that can be passed by the courts on heterosexual and homosexual paedophile offenders. The maximum sentence for anal intercourse (buggery) with a boy under 16 is life imprisonment whereas for unlawful sexual intercourse with a girl aged between 13 and 16 it is two years. (Life sentences can be imposed on heterosexual men only in cases involving rape and sex with girls under the age of 13.) The maximum sentence for indecent assault of a boy is ten years whereas for indecent assault of a girl under 13 it is five years and for assult on an older woman, two years.[6] These differences partly reflect an assumption that girls are less likely to be harmed by heterosexual experience, because it is 'natural', than boys by homosexual experience.

Home Office research[7] shows that these distinctions are carried on in the actual sentencing practice of the courts. Offences with boys are generally more likely to result in imprisonment than offences involving girls.

In cases of buggery between men and boys, the research showed that 90 per cent of the men convicted of the full offence with a boy under 14 were imprisoned. Just over 50 per cent of the men convicted of offences with 14- and 15-year-old boys (most of whom consented) were imprisoned.

Convictions involving penetrative intercourse by heterosexual men ranged over four categories: unlawful sexual intercourse with a girl (USI), rape, buggery and incest. Under 50 per cent of the men convicted of USI with 12-year-old girls were imprisoned, as against 75 per cent of those involved with girls under 12. Convicted men aged 17 to 24 often avoided imprisonment, regardless of the girl's age. Only 20 per cent of those convicted of USI with 13 to 15-year-old girls were imprisoned. Just over 25 per cent of women raped (whose cases were brought to court) were aged 10 to 15. Overall, 91 per cent of rapists were sent to prison. Six of the 22 men convicted of heterosexual buggery were imprisoned. Approximately half of the cases involved girls under 16. Incest by a father with a daughter under 13 was dealt with severely: 88 per cent of such offenders were gaoled.

For convictions not involving penetrative intercourse, i.e. indecent assault, one in five of the men convicted of the offence with boys was imprisoned. Prison sentences were rarely imposed on men convicted of indecent assault on girls – in only about one in eight cases.

The research also showed that in these cases of indecent assault about 20 per cent of the boys aged 10 to 13 had in fact consented to sex as had about 40 per cent of the boys aged 14 to 16. By comparison, about 20 per cent of the girls aged 10 to 12 had in fact consented as had about 33 per cent of the girls aged 13 to 15.

An explanation of sentencing practice relating to homosexual cases was provided by the English Court of Appeal in *R* v *Willis* (1975).[8] In this case, Lord Justice Lawton set out guidelines for the courts to use when deciding for how long to imprison a man convicted of a sexual offence with a boy. Much the same approach was said to be appropriate in cases of buggery as well as indecent assault. The court said that sentences should reflect the seriousness of the act constituting the indecent assault since the assault might amount only to touching or, on the other hand, might 'take the form of a revolting act of fellatio, which is as bad as buggery, or may be more so'. In general terms, the court thought that gaol terms of between three and five years were appropriate. Sentences could vary depending on whether there were aggravating or mitigating circumstances.

The four categories of 'aggravating' circumstances were: 'physical injury to the boy'; 'emotional and psychological damage'; 'moral corruption'; 'abuse of authority or trust'. It was said that the offender who uses violence should be discouraged from repetition by severe prison sentences. The court cautioned against assuming that emotional and psychological damage would be caused to a boy who had anal intercourse, or that anal intercourse in youth causes homosexuality to develop in later life. 'These are possible results depending on the make up of the boy rather than the physical act itself.' Although the court correctly stated that such a physical act does not cause homosexuality, it seemed to imply that it might be an aggravating factor if following his sexual experience a boy came to realise that he had a homosexual disposition. The court explicitly suggested that there is a link between moral corruption and homosexuality. 'Although the act of buggery itself probably does not predispose a boy towards homosexuality that which leads up to the act may do so as, for example, by gifts of money and clothes and the provision of attractive outings and material comforts.' Inevitably this will lead the courts to take the most jaundiced view of even innocent gifts made with genuine affection. The court warned that 'those who have boys in their charge must not abuse their position for the sake of gratifying their deviant sexual urges. If they do so, they must expect to get severe sentences.'

To be weighed against these factors were three kinds of mitigating circumstances: 'mental imbalance', 'personality disorder' and 'emotional stress'. With regard to 'mental imbalance', the Court of Appeal stated that judges should proceed from the assumption that the sexual act in question is simply a criminal one and not a symptom of a disease unless a specific mental or physical illness, such as senile dementia, is established by medical evidence. Turning to 'personality disorder', it was stated that the types of disorder may vary:

> 'At the one end of the scale there is the mentally immature adult who is in the transitional stage of psycho-sexual development; he can be helped to grow up mentally. At the other end are those severely damaged personalities such as the obviously effeminate and flauntingly exhibitionist types. Probably nothing can be done for these individuals – but their pitiable condition calls for understanding and mercy . . . At present little can be done by either doctors or welfare workers for most of them; they require management rather than treatment. If they cannot be managed, either because they do not want to be or are mentally incapable of accepting management, they may become a danger to boys at large in society. In such cases the public are entitled to expect the courts to keep this class of offender away from boys, in really bad cases for indefinite periods.'

With regard to the third mitigating factor, the court had in mind 'latent homosexuals' who have 'controlled their urges for years' and given way under stress resulting, for example, from a bereavement, or who have been seduced by an adolescent.

This ruling by the Court of Appeal appears at first to reject the idea that homosexuality is a disease, but then proceeds to represent homosexuality precisely so. The anti-psychiatric argument – 'at present little can be done either by doctors or welfare workers' – is deployed in favour of imprisonment, and because it is said 'they do not want to be or are mentally incapable of accepting management' the court claims that sentences given to paedophiles can be considered as merciful, taking into account personality disorder and emotional stress.

D.A. Thomas in *Principles of Sentencing*[9] found that in cases of buggery the trend of English Appeal Court judgments was to confirm prison sentences of up to ten years, but usually not more than seven years, where there were such aggravating factors as force or coercion, systematic seduction over a period of time, abuse of parental or other authority or extreme youth of the boy (in one instance 8 years old). Sentences of over three years for indecent assault were usually upheld only when there were aggravating circumstances such as 'corruption' of previously inexperienced children, inherently grave assaults 'such as masturbation', involvement of a large number of children, or where the offender had a substantial record of previous convictions. According to Thomas, so-called 'individualised measures' for men convicted of buggery were limited to people of proven mental disturbance or abnormality. Sentences ranged enormously from psychiatric probation orders, simple probation orders and hospital orders to life imprisonment. Similar sentences involving psychiatric treatment were applied in cases of indecent assault, although 'preventive' prison sentences were upheld where there was a long history of indecent assaults of a serious nature.

Evidence of 'similar facts'

This rule of English criminal evidence has a special history in relation to homosexual sexual offences, and more so in relation to paedophile cases. The judiciary conveys a scarcely concealed contempt for homosexuality. Judges view obvious and straightforward attempts at sexual encounters and common sexual practices as extraordinary, sinister or bizarre. This attitude is used to permit the jury to hear about circumstances or incidents which usually would be excluded because, although they may be 'relevant' and corroborative, they are unfairly prejudicial, showing in effect that a defendant has a 'criminal disposition' and not that he has in fact committed the particular crime with which he is charged. Until 1974 homosexual offences were effectively placed in a special category, with the result that there was seen to be a sufficient connection between two homosexual sexual acts (or indeed indications of homosexuality) so as to make evidence of one act admissible on a charge relating to another.

The rule was first applied to a reported case involving allegations of homosexuality in *Thompson* v *DPP* (1918).[10] The defendant was charged with gross indecency with two boys. His case was that his identity had been mistaken. In order to refute this, the prosecution were permitted to show the jury the defendant's powder puff and some apparently indecent photographs. These were admitted in evidence since they corroborated the boy's story that the defendant belonged, according to Lord Sumner, to a class of criminals that had 'abnormal propensities' such that 'not only takes them out of the class of ordinary men gone wrong, but stamps them with the hallmark of a specialised and extraordinary class as much as if they carried on their bodies some physical peculiarity'.

In *R* v *Sims* (1946)[11] four otherwise unrelated sexual encounters with the defendant were tried together because:

'not one but four men who admittedly had gone to the prisoner's house to spend the evening on different occasions, all said exactly the same advances had been made to them by the prisoner, and that exactly the same acts had been committed on them, which tended to show that the association which the prisoner had with the men was a guilty not an innocent one'.

The House of Lords ruling in *Boardman* v *DPP* (1974)[12] marks a watershed in these cases. Here the head of a school had been accused of enticing adolescent pupils to have anal sex with him. The various boys' accounts were all held to be admissible because in each instance:

'the homosexual conduct alleged against the accused was of an unusual kind involving a request by an older man to an adolescent to take the active part. There were other resemblances in the conduct alleged against the accused in each instance. Both boys said they were aroused from their sleep in the school dormitory at about midnight, they were addressed in a low voice and the ultimate invitation to commit the offence was made in the master's sitting room in both cases'.

Lord Salmon set out the general test of whether evidence of 'similar facts' should be admitted:

'whether or not evidence is relevant and admissible against an accused is solely a question of law. The test must be: is the evidence capable of tending to persuade a reasonable jury of the accused's guilt on some grounds or other than his bad character and disposition to commit the sort of crime with which he is charged? In the case of an alleged homosexual offence as in the case of an alleged burglary, evidence which proves thereby that the accused has committed crimes in the past and is therefore disposed to commit the crime is clearly inadmissible. It has, however, never been doubted that if the crime charged is committed in a uniquely or strikingly similar manner to other crimes committed by the accused, the manner in which the other crimes were committed may be evidence upon which a jury could reasonably conclude that the accused was guilty of the crime charged. The similarity would have to be so unique or striking that common sense makes it inexplicable on the basis of co-incidence'.

Lord Hailsham illustrated the principle:

'In a sex case . . . whilst a repeated homosexual act by itself might be quite insufficient to admit the evidence as confirmatory of identity or design, the fact that it was alleged to have been performed wearing the ceremonial head-dress of an Indian chief or other eccentric garb might well in appropriate circumstances suffice'.

Following this case there was a clutch of bewildering decisions by the Court of Appeal, each time constituted by a different set of judges. In *R* v *Novac* (1977)[13] the court said:

'we cannot think that two or more alleged offences of buggery or attempted buggery committed in bed at the residence of the alleged offender with boys to whom he had offered shelter can be said to have been committed in a uniquely or strikingly similar manner . . . if a man is going to commit buggery with a boy he picks up, it must surely be a commonplace feature of such an encounter that he will take the boy home with him and commit the offence in the bed. The fact that the boys may in each case have been picked up by the defendant in the first instance at amusement arcades may be a feature more nearly approximating to a 'unique or striking similarity' within the ambit of Lord Salmon's principle. It is a similarity in the surrounding circumstances and is not, in our judgment, sufficiently proximate to the crime itself to lead to the conclusion that the repetition of this feature would make the boys' stories inexplicable on the basis of coincidence'.

In *R* v *Johanssen* (1977)[14] a different set of Appeal Court judges came to different conclusions, using the same test. Here the defendant met boys in amusement arcades and similar places offering them money or a meal or treating them to a game, taking them to his home or on to the beach and having sex. 'His particular homosexual propensities were to handle the boy's penises and getting them to do the same with his, fellatio and buggery.' The Court of Appeal had 'no hesitation in deciding that there were striking similarities about what happened to each of the boys – the accosting in the same kind of places, the enticements, the visits to his accommodation, his homosexual propensities and his way of gratifying them.'

A still differently constituted court decided the appeal in *R* v *Scarrott* (1977).[15] In this case, the defendant had met boys on a towpath. He offered gifts and had sex in the vicinity. Lord Scarman in upholding the conviction said, 'It is necessary to repeat the features which are strikingly similar; the ages of the boys, the way in which their resistance was worn down, the location of the offences and the offences themselves.'

The decision in *R* v *Inder* (1977)[16] shows, if proof were now needed, that more rests on who comprises the court than on any overriding principle. In this case the strikingly similar facts were said to be that the offences were all committed when the defendant was living in institutional accommodation and sharing a bed with two or more boys. All the offences took place when the boys went to watch television in the defendant's room. He had entertained them, taken them to friends and to the 'Speedway'. The majority were little boys and, apparently, he did not mind which boy he had on any given occasion. In rejecting these so called similar facts Lord Chief Justice Widgery said, 'Looking at this list of similarities, it seems to us that these are the similarities which represent the stock in trade of the seducer of small boys and were not unique but appear in the vast majority of cases that come before the courts'.

According to the House of Lords, there is no relevant difference between English and Scottish rules on this point.[17] (See page 172.)

Despite apparently irreconcilable judgments, it is at least clear that evidence which merely shows general homosexual orientation is not now considered enough to justify its introduction. A different conclusion might be reached if the same facts as those of the *Thompson* case occurred today. Secondly, homosexual offences are not to be considered a special category as they were implicitly in the *Sims* case. However, so uneven is the knowledge and prejudice of the judiciary that quite usual methods of making sexual encounters may be considered unique or strikingly unusual so as to justify reference being made to them during criminal trials.

Conspiracy to corrupt public morals and the Paedophile Information Exchange (PIE)

Following an 18-month police investigation, five committee members of PIE were charged with conspiracy to corrupt public morals. It was alleged that the method of their conspiracy was to induce readers of PIE's contact sheets to give advertisers the opportunity to have sex with children (the first charge) and give advertisers a means of soliciting obscene material through the post (the second charge). One of the defendants died before the trial started. At the first trial in January 1981, one defendant was acquitted on both charges, two were acquitted of the first charge only, and with regard to the former chairman of PIE, Tom O'Carroll, the jury were unable to agree on a verdict on either charge. Following a second trial in March 1981, Tom O'Carroll was found guilty of conspiracy in respect of both allegations and sentenced to two years' imprisonment.

The defence case was that the sincerity of PIE was shown by the number of isolated and depressed paedophiles who found mutual support within the organisation. There was unchallenged evidence that former members had been suicidal. The work had been done despite the fact that PIE had attracted a great number of vicious attacks in the national press because of its political campaigning activities. Following brutal assaults by National Front members at a public meeting called by PIE in 1977, most of its meetings had to be held secretly. Nevertheless they were still infiltrated by sensation-seeking journalists. The precise content of members' correspondence was not known to the defendants, but in any event it was understood that these included matters of private fantasy and were exchanged between adults only. Correspondence and magazines were used to assist masturbation for pleasure and release. The correspondence was not, the defence said, used for any socially harmful purpose.

The basis of conspiracy to corrupt public morals is that society cannot exist without its moral code: if sexual morality is seriously undermined so is society at large. Hence it was claimed that what PIE had done was potentially 'destructive of the very fabric of society'. The prosecution sought to prove their case by producing former members of PIE who had become dissatisfied by the emphasis of some of their correspondents on pornographic fantasy and sexual material. The crux of the prosecution's case was that the committee had created a monstrous machine and, like Frankenstein, knowingly connived at its excess.

It was perhaps inevitable that PIE would be prosecuted. The group touched on an extraordinarily raw nerve among the general public: it rejected the common view that sex is harmful even to willing children.

Chapter Five
Obscenity

> 'I remember the very exciting feeling I got when I first saw one of
> these magazines before I came out. There I saw men kissing and
> holding and loving each other; something that I never thought pos-
> sible as the mainstream culture manifests itself in overwhelmingly
> heterosexual and macho terms. It was proof of a homosexual com-
> munity and it was through porn that I learned of its existence.'
>
> *Gregg Blachford*[1]

'Obscenity' – as represented in magazines, books, films, video or
live shows – is not a fixed or certain idea. One person's depiction of
open and liberated sexuality is another person's example of sexuality used to exploit, offend, oppress or invite crime. One person's
idea of a more publicly confident and assertive homosexuality is
another's nightmare of brutal machismo.

Generally speaking the simple purchase and possession of pornography does not give rise to legal problems for the consumer unless
child pornography is involved. The law is mainly concerned with
distribution and supply. For this reason (and because the subject is
discussed exhaustively in Geoffrey Robertson's excellent book
Obscenity[2]) what follows is limited to an outline of the obscenity
laws which have been used against depictions of, and reference to,
male homosexuality in publications and the arts.

Pornography

There are two types of legal censorship of pornography in the
United Kingdom: (1) the prohibition of 'obscene' material likely to
'deprave and corrupt' readers or viewers; (2) laws that permit the
police to confiscate 'indecent' material likely merely to embarrass
the 'ordinary citizen'. Obscenity is a serious crime. In England and
Wales it is punished under the Obscene Publications Act 1959
either after a trial by judge and jury[3] or by 'forfeiture' proceedings
whereby local magistrates are authorised to destroy obscene
articles discovered within their jurisdiction.[4] Because they are
based on loose definitions, forfeiture orders are subject to the incon-
sistent priorities and prejudices of local police forces in different

parts of the country. Distributors of 'indecent' material which is mild enough not to 'deprave and corrupt' its readers are within the law so long as they do not: send it through the post;[5] import it from abroad;[6] or display it openly in public places.[7] Ordering indecent material to be sent by post may be an offence, but otherwise possession of pornography for personal use is not a crime unless it is child pornography.

The central issue in any defence to a charge under the Obscene Publications Act is whether the publication is 'justified as being for the public good on the ground that it is in the interests of science, literature, art or learning or of other objects of general concern'.[8] The defence will attempt to establish this by calling expert evidence to the effect that the publication is for the public good.

In 1970 the Danish experiment in abolishing controls on sales of pornography was endorsed by the American Presidential Commission on Obscenity and Pornography which recommended abolition of all censorship for adults. Sexual orientation, it argued, was too deep-seated to be adversely affected by reading matter. Pornography was not merely harmless: it conferred therapeutic benefits by 'enhancing marital communication', provided pleasure for the lonely and acted as a safety valve for those with serious 'sexual dysfunction'. Between 1971 and 1976 arguments of these sorts were accepted in the English courts as amounting to a defence in that publication of pornography served 'an object of general concern'.

But because neither obscenity nor indecency is precisely defined in English law the definitions change as the views of judges vary and according to shifts in public opinion. Taken together the decisions in *DPP* v *Whyte* (1972)[9] and *DPP* v *Jordan* (1976)[10] reversed a tendency towards liberalisation. In the first case, the House of Lords ruled that 'depravity and corruption' was a condition of the mind, and books which aroused erotic fantasy without stimulating overtly anti-social behaviour could nonetheless be declared obscene. In the latter case, the court stopped 'therapeutic effect' evidence by limiting the 'public good' defence to material with intrinsic merit as literature or learning.

There is no defence of 'public good' in a case brought against a distributor of 'indecent' material through the post. In *R* v *Stamford* (1972)[11] where the defendant had posted gay magazines to customers, the English Court of Appeal ruled that the test of indecency was 'objective' and therefore the character and views of the recipients were irrelevant.

Obscenity laws are different in Scotland and are much more

strictly defined. The 1959 Act does not apply. The legal points are complex but it is clear that the requirement of 'intent to corrupt' is not proved by possession alone. Actual distribution must take place. Clubs with private membership can possess and distribute 'obscene' material within the confines of the club. Such action appears to be unlawful only when an innocent or uninvited third party obtains or buys material. In recent years attempts by the Crown Office to secure convictions in obscenity trials have been largely unsuccessful.

The law enforcement procedure adopted by the police in England and Wales is as follows. Having had a complaint from somebody or having seen something they object to on one of their regular visits to a porn shop, they will apply to a magistrate for a warrant to search for and seize any offensive book, magazine or film from the suspected premises. The items removed are then passed to the office of the Director of Public Prosecutions. The DPP decides whether to bring a criminal prosecution or apply for a forfeiture order or simply to return the material.

The police formulate their own internal guidelines for action on obscenity, and these generally provide some extra-legal restraint on the powers of individual officers. In the absence of more explicit guidance, Scotland Yard's obscene publications squad apparently has its own rules of thumb for identifying 'filth for filth's sake'. In 1978, erections and anal, oral, child, animal and group sexual depictions were among the main taboo subjects.[12] Well established gay porn shops in London have been raided by the police from time to time. Books and magazines have been removed and later destroyed under forfeiture proceedings.

Ad hoc prosecutions of distributors provide no real control. Publishers can switch their operations to other areas. The DPP maintains some centralised control over the obscenity prosecutions by reading material seized by London and provincial forces (or submitted by members of the public), advising whether its publisher should be prosecuted and if so under what section of what Act, and keeping records of the results of prosecutions in an attempt to identify patterns of jury verdicts.

Protection of Children Act 1978

During the second half of 1977, a great deal of press publicity and police action was directed against men allegedly taking indecent photographs of boys or those who knew such men or boys. At the beginning of 1978, a Conservative MP successfully promoted a private Bill – which became the Protection of Children Act 1978[13] – aimed at suppressing an allegedly proliferating market in child (or paedophile) pornography.

Because children are presumed by the law and society at large to be sexually innocent, most concern is focused on the effect of sexually explicit photography on child models. The promoter of the Protection of Children Act had collected some accounts of children distressed by having been photographed for commercial pornography. That upset was no doubt real, though it seems less clear whether it was caused by the modelling itself or parental hysteria because of 'society's attitudes'. In the end, because the Act made it an offence to possess child pornography in most instances, even for personal use, it is far wider than is necessary to protect children.

The Act allows the prosecution not only of those exploiting children, but of a whole class of people whose sexual preference is disapproved of, and appears to permit prosecution even where the use of child pornography is recommended as therapy by doctors.

It is an offence to take (or permit to be taken) any indecent photographs of a child (defined as a boy or girl under 16 years) (section 1 (a)); or distribute or show such indecent photographs (section 1 (b)); or have in one's possession such indecent photographs, with a view to their being distributed or shown (section 1 (c)), or publish (or cause to be published) any advertisement likely to be understood as conveying that the advertiser distributes or shows such indecent photographs (or intends to do so) (section 1 (d)). Offences are punishable by magistrates with six months' imprisonment and/or a fine of £1000 or by the crown court with up to three years' imprisonment and/or an unlimited fine.

There is no defence to a charge under section 1(a) other than that the photographs were not indecent, or if they were, they were not of children under 16, or that the defendant had no part in their production. Under section 1 (d) it is unnecessary for the photographs on offer to be indecent. It is enough if wording indicates a willingness to sell or show pictures of nude children in the prohibited age bracket. Distributors or exhibitors charged under section 1 (b) or (c) should be acquitted if they can establish on the balance of probabilities that either they had a legitimate reason for distributing or showing the photographs or having them in their possession; or that they had not themselves seen the photographs and did not know or suspect them to be indecent.

Although the DPP must institute prosecutions, the police have an independent power to search premises and seize any photographs, films or video 'reasonably suspected' of contravening the Act and have them destroyed by magistrates in proceedings similar to the forfeiture process under the Obscene Publications Act.[14]

In 1977 the Home Secretary set up a committee to 'review the laws concerning obscenity, indecency and violence in publications, displays and entertainments in England and Wales, except in the field of broadcasting, and to review the arrangements for film censorship in England and Wales'. This committee, chaired by Professor Bernard Williams, reported to the government in 1979, recommending a total rewriting of the laws on obscenity and indecency.[15] It concluded that the law should concentrate more strongly than at present on protecting the general public from offence, and that a legal definition based on what is 'offensive to reasonable people' should replace the present tests of 'obscene' and 'indecent'. The argument that pornography acts as a stimulus to sexual violence was rejected. The only convincing evidence of harm it claimed was in relation to the participation in pornography of those who are too young properly to consent or who receive physical injury in the process. It was concluded that the legitimate interest in protecting 'public decency' justifies restrictions on the open sale of pornography. Otherwise the evidence of harm to the consumers of pornography was not such as to justify the further suppression of material available only to the willing customer.

On the control of publications, the Williams Committee recommended that there should be a ban on the sale of pornography — not just on its display — in shops into which children or unsuspecting adults are liable to go. The committee concluded that such terms as 'indecent', 'obscene' and the 'tendency to deprave and corrupt' had outlived their usefulness. So the control or restriction of publications should be based in future on whether the unrestricted availability of a publication is offensive to 'reasonable people on account of a particular type of content'. Restricted publications should not be sold in any shop other than one with blank windows which does not admit people under 18 and which displays a warning notice which customers have to pass before they can see what is inside the shop. In the committee's view, restricted publications could be sold through the post, so long as neither the publication nor advertisements for them are sent to people under 18 or those who have not asked for them.

In addition, there should be a total ban on any kind of material involving the sexual exploitation of a person under 16 or of any other person on whom physical harm was inflicted. It would be for a court to decide whether material fell into this prohibited category.

These proposals were castigated as perverse and dangerous by the moral order campaigner Mary Whitehouse. In 1981, the government said that there was no early prospect of reforming the law on obscenity, but it agreed that the present controls over film clubs were unsatisfactory and thought some limited action might be taken. The Home Office minister of state appeared to reject one of the central conclusions of the Williams Committee and stated: 'There is a great deal of concern about the increase of violent sexual crimes. Is it unreasonable to think that these may be due in some part at least to acting out what is seen in pornographic publications?'[16]

Subsequently the government has supported three new laws to control sex shops and cinemas. The Indecent Displays (Control) Act 1981 makes the display of 'indecent' material in public a criminal offence. Pornographic magazines may be lawfully displayed in 'corner shops' provided that they are put in a separate place marked off by a warning sign. Sex shops are only required to display a notice on the shop front that they sell material which might offend. The Local Government (Miscellaneous Provisions) Act 1982 and the Civic Government (Scotland) Act 1982 give local authorities powers to control the siting of sex shops and cinemas. The Acts changed the law whereby sex shops opened in premises previously used as ordinary shops did not require planning permission. Now they must apply for special licences, the granting of which will depend on the suitability of the applicant and the locality. The Cinematograph Amendment Act 1982 subjects video cinemas or lounges to the same fire, safety and licensing controls as ordinary cinemas. This closed a technical loophole in the Cinematograph Act 1952 which did not apply to video.

Censorship of the media

Newspapers

In England and Wales, the law of blasphemy punishes a particular kind of obscenity in a way which circumvents the limited protection given to the publisher under the 1959 Act. The test is whether the material is 'indecent' rather than whether it has a 'tendency to corrupt'. The work need not be considered as a whole or in relation to likely readers. Nor is there a defence of publication for the 'public good'.

The House of Lords in *Whitehouse* v *Gay News Ltd and Lemon* (1979)[17] upheld the conviction of the editor of *Gay News* for blasphemy in publishing a poem by a professor of poetry which described a centurion's homosexual fantasies about the crucified Christ. Six months after publication of the poem Mary Whitehouse had obtained permission from the court to bring a private prosecution against both the editor and the publishing company for the offence of blasphemous libel, in that they 'unlawfully and wickedly published or caused to be published in a newspaper called *Gay News* No. 96 a blasphemous libel concerning the Christian religion, namely an obscene poem and illustration vilifying Christ in his life and in his crucifixion.' The defence had maintained that it was not blasphemous because it did not attack but glorified Christ by asserting Christian beliefs and speaking of a love for Christ through the emotional and sexual experience of gay men.

Gay News and its editor were convicted and their appeal against the trial judge's directions to the jury was unsuccessful. The House of Lords decided that guilt for this offence does not depend on the defendant having an intent to blaspheme but on proof that the publication was intentional (or in the case of a bookseller, negligent) and that the matter published was blasphemous. Most offences require a much higher burden of proof with regard to criminal intention. Nevertheless limits appear to have been set to the use of blasphemous libel. According to Geoffrey Robertson the offence is limited to indecent or offensive treatment of subjects sacred to Christian (and in particular Anglican) sympathisers.[18] It has however extended the bounds of censorship to serious literature, which is endangered whenever it combines talk of sex, particularly homosexual sex, with religion, irrespective of its purpose. In 1981, the English Law Commission suggested that the crime of blasphemy should be abolished.[19]

It seems that the crime of blasphemy does not exist in Scotland.[20] Also private prosecutions, such as the one brought by Mary Whitehouse, are almost impossible to bring in Scotland. This is because, unlike in English law, a private individual must show some special personal interest in the matter rather than simply being an offended member of the general public.

Contact advertisements

It is clear that advertisements for sexual partners placed by and aimed at gay men, even if over 21, are unlawful. In *Knuller* v *DPP* (1973) (see page 73 above) the publishers of a newspaper which carried explicit gay contact ads were convicted of conspiracy to corrupt public morals. Nowadays gay contact ads are very common, even if a little less explicit. The authorities appear to have lost interest in the subject and use their discretion not to prosecute. It remains possible of course that the DPP could be persuaded to take action where lurid public attention had been focused on a particular paper and there was a good chance of convincing a jury to convict.

Theatre, cinema, broadcasting

Until 1968, English and Scottish stage plays were censored by the Lord Chamberlain's office. For many years the Lord Chamberlain maintained an absolute ban on all references to homosexuality. In 1946 and again in 1951, having secretly consulted prominent people in the clergy, law, universities, medical profession, government and judiciary and artistic circles on the merits of lifting the prohibition, he decided it should stay. In 1958 he indicated that serious plays on homosexual themes would at last be considered for licensing, but only if homosexual characters were essential to the plot, and the play was not written to propagandise for changes in the law. 'Extracts or practical demonstrations' of love between homosexuals were not allowed.[21] This pre-performance vetting of play scripts was abolished by the Theatres Act 1968.

Nowadays the Attorney General may sanction a prosecution if a performance of a play is thought to be 'obscene' i.e. if 'taken on the whole, its effect was such as to tend to deprave and corrupt persons who were likely, having regard to all relevant circumstances, to attend it'. It was in order to sidestep this requirement that Mary Whitehouse brought a private prosecution under section 13 of the Sexual Offences Act 1956 against Michael Bogdanov, director of Howard Brenton's *The Romans in Britain* staged at the National Theatre.

The prosecution complained about an act of simulated buggery, a scene which lasted about 30 seconds in a three-hour play. The case was possible because of a loophole in the Theatres Act 1968 and the special nature of the offence of gross indecency. The Theatres Act exempted from prosecution sexual offences under the common law or under the Vagrancy Act but had failed to include similar statutory offences such as gross indecency. Secondly, since there is no offence of gross indecency between members of opposite sexes, had the victim of the scene of simulated rape – a young Celtic priest – been a woman, the director could not have been prosecuted under the Sexual Offences Act. A final bizarre twist is the fact that had the director been a woman, she could not have been prosecuted for procuring an act of gross indecency since the statute provides that the offence may be committed only by a man.

At the Central Criminal Court in 1982, Mr Justice Staughton ruled at the end of the prosecution case that there was sufficient evidence of an offence for the trial to continue. It was stated that the Sexual Offences Act could apply to events on stage; that a simulated sexual act could amount to gross indecency; and that the motive of 'sexual gratification' was not an essential part of the offence. Having obtained this ruling, counsel acting for Mrs Whitehouse obtained from the Attorney General an official withdrawal of the private prosecution in the public interest – a rarely used device known as a *nolle prosequi*. Although Mrs Whitehouse claimed that the case was a victory, it was a shallow one. The judge's ruling did not create any binding precedent for other courts. This could have happened only if the case had been allowed to run its full course and the legal issues had been taken subsequently to the Court of Appeal for a binding ruling. The law remains uncertain. At the time of writing the Attorney General has declined to give any undertaking either to amend the Theatres Act or to enter a *nolle prosequi* in any similar case.

Film censorship operates at four different levels. The distributors of feature films risk prosecution for obscenity by the DPP; exhibitors may be refused a licence to show a particular film by district councils; the British Board of Film Censors (BBFC) may insist on cuts being made before certifying a film's fitness for the public screen or for certain age groups; and customs officers are empowered to refuse entry to any foreign film classified as 'indecent'.

The fate of a progressive gay film from West Germany, *Taxi Zum Klo*, illustrates the current attitude of the BBFC to gay sex. There were about three minutes of explicit sex integrated into the 92-minute film. Permission was given to show the movie unlicensed in several London cinema clubs. It was also uncut save for two brief shots which probably contravened the Protection of Children Act. These shots were extracts from a film entitled *Christian and His Stamp Collector Friend* – which is apparently required viewing in some Berlin primary schools – and show a man placing a little boy's hand inside his flies, then touching the boy's crotch. However outside club conditions the BBFC insisted that most of the sex scenes in the rest of the film be excised, including a sequence in a VD clinic in which a doctor is examining his patient's anus.[22]

The consent of the DPP is needed for any prosecution of feature films and no order can be made to forfeit such a film when it is seized under a warrant applied for by the DPP. In this way licensed cinemas, and film clubs and societies are protected from the sort of arbitrary police harassment endured by booksellers and news-agents. However in relation to 8-millimetre 'blue movies', the police have wide powers of search and seizure. A video cassette is an 'article' within the meaning of the Obscene Publications Act 1959 and thereby subject to control.[23]

Extensive censorship operates both at the BBC and in commercial television. In 1964, the Board of the BBC accepted that:

'... the programmes for which they are responsible should not offend against good taste or decency, or be likely to encourage crime or disorder or be offensive to public feeling. In judging what is suitable for inclusion in programmes they will pay special regard to the need to ensure that broadcasts designed to stimulate thought do not so far depart from their intention as to give general offence.'

IBA members have a similar obligation under the Independent Broadcasting Authority Act 1973, section 4.

In 1973 the IBA was criticised by three Appeal Court judges for its decision to broadcast 'tasteless and offensive' scenes in a pro-gramme about Andy Warhol.[24] Lord Denning stated that the pro-gramme had to be judged, 'not as a whole, but in several parts, piece by piece'. He also commented that the IBA 'should always remember that there is a silent majority of good people who say little but view a lot. Their feelings must be respected, as well as those of the vociferous minority, who, in the name of freedom, shout for ugliness in all its forms.'

The arguments of the moral authoritarians against the depiction or description of homosexual sexuality or lovemaking are broadly as follows. First, homosexual practices are sins; therefore to right-minded people, nude men, explicit references to homosexual fantasies or love are deeply offensive and inherently indecent or pornographic. Second, pornography does harm to consumers particularly adolescents and young men) in two ways: it makes it difficult for them to have 'normal' sex i.e. marital intercourse; it makes it easier for them to contemplate or actually perform 'abnormal' or 'perverted' sexual acts or acts of sexual violence. In particular it is deeply damaging to the 'normal' development of heterosexual sexual relationships of young people who are exposed to pornography either as consumers or models. The moral authoritarians would say that in the long term the effect of uncontrolled pornography would be to degrade and seriously undermine the present moral order that confines 'healthy' sexual expression to private encounters between married couples. It is argued that in the short term pornography contributes towards personal unhappiness and sexual violence, while in the long term it weakens the marital family and contributes to the increase of promiscuity and crime.

These assumptions fire those who have the power to use the law, including chiefs of police.[25] In recent years the 'moral crusade' against pornography in this country has been led in the media by the Festival of Light organisation and the National Viewers and Listeners' Association. It is a campaign that has been most successfully articulated by Mary Whitehouse.

This political movement appears to have taken upon itself the suppression of 'lewdness' where central government has hesitated. The early seventies had seen a spate of prosecutions and confiscations (supported by the government) of underground publications (in particular *International Times, Oz* and *The Little Red Schoolbook*) all of which had explicit positive references to homosexual love and in the case of the two papers, gay personal advertisements. By the mid-seventies gay nude magazines were being printed for a newly emerging consumer market and were greeted by seizures and prosecutions. In 1974-75 the police raided the publishers of *Gay Circle* and *Him Exclusive*.

However the victories of the 'Whitehouse lobby' referred to above seem to be pyrrhic. In practice very few obscenity trials take place under the Obscene Publications Act because juries are so reluctant to convict; this is one of the reasons why the police prefer to use their powers to have pornographic material forfeited.

Within the women's movement there has been an increasing rejection and rigorous criticism of *all* types of pornography and imagery that exploit sexuality. Feminists are not opposed to sex, but to any activity, including pornographic reproduction, that mimics the worst aspects of alienated male heterosexuality.[26] Gay porn cannot be dismissed so easily as its heterosexual equivalents; although it obviously exploits sexuality, the images are important to many gay men because at least they show that positive gay male sexuality actually exists in a society which rarely admits that fact.

Chapter Six
Employment

'A woman teacher, whose new employers were somewhat slow in completing the normal formalities, had been working for two months when she was informed that she was "medically unfit" to teach. She had mentioned in completing her medical history form that she was suffering from a mild form of depression. She told us: "After some investigations, I discovered that my GP had revealed that my mild depression was due to marital troubles as a consequence of my having had lesbian affairs." She confronted her occupational health officer who told her: "A lesbian cannot be trusted to teach in a girls' school, where some of the girls are quite well developed." The same fears, however, did not apply to the employment of male teachers in the same girls' school, for heterosexual men were "not in question". Had the school been more prompt in contacting her GP, of course, the case would not have arisen, for she would have been rejected as unsuitable at the outset, for reasons which she would not have known.'[1]

There is no legislation to protect gay women and men in employment. Employers may therefore refuse to hire, refuse to promote and may even dismiss or demote gay employees solely on the grounds of common prejudice. Fellow workers sometimes make complaints to employers which lead to dismissal. In this situation, gay workers are doubly handicapped, having neither the protection of the law nor support from their workmates.

Some people do not believe that there is any discrimination against gay workers. The gay movement has helped to expose its existence and the extent to which it has affected the employment opportunities of lesbians and gay men. It follows from the fact that most gay people's orientation is hidden that homosexual oppression is also concealed until some crisis arises. For many gay people an open affirmation of their life style has spelled the immediate threat of or actual loss of a job or opportunities for promotion. Those who decide to remain secret about their sexual orientation find their jobs jeopardised by rumours that they are gay; this also happens to those who do not fit the stereotypes of the masculine man or the feminine woman. Because popular mythology links homosexuality with sexual interest in children, school and college

teachers and others who work with young people face a particularly invidious type of discrimination. Dismissal often follows when
a (male) teacher has been convicted of a homosexual sexual
offence. These dismissals have usually been upheld as fair by
industrial tribunals.

Evidence of discrimination is not limited to reported cases. Most
lesbians and gay men do not go to industrial tribunals either
because they do not qualify (see page 101 below) or because they
want to avoid publicity. And looking at all the reported cases,
there seems little point in going to them. With a very strong case it
is useful to go to a tribunal, because if it is well argued from the
beginning a new precedent may be established. Otherwise a gay
person's best remedy is to gain the support of fellow workers to persuade the employer to change the decision.

People have been dismissed because of their homosexuality after
they have come out at work, or after they have been convicted of a
homosexual 'offence', or after they have been identified as homosexual, for example, by antagonistic fellow workers or neighbours,
or as a result of having been seen on television or reported in the
press.

The police often notify employers or professional associations of
the names of persons convicted of homosexual offences, however
minor. This is particularly likely in the case of anyone who works
with young people. For most purposes people given fines or short
prison sentences become 'rehabilitated' after a certain number of
years[2] and are regarded as not having been convicted, charged
with, prosecuted for or having committed an offence, but this does
not apply to all occupations. Those excluded are medical practi-
tioners, lawyers,[3] chartered and certified accountants, dentists,
vets, nurses and midwives, opticians, chemists, employees in the
courts, police or prison service, some social workers, workers with
children and young people under 18, some workers in insurance
and unit trust companies, firearms testers and civil service
employees subject to positive vetting. Such people can be refused
employment or admission to a profession, or dismissed for failing
to reveal a spent conviction; they are supposed to be told when
applying for a job, or at an interview, that any spent convictions
must be disclosed.

Anyone disciplined or dismissed following a conviction should
contact their union and the NCCL, make use of any internal
appeals machinery, and where appropriate consider legal action
for unfair dismissal.

Protection from 'unfair dismissal'

Since 1972 employers have been unable to dismiss workers without a specific reason and a justification for the decision. In order to claim this protection against unfair dismissal, an employee must have worked for the same firm for at least 52 weeks (for a minimum of 16 hours a week, or eight hours per week if they have worked five years or more). If the firm employs 20 or fewer, the employee must have been there for at least two years. These qualifying periods do not apply to workers who claim they were sacked because of race or sex discrimination or being a member of or taking part in the activities of an independent trade union.

'Unfair dismissal' is not a commonsense expression; its meaning can really only be decided by the industrial tribunal which hears the case. Under the Employment Protection (Consolidation) Act 1978 (as amended) the employer is required to prove that the employee was dismissed for one of the following potentially 'fair' reasons. For it to be potentially fair the reason must: (1) relate to conduct, or (2) relate to capability (i.e. skill, aptitude, health, physical or mental capabilities), or (3) relate to qualifications (i.e. those relevant to the job in question), or (4) be that the employee could not continue in the job without contravening a legal duty or restriction, or (5) be 'some other substantial reason' which could justify the dismissal of someone in the type of job in question.

Having fitted the reason into some of these very broad categories, in practice the employer also has to show – though technically s/he does not have the burden of proving – that in the circumstances s/he acted reasonably in treating this as a sufficient reason for dismissing the worker, i.e. that any reasonable employer would have acted as s/he did. It is up to the industrial tribunal to decide on the evidence from both sides whether the dismissal was in fact reasonable.

Claims for unfair dismissal on the grounds of race or sex discrimination can be brought under the Race Relations or Sex Discrimination Acts. In Northern Ireland, claims for dismissal on grounds of religious discrimination can be brought under the Fair Employment (Northern Ireland) Act 1976.

If dissatisfied with the decision of an industrial tribunal, the employee or employer can appeal on a point of law to the Employment Appeal Tribunal (EAT) which sits in London and Glasgow, and to the Northern Ireland Court of Appeal in Belfast.

Financial compensation is the main remedy in most successful cases. Cash awards made by tribunals are not large, most usually limited to three figure sums. Very few dismissed employees who win their cases are reinstated in their old jobs.

Since the mid-seventies a body of decisions by industrial tribunals and the EAT has been built up. This gives a general impression of how tribunals deal with employees who claim their dismissal was because of their homosexuality. Obviously the picture is not static. Attitudes and personnel differ and change from place to place and from year to year. Tribunals see their job as being not to substitute their own decision for that of the employers, but to consider what could have been the decision of the 'reasonable employer' in those circumstances. In practice this has meant taking far too much account of employers' prejudices.[4]

The most significant issue of principle, which comes out in many of the cases, is that the 'general public' is entitled to have 'strong views' (i.e. prejudices) against homosexuality – and the actual or supposed hostile views of parents, fellow workers, or customers can justifiably be acted upon by an employer who wants to get rid of a gay or lesbian worker. This issue is refined according to the particular nature of the employment. In relation to employees working with children and young people the hostile views blatantly relate to the risk of corruption and assaults on juveniles and the responsibility of the employers to uphold the good name of their institution. With regard to workers who have contact with the general public, the reputation of the firm or the risk to profitability are given as justifications.

Working with young people

The gay workers most vulnerable to discrimination on grounds of homosexuality are those who work in proximity to young people. It is assumed, particularly by employers within public authorities, that there is a widely held view among the general public that a conviction for 'cottaging' means that a gay man is not to be trusted with children. It is presumed that gay men are sexually uncontrollable and that young people in their care are at risk. Lesbians are also oppressed by similar prejudices. Industrial tribunals are not impressed with evidence that individuals have been responsible, upright citizens and employees. In the *Saunders* case (see page 105 below) the mere fact that a man was homosexual was considered sufficient reason to believe that children were at risk from him.

As yet there has been no case involving a gay worker who dealt with young people which has finally been won either before an industrial tribunal or the EAT. Tribunals consistently reinforce the lowest common denominator of prejudice.

The earliest case to go to an industrial tribunal was *Gardiner* v *Newport County Borough Council* (1974).[5] Here the Cardiff industrial tribunal decided that a lecturer at a college of art and design (who taught on a foundation course mainly for 16 to 18 year olds) was fairly dismissed because of a conviction for gross indecency. This was so despite the fact that the employers had misconducted the disciplinary proceedings by hearing vague and unsubstantiated allegations; the procedure was also unsatisfactory because it did not provide for an appeal. Nevertheless, it was held that on the basis of the conviction alone any 'reasonable employer' would have been driven to the same conclusion. The tribunal decided that:

> 'the principal fact is that he had been convicted of a particularly revolting offence, and one obviously relevant not only to his character as a teacher in general, a member of an honourable profession, but in particular also having charge of quite young people of both sexes.'

The arguments that have been put forward on behalf of gay applicants have become more sophisticated since then, but the findings of tribunals are barely more sophisticated in terms of their prejudice.

In *Jarrett* v *Governors of the Bishop of Llandaff Secondary School* (1977)[6] Mr Jarrett was a geography teacher employed for 12 years at a school run by the church in Wales for pupils between the ages of 11 and 18 or 19. He had a senior position, was very highly regarded and at no time had there been 'any breath of suspicion concerning his sexual morality or against his behaviour with the children or with any member of staff'. His career was destroyed when he pleaded guilty to a charge of gross indecency in a toilet. Although he denied being involved, he said that he had pleaded guilty to avoid publicity. The school found out, and there was a hearing before the board of governors. They decided to dismiss him because it was 'inappropriate for a man to continue as a teacher with a conviction for gross indecency'. The industrial tribunal decided that he had been fairly dismissed for a substantial reason and that in reaching that decision the employers had acted reasonably.

'In all the circumstances the only reasonable decision was not to take a risk. If the comparatively small risk of the applicant behaving in some improper way with the children in the school had been realised the parents of the children would have been up in arms, and legitimately up in arms.'

The theme of parental fears has been continued and applied by industrial tribunals to the present day. No substantial evidence has ever been presented by an employer to demonstrate that these fears exist in relation to the *particular* individuals before the tribunal. Tribunals have recognised that the actual gay men involved constitute no risk at all.

McNamee v *St Monica's Roman Catholic Primary School* (1977)[7] is an example of this. Here the Liverpool Industrial Tribunal decided that Mr McNamee, a 'completely dedicated teacher' was fairly dismissed for misconduct on account of a conviction for gross indecency.

'... for a greater part of the day during term time, the teachers are having the children under their charge and are *in loco parentis* to them. One can imagine the sort of criticism that could have been levelled at the managers of this school if they had allowed the applicant to continue in his employment after this had happened, and after it had been quite well known that it had happened, if there had subsequently been an incident with one of the children at the school, unlikely though that may perhaps have been.'

The first case to go on appeal to the Employment Appeal Tribunal was *Nottinghamshire County Council* v *Bowly* (1978).[8] In this case a much wider range of evidence was put to the original industrial tribunal and the arguments put more coherently. Already in the judgment of this case, the tribunal expressed doubt that someone who is gay and convicted on a cottaging charge is in fact a risk to children. The majority of the original tribunal thought that the school's disciplinary sub-committee had behaved unreasonably and were influenced by innuendoes about the possibilities of relationships with pupils. The EAT thought that was wrong. The industrial tribunal should not have substituted its own decision for the sub-committee's when the facts fell into 'a grey area', where it could not be shown that the sub-committee were prejudiced, failed to keep an open mind or made a procedural error.

Saunders v *Scottish National Camps Association Ltd.* (1980)[9] is the most important case in which the implications of previous decisions were amplified and extended. Mr Saunders was not a teacher, he was a maintenance man. He had not committed an offence, but his employers were tipped off that he was gay. Although it was accepted that gays are not in fact a greater risk it was held sufficient justification for an employer to act on the basis of popular prejudice concerning the risks of employing homosexuals working with children.

The camp at which Mr Saunders had worked for about two years was attended by young people of both sexes from the ages of 10 to 18 for 'social, physical and mental training'. One evening he had been robbed by someone he met at a gay pub, well away from his workplace. He reported the incident to the local police and during his interview freely admitted that he was gay. Soon after, his employers were unofficially informed that Mr Saunders was homosexual. Having confirmed the information, interviewed Mr Saunders and looked up the word 'bi-sexual' in the dictionary, the camp manager sacked him. The manager's decision was later confirmed by the Association's secretary following a further interview with Mr Saunders. The Glasgow industrial tribunal commented that this procedure for dismissal was 'not entirely satisfactory' but that given the size of the organisation it did not matter.

Mr Saunders was given a written explanation for his dismissal; 'the reason is that information was received that you indulge in homosexuality. At a camp accommodating large numbers of schoolchildren and teenagers it is totally unsuitable to employ any person with such tendencies'. It was accepted by all that none of Mr Saunders' relationships had involved residents at the camp.

The EAT decided that it was proper for the industrial tribunal to take account of the fact that there was a

'considerable proportion of employers who would take the view that the employment of homosexuals should be restricted, particularly when required to work in proximity and in contact with children. Whether that view is scientifically sound may be open to question but there was clear evidence from the psychiatrist [who appeared before the tribunal at the original hearing] that it exists as a fact. That evidence the tribunal were entitled to accept and it appears to have coincided with their own knowledge and experience. Some employers faced with this problem might have decided not to dismiss –

others, like the respondent, would have felt that in the interests of young persons for whom they were responsible to parents it was the only safe course. Neither could be said to have acted unreasonably'.

The industrial tribunal was therefore correct in deciding that the dismissal was fair. The Court of Session in Edinburgh similarly dismissed Mr Saunders' appeal and upheld the rulings of both the tribunal and the EAT.

In *Wiseman* v *Salford City Council* (1981)[10] the same issues were raised in relation to a teacher in a college of further education. The Manchester industrial tribunal decided that a lecturer in drama therapy at the local college of technology had been fairly dismissed following a conviction for gross indecency. Although the principal of the college accepted that 'there was no evidence to suggest that Mr Wiseman's "inclinations" had affected his teaching duties in the past or in his attitudes towards his students' he decided nevertheless that 'there was a risk element – the applicant's work involved close contact with young people', and he did not think that a responsible authority would be justified in taking such a risk once it was known that 'the applicant had on two occasions given into the temptation of this sort, albeit he had not been convicted of gross indecency on the one occasion'. Further, the local authority was 'entitled to expect certain standards from their lecturers and for them to set examples to their pupils particularly young persons'. The majority of the industrial tribunal members considered that the college had been unprejudiced, open-minded and had reasonably come to the conclusion to dismiss. A dissenting member disagreed:

'Are these offences in themselves such that reasonable, fair employers would take as grounds for dismissal? As in all these grey areas of moral judgment and sexual predisposition objectivity is difficult to achieve, but it is helpful to gain a perspective by asking the question: "would a male or female heterosexual lecturer have been dismissed if discovered soliciting or indulging in promiscuous behaviour?" We have no evidence, certainly but we find it difficult to imagine that this would be the case. In treating a homosexual male more harshly because of his homosexuality, the governors showed themselves to be less than "unprejudiced" and "open-minded" as the Employment Appeal Tribunal requires them to be.'

Although industrial tribunals say they examine each case on its merits, they had not really done so in previous cases. This point had never been strongly argued at an employment appeal tribunal and became the central question in *Wiseman*'s case. No evidence has been presented as to whether homosexuals in general were likely to be more interested in teenagers or children than heterosexuals are. Indeed his employers had never suggested that he was interested in young people and never suggested that he had shown sexual interest in his students. It was argued that a reasonable employer would look at his/her employee's particular circumstances. It would therefore be unreasonable and sheer prejudice to dismiss an individual because of stereotypes and mythical beliefs about the class of person to which he belonged.

However, the EAT confirmed the majority decision:

'The real question raised before us is: is it a self-evident proposition that someone who has done what Mr Wiseman told the disciplinary bodies and the industrial tribunal he had done, and takes his view about his own conduct, cannot be a risk to teenage boys in his charge? Whether that proposition is right or wrong, in our judgment it is not self-evident. It may well be that there is a responsible body of opinion which supports it. But it is a highly controversial subject, and in our judgment the disciplinary bodies, and the majority of the industrial tribunals, are not making an error of law if they do not accept that view but conclude that there is a risk. Short of [the] proposition being self-evidently right then it is for the industrial tribunal to evaluate the reasonableness of the employer's action in treating Mr Wiseman's conduct as a reason for dismissal in the circumstances, having regard to equity and the substantial merits of the case.'

The particular circumstances, characters and reputations of Mr Saunders and Mr Wiseman were never really considered by the tribunals. They simply belonged to a class of person – homosexuals – and were therefore not suitable employees. This approach contrasts sharply with the application of the Sex Discrimination Act in relation to women with children. In *Hurley* v *Mustow* (1981)[11] the EAT decided that an employer's refusal to engage a woman because she had young children was unlawful. It emphasised that a condition excluding all members of a class from employment cannot be justified on the grounds that some members of that class are undesirable employees.

'We are not deciding whether or not women with children (as a class) are less reliable employees. Parliament has legislated that they are not to be treated as a class but as individuals. No employer is bound to employ unreliable employees, whether men or women. But he must investigate each case, and not simply apply what some could call a rule of convenience and others a prejudice to exclude a whole class of women or married persons because some members of that class are not suitable employees'.

In fighting discrimination workers must get advice at the earliest possible stage. Trade union officers, if involved, need to be advised by lawyers experienced in arguing this kind of case and to maximise the chance of eventually winning the case at an industrial tribunal the full arguments should be put at the first disciplinary hearing. Whether young people are in fact at risk from gays never seems to have been questioned. The EAT has used loopholes in the arguments for employees to reinforce their own prejudices, which are the widely held prejudices of society.

The situation of people working with the mentally handicapped is analogous to teachers in so far as they both have a special responsibility to people in their care, often acting *in loco parentis*. *Stancombe* v *Devon Area Health Authority* (1979),[12] concerning a mental hospital ward orderly, is a rare case. Here the Exeter industrial tribunal decided that Mr Stancombe had been unfairly dismissed after his employers had read about his plea of guilty to an act of gross indecency unconnected with work. At no time did his employers have any greater knowledge of the offence than was contained in a minuscule press report which was a 'very badly printed report, some of the sentences being incomprehensible'. The tribunal considered the matter to be 'a very minor offence, one which may very well have been more of a medical than a criminal matter'. The health authority were found to have been seriously at fault in not following their own disciplinary procedures before reaching a decision. The tribunal also decided that although the criminal conviction was sufficient to prevent Mr Stancombe from continuing to work at the mental hospital, a reasonable employer would have transferred him to an appropriate vacancy in some other hospital in their area.

The DES blacklist

The DES (Department of Education and Science) maintains a blacklist – called List 99 – of people not allowed to be employed anywhere in Britain as teachers or youth workers. If the DES consider placing someone on List 99 – for instance, following suspension or dismissal after a criminal conviction – that person has the right to make representations, in writing or in person. This right should be used. Even if blacklisted a person may be told that the prohibition on their employment is temporary and that they can apply to have it reconsidered after a certain period. There are also degrees of blacklisting. Some people are blacklisted for particular kinds of jobs. Individuals whose cases involved young children are usually deemed totally unsuitable. In most other instances, the DES will accept assurances that the offence took place out of working hours, away from work, that no students or adolescents were involved, so that no implications can be drawn from the fact of conviction as to an individual's suitability as a teacher or youth worker. According to the NCCL, in virtually all recent cases where such submissions have been made the DES has not blacklisted.

Office, shop and industrial workers

Employers have considered it a sufficient reason to dismiss homosexual workers who, it is claimed, may give offence to the public or to other workers (and again, where it can be dragged in, may constitute a potential risk to children). In the main, people who have lost cases were working in the private sector, had not been unionised, and complaints had been made by fellow workers. Cases that have been won were brought by public sector workers who are more powerfully organised.

These results could just be coincidental, but a strong stand by a union undoubtedly does change the atmosphere of employer/employee relations. Where a trade union has a strong gay rights policy it is unlikely that fellow workers will complain about someone being gay. If this does happen, a union with such a policy is far more likely to give the lead to its membership.

In *Z* v *Portsmouth City Council* (1980)[14] the Southampton industrial tribunal found in favour of the gay applicant because his employers had failed to follow the proper procedure agreed with the unions. No implications could be drawn about his having a 'homosexual condition' but he should at least benefit from the procedures affecting all workers. Mr Z had been given a conditional discharge after he pleaded guilty to a charge of soliciting. Later a disciplinary committee of the council voted by a majority of five not to dismiss him. However it decided that his reinstatement as city arts director would not take effect until his superior Mr W had made appropriate arrangements. W then apparently received a number of letters from staff. One threatened to resign, others asked for transfers if Z was reinstated. Although W should have attempted to resolve the staff problems he in fact made no attempt to do so. Instead of making arrangements to reinstate Z, W convened a further meeting of the disciplinary committee. At this meeting (which considered the staff objections) there were three members who were not on the original committee and had not heard the evidence given to that committee. Additionally there was a pre-meeting caucus of Conservative Party members who, it was found, were expected to vote in accordance with the chairman's line. In the end, the meeting voted by a majority of two to dismiss Z. Those who were dissatisfied with the first committee's decision to reinstate Z simply reconstituted another committee to give them the result they wanted.

The tribunal held that the decision to dismiss at this meeting was taken in breach of natural justice. The committee was acting in quasi-judicial capacity and, therefore, was obliged to follow the principles of natural justice; in particular someone should not participate in a decision if s/he has not heard all the oral evidence and submissions.[15] A further breach was constituted by the climate created by the caucus held immediately before the council meeting. 'It is unnecessary to establish the presence of actual bias . . . it is enough to establish a real likelihood that in the circumstances of the case an adjudicator will be biased.'[16]

The case of *Bell* v *Devon and Cornwall Police* (1978) (for facts see page 45 above) was won by the gay applicant because of the extraordinary nature of the complaints made by fellow employees. The case is interesting because of what it demonstrates about the attitudes of the police. The decision was not significant except in showing limits beyond which industrial tribunals will not go in supporting prejudice.

Security clearance in the civil service is another major area of discrimination in public sector employment. A case illustrating this issue as it affects gay civil servants is cited in *Queers Need Not Apply*.[17]

'A civil servant was — unusually — working in a "sensitive" area of the civil service department (the Minister's Office) before his "positive vetting" (security clearance) was completed. A matter of days after he mentioned his homosexuality in a security interview he was abruptly transferred to another section. This was not because he was thought to be a security risk (management in the civil service believes it does not discriminate, because homosexuals are treated just like a heterosexual with a "personality defect") but because his department felt it could not defend its employment of a gay man should there be a leak of classified information. He appealed against the decision, which would not help his career; and it is quite clear that whatever action he took it was unlikely he would ever be allowed to work in a "sensitive" area again. He lost the post which was particularly interesting and rewarding, and which had potential career implications.'

The private sector

As a general rule, industrial tribunals are unprepared to find against private employers if the underlying reason given for dismissal is to protect business interests and efficiency. Certainly embarrassment to an employer could support a fair dismissal (or a refusal to employ a gay person) even if the embarrassment arises from unreasonable public prejudice. Under present social and political conditions little security is available to those who choose to be open about their lesbian or gay life style.

In *Boychuck* v *H.J. Symons Holdings Ltd.* (1977)[18] both the industrial tribunal and the EAT claimed the fact that the applicant was lesbian was irrelevant. The issue as they saw it was whether the wearing of a badge, which allegedly could give 'offence to the public', was reasonable. It was decided that the employer had acted reasonably in considering the wearing of a badge about lesbianism was offensive. There was no evidence that any member of the public was actually offended. As in the *Saunders* case (see page 105), the EAT came to a decision on the basis of possible beliefs of third parties who were not there to give evidence. The employer's paranoia was sufficient.

During the winter Ms Boychuck, who was employed by a City insurance company as an accounts clerk, had worn lesbian badges on her overcoat to work. For three or four months of the summer before she was sacked she wore a badge on her work clothes. Things suddenly escalated when the managing director noticed Ms Boychuck was wearing a badge which said 'Lesbians Ignite'. She was told that he found it personally offensive, it would 'offend the decencies of other people' and was 'not a thing for the clients to see'. Normally her job would only involve seeing clients about one day a week when she worked on the company's reception. He warned her to remove it or be dismissed. Later in the day her immediate superior asked her to wear a less explicit badge as she had previously done (such as one with the lesbian symbol or with the word 'Dyke' on it – 'recognised' according to the tribunal 'as a lesbian indication only to the initiated'). After a few days consideration Ms Boychuck decided that the company was being unreasonable; she would continue to wear an unambiguous badge. She was then dismissed.

The bizarre logic of an evidently confused tribunal chairman is amply shown by the following verbatim exchange noted by the NCCL lawyer who conducted the case.

Chair: 'Aren't you trying to propagandise, encourage others to be lesbian?'

LB: 'No you can't do that because it is an ongoing process of growth and development; it is slow overcoming prejudice.'

Chair: 'Why not a less explicit badge?'

LB: 'Because people would not know what it meant.'

Chair: 'Weren't you trying to encourage others?'

LB: 'No. Trying to show what lesbian was, trying to dispel myths.'

Chair: 'You wore all these badges?' [meaning Gay Switchboard, Lesbians Ignite, among others.]

LB: 'Yes'

Chair: 'With telephone numbers?'

LB: 'Yes'

Chair: 'Weren't you trying to bring other women into the cult . . . Gay Switchboard is an introduction service isn't it? Why would you be wearing a Gay Switchboard badge unless you were propagandising?'

The industrial tribunal rejected her case, stating that it was properly within an employer's discretion to instruct an employee not to wear some sign or symbol that 'could be offensive to fellow employees and customers'. In dismissing her appeal against that finding, the EAT ruled that what the tribunal had meant by 'could' was 'could be expected to be'.

> 'That does not mean that an employer by a foolish or unreasonable judgment of what could be expected to be offensive, can impose some unreasonable restriction. It does mean that a reasonable employer, who after all is ultimately responsible for the interests of the business, can be allowed to decide what, upon reflection and mature consideration, could be offensive to the customers and to fellow employees. We do not think that it can be said to be necessary for him to wait and see whether the business is damaged, or what disruption is caused, before he takes steps in those circumstances.'

The outcome in *Burman* v *Trevor Page Ltd.* (1977)[19] emphasises the need for support from fellow workers. Mr Burman worked as a delivery driver for an old established furnishing company employing 16 people. He pleaded guilty to a charge of buggery with an older man; he was fined £25. After the case was reported in the press some of his fellow employees became very antagonistic, saying it was 'horrible', they were 'repulsed', and threatened to leave. The bad working relationship which ensued was accepted as the main reason for dismissal.

The majority of the tribunal decided that:

> 'it was Mr Burman's responsibility and no one else's that tension arose in a working organisation which had hitherto been harmonious. To us it seems misconceived that long serving and loyal employees should be expected, as Mr Burman put it, to 'overcome their hostility'. In our view there was no hope at all after the publicity of the two court appearances that the situation could ever again be what it had formerly been . . . parliament [in 1967] did not declare [homosexual] conduct to be normal or desirable. Members of the public are entitled to hold what views they like on the subject and strong views are indeed held both in favour of and against homosexual conduct. What is significant in this case is that Mr Burman's homosexuality became public by his own act. Thereafter it was inevitable that public opinion would be formed and expressed.

... In this case [we] consider that Mr Burman's offence was not private conduct at all, but public conduct because it led to a criminal conviction. Further, it was not only capable of damaging his employer's business but actually damaged it, because a good working relationship between the members of staff was markedly worsened. It was capable of damaging the business because there was concern that the high reputation which the company enjoyed with their customers might be damaged either through tension between Mr Burman and other employees becoming apparent to customers, or which would have been worse, Mr Burman making use of his opportunity when visiting customers' houses to interest members of customers' families in homosexual activities with him. His conduct was also intolerable to a significant proportion of fellow workers.'

There have been a large number of dismissals from private concerns, reported to advice and campaigning agencies or in the gay press. These gay employees have usually been dismissed before they were qualified by length of service to take a case to an industrial tribunal. They have been working in areas not strongly unionised, so their employers could operate arbitrarily, their prejudice having free rein.

So far, no 'blue collar' worker has taken a case to an industrial tribunal. Employers do not seem concerned about any alleged disruption caused by the presence of a gay blue collar employee. Fellow workers rarely complain, just abuse the gay employee.

In two cases, both on the files of the NCCL, a car worker (whose criminal conviction for an indecency offence was discovered by fellow workers) left his job because of the abuse he received. Having moved to another town and found new employment, the same thing happened again. Another case concerned a coal miner who came out at work. After several months of serious abuse and ostracism he was gradually accepted back into the social network of the mining community. In the present state of employment law this does not raise legal questions. Legal remedies are not appropriate – what is needed is a lead by trade unions.

'Getting it together'

Working with young people: personal experience

Some of the problems of being an openly gay teacher (that is, open to the pupils) are explained by a former ILEA teacher, John Warburton.[20]

'Perhaps the only area where I felt dubious about being openly gay was school. I had never hidden my gayness from staff, but on the other hand I had never made it clear to all staff, only to colleagues I felt I related to as friends. I never came out to kids, believing, firstly that I would not be able to cope with, as I felt then, the inevitable hostility such a revelation would produce, and secondly that my job would be put in jeopardy by so doing. (I can recall occasions when I avoided conversations with kids that I knew would, if I had been honest, have led to the issue of my homosexuality; more than once I lied for the same reason.)

It is, I think, important to expand here on the roots of this attitude. I felt then that my gayness was something that could only be accepted by a rational adult. I was seeking acceptance, and thus I was prepared to be seen as heterosexual by people I worked with whose personal attitudes were unknown to me or who I felt were not sufficiently sophisticated to be able to accept my gayness. Thus at a time when I considered myself to be open about my sexual orientation, I was still adhering to an oppressive self-image, and at the same time holding a condescending attitude, especially towards the kids I taught. This attitude changed in June 1974 when I worked as a supply teacher at Mary Boone School in Hammersmith. In one of my classes, a group of girls was giggling over a magazine article about lesbians. From an attempt to counter their prejudice in a detached way, I moved to 'some of my best friends are gay' to 'yes I am gay'. That was the first time I had discussed gayness in a classroom and I was amazed at the kids' ability to quickly accept the fact, admittedly after an immediately hostile reaction on the part of at least some of the kids. For some reason the news was not spread around the school and after a further discussion with that class next time I taught them, I continued teaching till the end of term as before. The only obvious change was a definite improvement in relations between myself and that particular class.

That occurrence made me realise two things. First, I could come out to kids without detrimental results, and second, I had underestimated the sensibility of the kids I had taught. (I often wonder how many of the teachers who appear aloof and distant to the kids they teach are in fact gay.) This view was strengthened when one girl came to me after the second lesson, thanked me for saying what I did, and after making me promise not to tell anyone else, told me her sister was a lesbian. She really needed to tell someone that. That revelation made me appreciate that gay teachers, rather than being discreet, should be open and positive about their gayness in school. It is necessary if the prevailing view of gays is ever going to be that of equality with non-gays, It is not only important for gay kids to have a positive role model, but also important that non-gay kids have an opportunity to question their prejudice about us.

Thus I knew when I started teaching at St Marylebone that I would be able to cope if and when the kids realised I am gay. I was surprised it took so long and was even more surprised at the way I eventually did come out – by meeting a pupil whilst on a gay rights march. Apart from the initial unnerving awareness that half the school seemed to have been informed of the news, I was right – I did cope well.

My first class greeted me with a chant of "homo-homo" and various other insults. I could not teach them geography until I had sorted it out, and thus told them that I am homosexual, that it was insulting to call me "queer", "bent", "poof" etc. and why, what the demonstration I had attended was about and other ways that homosexuals are oppressed in society and answered their questions. The talk and discussion lasted about 15 minutes. Although I could have easily devoted the next few weeks to the subject, my only concern was that I should regain the respect that the kids had for me and I for the kids which produces an environment conducive to teaching my subject. Similar discussions occurred in my other two second year classes when I subsequently took them, for the same reasons'.

Sometime later these discussions were reported to the school's administration. Mr Warburton was given an ultimatum by the ILEA: either undertake 'not in future to discuss homosexuality with pupils, except in the course of a completely structured programme of sex education of which the headmaster/headmistress has full knowledge, and with which he/she is in full agreement' or be banned from teaching in any inner London school. Mr Warburton refused, he rejected the argument that he should not be as open about his sexual orientation as the majority of heterosexuals are about theirs. He was banned.

Many schools and education authorities would agree with the

position that the ILEA took at this time. Some schools have not taken such a hard line attitude. They have not taken any action against gay teachers discussing homosexuality and those teachers have not been required by the ILEA to sign any undertaking. In 1982 the new Labour administration of the ILEA reversed this previous policy and confirmed that Mr Warburton could be considered for teaching posts. A GLC councillor and former vice-chair of the ILEA schools sub-committee stated:

'It is quite acceptable for most teachers to divert from their subject matter if questions arise naturally from pupils. Homosexuality should not be treated as abnormal, because it isn't if you are homosexual. Homosexuals have the same right to be open about their private lives as heterosexuals do.'[21]

Trade unions[22]

Some trade unions have been very strong on gay rights, for example the National Association of Local Government Officers (NALGO), the National Union of Public Employees (NUPE), the Civil and Public Servants Association (CPSA) and the Society of Civil and Public Servants (SCPS). NALGO and the SCPS have suggested that sexual orientation should be included in the TUC model equal opportunity clause (see page 119 below). The Scottish Trades Union Congress, the Institute of Education in Scotland and a host of Scottish trade union branches gave support to John Saunders, (see page 105) dismissed because he was homosexual. However, until gay rights are taken up by a much larger section of the trade union movement there is little chance of specific protective legislation.

The Gay Teachers' Group (see Appendix V) campaigns for the rights of gay teachers and students. It is important work considering the ambiguous attitude adopted by teachers' unions towards gay staff. No case which has gone to a tribunal has been taken on by a teachers' union, who when faced with intransigent employers recommend resignation to the employee. The official line of teachers' unions has been that a teacher's sexuality has nothing to do with a teacher's professional life. This means they do not support discussion of homosexuality in school, even when gay teachers are questioned by pupils. The National Union of Teachers recommends that students asking such questions should be referred to the biology teacher. However, NATFHE, the union for teachers in further and higher education, has a policy to give 'full and appropriate support' to all gay members.[23]

In June 1976, NALGO decided to seek agreement with employers to a commitment to equal opportunity in employment regardless of sexual orientation. The motion adopted by NALGO added sexual orientation to the TUC clause on equal opportunities in employment (TUC Circular No. 100, 1974-75) which is a model for inclusion in all relevant collective agreements between trade unions and employers. This amended model clause reads:

'The parties to this agreement are committed to the development of positive policies to promote equal opportunity in employment regardless of workers' sex, sexual orientation, marital status, creed, colour, race or ethnic origins. This principle will apply in respect of all conditions of work, including pay, hours of work, holiday entitlement, overtime and shift-work, work allocation, guaranteed earnings, sick pay, pensions, recruitment, training, promotion and redundancy.

The management undertake to draw opportunities for training and promotion to the attention of all eligible employees, and to inform all employees of this agreement on equal opportunity.

The parties agree that they will review from time to time, through their joint machinery, the operation of this equal opportunity policy.

If any employee considers that he or she is suffering from unequal treatment on the grounds of sex, sexual orientation, marital status, creed, colour, race, or ethnic origins, he or she may make a complaint which will be dealt with through the agreed procedure for dealing with grievances.'

NUPE has adopted a similar policy to that of NALGO. At central government level in the civil service, the CPSA, the SCPS, the Institute of Professional Civil Servants (IPCS), and the First Division Association (FDA) – who together represent over 75 per cent of the non-industrial civil service – have all been mandated by their memberships to oppose discrimination on grounds of sexual orientation.[24]

The TUC has declined to amend its model clause and has stated that to include sexual orientation would weaken its effect: 'There are perhaps other minority groups that could argue for inclusion.' In response to the *Saunders* case (see page 105) the SCPS renewed the request for sexual orientation to be included in the model clause. If the TUC were to adopt this amendment gay people would be placed in a much better position to deal with employers.

Chapter Seven
Lesbian and gay parents and children

'Lesbian mothers: "moral danger"
Warp the child, contaminate it
Hail the Judge our overseer
See the father pale and pining
Hardly knows his frightened daughter
Prick too proud to pass this battle
Property – his right to fight for
Prejudice his moral armour
Patriarch the social norm'
    Sarah Hardy,
    from 'The Trial of a Lesbian Mother'[1]

To many people, the idea of a person being both homosexual and a parent is inherently contradictory. In fact there are many lesbian and gay parents but until recently there were almost no reported court decisions dealing with our rights as fathers and mothers. There are two reasons. Firstly, most lesbian and gay parents have worked hard to conceal their sexual orientation from their children, their families and their ex-spouses and, secondly, if someone discovered or suspected that a parent was gay, the parent has often given up custody or access 'voluntarily' rather than face a long, expensive and public court case. It has generally been assumed not only that the lesbian or gay parent would eventually lose the case, but also that the inevitable publicity would jeopardise other aspects of the parent's life, such as their employment, their home life or their social position.

Since the mid-1970s, more and more parents in Britain have been unwilling to keep their homosexuality secret and have refused to concede their parental rights. For whatever reason – the emergence of support and pride from the women's and gay movements, or some other cause – fewer parents are accepting without a fight that they must choose between their sexual orientation and the custody of their children.

'Custody' is the right to make the major decisions concerning a child. The parent with physical custody, called 'care and control', has the greatest decision-making power. The majority of reported custody cases concern lesbian mothers. Most of the cases involving gay fathers deal with their right to visit their children – the legal term used is 'access'. The different types of custody and access are explained more fully below on pages 135-137.

Court attitudes

The legal system in the United Kingdom has not accepted the notion that a good parent may also be homosexual. The system is dominated by judges, lawyers and legislators – most of whom are white, male, heterosexual and middle class and who support popular social values. The obvious result is that society's assumption and prejudices regarding both homosexuality and the proper way to bring up children are reflected in the law and court decisions. Several recurring themes emerge from the court decisions on child custody involving lesbian parents.

First, there is the concern that being brought up in a lesbian household will stigmatise a child and create conflicts between the child and the child's friends. Even in cases in which a child has not experienced problems, judges, court welfare officers and psychiatrists have assumed that trouble will develop in the future, and therefore that the child would be better off living in a heterosexual home.

> 'It will be difficult to imagine that this young boy could go through his adolescent period of development without feeling shame and embarrassment at having a mother who has elected to engage in sexual practices which are statistically abnormal.' (Psychiatrist's report)[2]

Second, there continues to be a substantial fear, despite the absence of any supporting evidence, that children brought up in a gay home will grow up to be gay themselves or will develop 'improper' sex role behaviour. It has been openly suggested by the heterosexual parent that (in the case of a lesbian parent) the woman's lover will emasculate male children and seduce female children. Courts refuse to listen to the argument that heterosexual lovers might seduce the daughters of their lover. Use of sympathetic psychiatric evidence against this fallacy is crucial. (See pages 131-132 below.)

> ' A reasonable man would say "I must protect my boy, even if it means parting from him forever, so that he can be free

from this danger." Judge Noakes, Deptford County Court, approved by House of Lords in *re D (an infant)* (1977)[3] (referring to a gay father).'

Third, it is widely presumed that, given a choice between a heterosexual and a homosexual home environment, the heterosexual home is unquestionably better for a child. Once again, no specific reason is provided to support the presumption. Occasionally courts take the position that a heterosexual home provides a better 'role-model' and a better moral environment than does a lesbian home. In *W* v *W* (1976)[4] the Court of Appeal made it clear that the lesbian mother was to be given custody of her two daughters only because the father had no suitable home to offer.

Fourth, although it is the general practice of the legal system to treat the parent-child relationship with respect and deference, the courts have the duty to intervene for the welfare and protection of the child. Unfortunately, in applying this principle a court may conclude that the child's welfare requires removal from the custody of a gay parent. In effect the courts are expressing fears concerning the challenge presented by an alternative home environment to the idea of an isolated heterosexual family unit.

The result is that lesbian mothers and gay fathers live with a constant threat of losing their parental rights. The most common occasion for dispute is between parents during the break-up of a marriage. The right to custody may also be challenged by other relatives (for example grandparents) or by local government social services departments.

Custody disputes

Disputes following marital breakdown

The question of child custody and access usually arises when a marriage has broken down, though it can arise as soon as a couple separate and before a divorce is granted. A married couple can be judicially separated (by the court or by mutual agreement) at any time. This means they are no longer legally bound to live together and so arrangements will have to be made for any children. After three years, a marriage may be ended in divorce if it has 'irretrievably broken down'. This is the sole ground for a divorce in the United Kingdom.[5] In extreme circumstances of 'exceptional depravity' and 'exceptional hardship' a spouse may be allowed by the court to petition sooner than the three-year minimum period. It has been decided that if a wife wishes to divorce her husband within that period, the fact that he has come out as gay does not, in itself, constitute 'exceptional depravity'. However in these circumstances, a wife may be allowed to petition on the alternative ground of 'exceptional hardship'.[6]

'Irretrievable breakdown' can be proved by one of the following five circumstances: (a) one spouse has committed adultery (that is, penetrative intercourse with someone of the opposite sex) and the other finds it intolerable to live with that spouse; (b) one spouse has behaved in such a way that the other cannot reasonably be expected to live with that spouse; (c) one spouse has deserted the other for a continuous period of at least two years prior to petitioning for divorce; (d) the spouses have lived apart for a continuous period of at least two years immediately prior to petitioning for divorce and the respondent (the spouse who is served with the divorce petition) consents to the divorce; (e) the spouses have lived apart for a continuous period of at least five years immediately prior to petitioning for divorce.

Very few divorce cases are ever defended. If one spouse says that they cannot abide living with the other to the extent that they find life intolerable, no divorce court will force them to become reconciled.

So if one partner knows the other is gay and finds that sexual orientation and the change in the other's life objectionable that is sufficient. Since allegations need only be of instances of 'unreasonable behaviour' it is not necessary to prove actual sexual acts (as it would in cases where heterosexual adultery is the source of the breakdown). Allegations of anything connected with a lesbian or gay lifestyle or relationships would probably do, especially those that suggest that the children of the marriage are being neglected, for example by staying out late or all night at gay discos, going to women's meetings, bringing home gay friends who are trying to influence the children about women's or gay rights.

At the time of a divorce, legal provision must be made for the custody of any daughters or sons under the age of 18. If the parents agree who will be the one to have physical custody and what visiting rights the other parent will have, the process is relatively trouble free. It is far better to bargain if possible and keep out of court. (See page 135 below.) If, however, parents cannot agree, a court hearing will be arranged at which a judge will order where the children will live and what rights each parent will have. Such orders can be appealed against or reviewed and altered at a later date.

In disputes between two parents, both are presumed to have an equal right to custody of the children.[7] In deciding between the parents, the judge is given an enormous amount of discretion and the decision is rarely reversed on appeal. The sole principle guiding the judge, overriding any other, is that the 'welfare of the minor is the first and paramount consideration'.[8]

This concept of the child's welfare has no legal definition. There are no hard and fast objective considerations or settled rules, but common factors viewed as important by the courts include: (a) with whom the child has been living since the parents separated, (b) the home environment of both parents, (c) the financial abilities of both parents, and (d) whether one parent is better able to provide for the health or special needs of a child. The judge may also hear evidence on any other issues considered relevant, including the sexual behaviour of the parents, for example: will being brought up in an 'abnormal' (gay) household harm the child?

The homosexuality of a parent is a powerful weapon that can be used to prevent or limit rights to custody or access. Typically, once it has been brought to the court's attention that the mother is lesbian or the father is gay, almost all other evidence becomes secondary. The trial thereafter is liable to focus almost exclusively on the issue of homosexuality, with the lesbian or gay parent trying to convince the judge that there will be no detrimental effect on the child and with the other parent arguing that the child will surely be stigmatised, traumatised, molested, perverted and sexually confused if allowed to live in (or visit) a homosexual environment.

Although there have been a few cases in which the courts (including the English Court of Appeal) have held that a mother's lesbianism does not *in itself* make her an unfit parent, these cases have not had a great impact on child custody litigation. This is because in applying the test of the child's welfare as the 'first and paramount consideration' it is not necessary for one parent to be found unfit. In deciding which of the two parents should have custody, a judge can simply order that it is in the child's best interests to be with the heterosexual parent. There is no requirement that a judge articulate a specific connection between the mother's lesbianism and its effect on her children before denying her custody on the basis of her sexual orientation.

The outcome of a lesbian mother's custody case is often unpredictable. Some lesbians have been successful in their legal battles to retain the children, while others have lost custody of their children after years of being the main parent. Even when a lesbian mother is granted custody of the children, it may be on the condition that she agrees not to live with her lover or not to have gay friends round or to participate in certain public political or social events. The English Court of Appeal has however ruled that judges should not grant custody whilst making conditions about whom the lesbian mother will bring into contact with the children. In *W* v *W*[9] the Court of Appeal reluctantly gave the lesbian mother custody and refused to impose conditions which could not be enforced.

The extreme fear and prejudice triggered by the notion of a homosexual parent is shown in a number of cases involving the right of non-custodial parents to visit their children. It is not uncommon to find, particularly in courts outside London, that the right to visit is given on an undertaking that the lover or any gay friends will be absent during the visit, or in some instances that a heterosexual adult will be present while the parent is visiting the children. However, in *M* v *M* (1977)[10] the Court of Appeal refused to impose a condition on a staying order that the mother's lover, who jointly owned the home, had to be absent.

In *re D (an infant)* (1977)[11] the House of Lords ruled on an application by a mother and her new husband to adopt the child so as to stop all contact between him and the gay father. (For adoption and fostering by gay couples, see page 145.) The father, who was now living with another man, had access to his son by agreement at the mother's home once a week in the presence of the mother and her new husband. The boy was now eight and they were concerned that he might be subjected to homosexual influences by continuing contact with his father and meeting his gay friends. In order to cut him out, the mother and stepfather applied to adopt the boy.

As a general rule 'it is only where the welfare of the child so overwhelmingly requires adoption, that the father can and should be deprived of his parental status'. At the original hearing in this case the gay father explained his objection to the proposed adoption. He told the judge that he loved his son and that he genuinely wanted to see him, and he proposed that there should be access in the home of his parents, but when the boy was older there should be a broader form of access. Yielding to social pressure he said that he did not think it right that the child should be subjected to homosexual influences, and could guarantee that would not happen. He acknowledged that he was likely to have gay friends and to live with men, and possibly his son would find this out. He thought this would not do the child any harm.

The judge decided that his objections were unreasonable: the father's influence was likely to be harmful. The Court of Appeal overruled that decision. They ruled that in order to decide whether this father's objections were reasonable the standards of the hypothetical homosexual father should be used. The mother and stepfather appealed against that judgment to the House of Lords. They won and the original judgment was restored. It was decided that the Court of Appeal was completely wrong. The House of Lords supported the original judge's finding that the fact that the father was homosexual 'destroys at once the main argument which is strong in normal cases that the maintenance of the tie with the possibility of parental influence is valuable to a child and should not be cut off'.

Lord Wilberforce said:

'Whatever new attitudes parliament, or public tolerance, may have chosen to take as regards the behaviour of consenting adults over 21, these should not entitle the courts to relax, in any degree, the vigilance and severity with which they should regard the risk of children, at critical ages being exposed or introduced to ways of life which, as this case illustrates, may lead to severance from normal society, to psychological stresses and unhappiness and possibly even to physical experiences which may scar them for life. I think that the reasonable parent in the circumstances here shown would inevitably want to protect his boy from these dangers, that this parent, to his credit recognised this, and the trial judge so decided.'[12]

Emphasising the point, Lord Edmund Davis said:

'It is only fair to the learned judge to say that he clearly (and rightly) did not regard the fact that the natural father is a homosexual as sufficient per se to establish that his refusal was unreasonable. Thus, he stressed that the case was not one where the father was only occasionally involved in homosexual incidents but that his life-style is to keep a homosexual establishment.'[13]

Having a stable home with a gay lover, accepting one's gayness fully are to these judges factors which are to count against the homosexual parent.

The nature of the remarks in this case shows the general attitude likely to be adopted by the courts in cases involving gay fathers. However, should a gay father make an application for access or custody, his lawyer would seek to draw distinctions between his

case and *Re D*. This judgment was made in very different circumstances, since parental consent to adoption was being withheld
where the father had not been looking after his son and had not
had very close contact with him. A great deal also turned on the
fact that the father was living with a man aged 19. Lord Simon
pointed out that the law did not regard such relationships
neutrally. The situation might be different for a father living with
a man in his twenties or thirties.

Re D is a startling example of the prejudices judges hold against
gay people. It was conceded that the father did not constitute any
danger to his son, but nevertheless should be separated from him.
A more positive point is that four out of the five law lords specifically stated that this case was not a general precedent for dis-
pensing with parental consent on the ground of homosexuality
alone.

Disputes with relatives

It is possible for a parent or indeed for both parents to be involved
in a legal dispute about the care and control of their own children
with another relative, often a grandparent. Whereas a mother and
father are equally entitled to have custody of their children, a
parent is generally considered to have a greater right to custody
than any other relative. Therefore, before a child can be taken
from a parent (by way of guardianship proceedings)[14] and placed
in the custody of a relative, a judge must decide that it would be
detrimental to the child to continue living with the parent, or that
the parent is unfit.[15] There is in effect a greater burden of proof on
other relatives challenging the parents' right to custody than in
cases where one spouse is challenging the other spouse. However,
the courts retain the discretion to presume that it would be
detrimental to the children to allow them to live with gay parents,
and judges are free to apply their own values in deciding what is
detrimental.

Disputes with local authorities

Action by local government authorities to remove a child from the
custody of its parents is generally recognised as a very serious
matter – the last resort. It is action to be taken only when some

behaviour, such as neglect, abuse by the parent, or 'exposure to moral danger' severely harms the child.[16]

Sometimes situations arise where a parent is arrested or goes into hospital and the social services department intervenes to ensure that the children receive proper care during the parent's absence from home. If for example, in the course of this process, a mother's lesbianism is discovered, there may be an attempt to place her child or children in foster care.

Despite the gravity of such intervention, there have been cases in which children were removed from the home and placed in foster care because the court believed that exposure of the children to a continuing lesbian relationship involved the likelihood of serious 'adjustment problems'. However in a recent unreported case where neither parent of a 15-year-old girl was capable (both through alcoholism) of looking after her, her 19-year-old lesbian sister and her lover were supported by a London local authority in their application for custody. The sister was allowed to become an 'intervenor' – a kind of party in the divorce proceedings – and eventually, as both parents and local authority agreed, the court consented to her being given the custody of her sister.

Issues at the hearings

Once a lesbian parent becomes involved in a child custody dispute, every facet of her life is open to scrutiny by the court. It is common for the judge or for the other parent's lawyer to ask questions about the gay parents' sexual partners, about the amount of affection the parent shows to a lover while the children are present, whether the parent is active in feminist or gay organisations, whether the children play with the toys 'appropriate' to their biological sex and even whether or not they share a bed.

Judges and lawyers will often insinuate or directly accuse lesbian parents of molesting their own children, of not caring about them, or of having sexual relations in front of their children. The affront to a parent's dignity is constant throughout the court proceedings. Almost all of the parent's strength and energy are consumed in dealing with the legal system, leaving her to feel she has little remaining to offer a lover, children or friends. Even when cases have been won, this has sometimes been at the cost of the relationship with the lesbian parent's lover.

In one case, a barrister reported that the court

'dwelt on the minutiae of who was in which bedroom, whether
or not the woman slept in the same bed – and whether the ex-
husband had found a depression on the second pillow that
indicated his wife's promiscuity and that the other woman had
been in the house. In five days of hearings during which this
aspect of the case was emphasised, the education of the children and the standard of living that they were going to enjoy
were very much minor issues. Also when the mother challenged
the judge to acknowledge that she wanted to bring up her
children to accept the possibility of life styles other than the
norm, he rejected the challenge and allowed the father's barrister to continue on cross examination centred on details of
the mother's sexual life.'[17]

Perhaps the most devastating blow comes when a lesbian mother
is told she may have custody of the children only if she does not live
with her lover. Except in the most extreme case of physical abuse
no court would tell a heterosexual person to choose between a
spouse and children. But it is not uncommon in lesbian mother
cases for the children and the mother to be denied the right to live
as members of a family headed by two women.

Even in situations in which gay parents have been granted access
or custody rights, the matter is never finally over. Child custody
orders are subject to variation and the possibility remains that a
case may be reopened at any time. If the custody or visiting rights
are accompanied by any conditions, such as the presence of
another adult during the visit, the gay parent must be unswerv-
ingly diligent in abiding by those conditions. However, the fact
that nothing is ever final in custody proceedings means that a gay
parent can apply to the court once regular access is established and
ask for conditions such as having a supervisor, or the absence of a
lover, to be reviewed: an example of this is *M* v *M*.[18] They can also
ask for longer, staying access and eventually custody.

The wishes of the children

The court generally regards it as in the best interests of the children
for them to remain with their mother until the age of about nine.
Around that age, the court considers it acceptable for children to
go to live with their father. This is particularly true when courts are
considering the custody of boys.

Children's wishes can be taken into account after the age of seven or eight. The court welfare officer prepares a report for the court and this officer is more likely to be guided by the child's wishes from the age of ten upwards. By the age of 14 or 15, children would probably be able to choose for themselves, but below that age the court would be likely to impose its own view of what was good for the child. Even if a child of ten were to state its choice, there may be a dispute over who had influenced the child.

In one successful case, a lesbian mother was awarded custody of her daughters. They were 11-year-old twins — one of whom said she wanted to be with her mother, the other was uncertain — and a 16-year-old daughter who very definitely wanted to be with her mother. It had been accepted all the way through the case that the eldest daughter could stay with her mother at that age. In this case it was the ages and the wishes of the younger children that counted, together with the question of accommodation for the mother and the 16-year-old. The Court of Appeal had been critical of the lesbian mother who, they said, was 'obsessively involved in herself and the feminist cause': *W* v *W* (1976).[19]

The psychiatric issues

At the custody hearing the judge will usually ask for a report from the court welfare office to be presented. In addition, the judge or either parent may ask for psychiatric reports. The psychiatrist will see the lover (especially if living with the gay parent) and the ex-spouse. If a gay parent decides to get their own report, the ex-spouse will have to be informed since some judges do not like to see only one side having such a report. The drawback of both sides having reports from different psychiatrists is that each parent then has an 'expert' witness, who is likely to produce a report favourable to their own client. It is advisable to find a psychiatrist through someone known to be sympathetic.

A common question asked of psychiatrists at the hearing will be whether it seems likely that the child will be homosexual if he or she continues to live with or visit the lesbian or gay parent. The psychiatrist will also be asked whether the child is over-anxious about the parent's homosexuality — being embarrassed or distressed by it. Finally, a psychiatrist could even be asked whether the child will be molested by either the parent or the parent's gay friends.

All of these questions may be answered favourably for the gay parent by the examining psychiatrist. However, some psychiatrists are more expert than others on the question of the development of children's sexual orientation and the adjustments children make to a parent's homosexuality. Most psychiatrists believe that a child's sexual orientation is determined by the age of four-and-a-half to six and that exposure to homosexual parents will not influence their development after that age. Prior to that age, it is believed that there are innumerable environmental as well as physiological (in certain instances) causes for homosexual orientation. Having homosexual parents is certainly not a conclusive nor even a primary contributory reason for homosexual orientation. It is also commonly believed by many experts and by gay people that homosexual orientation is almost impossible to reverse. There are few cases where psychiatrists claim reversal, and long term reversals are rarer still. There are greater benefits – short and long term – to be gained from making gay youngsters more easily adjusted to their sexuality by seeing gay adults who can lead a happy life.

Research conducted by the Institute of Psychiatry in London, comparing children growing up in the households of lesbian and single female parents, has concluded that no dire effects were detectable in respect of children being brought up by mothers who are openly lesbian.[20] The myth about homosexuals molesting children has been extensively researched. It has been proven that gay men are less likely than heterosexual men to molest children; lesbian women are the least likely to do so.[21]

The line between compromise and personal politics is often a thin one. For example, while a parent might actually prefer his or her daughter, say, to be lesbian, such candour is unlikely to impress a judge favourably.

Children may well be embarrassed if their friends discover that one of their parents is gay. This argument should carry little weight considering the long-term suffering that young people endure through enforced separation from the parent of their choice. It is obviously helpful in such a case to call a psychiatrist to make this point.

The welfare issues

The court welfare officer will investigate and report to the judge on the following issues: the size of the home, its cleanliness, furnishings, decorations, presence or absence of political posters and so on; the rooms for the children; proximity to school and other children's activities; how the child is doing at school. The officer may speak to the head teacher. Additionally, the officer will report on their parent's relationships — with their child, with their lover, and their lover's relationship with the child. Thus for the welfare officer's visit, the home should be made to appear as conventional as possible, by removing, for example, anything that suggests an interest in 'contentious' living.[22]

Keeping out of court: advice about custody agreements

Why try to make an agreement?

Despite a wide variety of backgrounds we all grow up with notions, continually reinforced, of what is 'normal' in our society. The 'normal' British family is composed of a mother, a father and 2.4 children. This 'normal' family will want to buy a house in the suburbs — if it does not already have one. This image of 'normal' families excludes extended families, communal households and single-parent families. 'Normal' is a dangerous standard in our legal system when it is equated with 'better' or 'desirable'. Judges are accustomed, as pointed out earlier, to enforcing the values and lifestyles of mainstream society. They will look for the 'better' solution or, rather, the family environment which looks most 'normal'. Since a lesbian or gay parent does not generally fit the judge's image of 'better' when it comes to providing a home for the child, it is advisable to keep out of court whenever possible and to resolve custody issues by negotiation.

In order to win by negotiating, a case should be thoroughly prepared from the outset since it may be necessary to contest the issue in court as a last resort. Thorough preparation involves defining what is wanted, knowing what compromises can be made, and knowing which arguments the other side is likely to present. A lawyer is almost certainly needed for such a negotiation. But it is important to have one who will share the decision-making process. In the end the parent is the expert when it comes to deciding what is best for the child, and will have to live with the final arrangement.

Because the legal struggle can be long and frustrating a parent will need active support. The choices that are made about where to look for this support — to friends, family or community and political groups involve important decisions. The chances are that the more support one gets from gay or feminist groups, the more sexuality will become a central focus of the case if it goes to trial. (See pages 173-174 below.)

Reaching agreement

There is no fixed formula for negotiating, but the goal is clear: to retain decision-making power. A number of concerns will arise in any custody case. The first concern is which parent should have custody. A number of different types of custody and visiting rights are explained below. A second concern involves the property and financial support of the children and the parent who has custody. A third concern involves the disclosure or concealment of sexual orientation or private information from the other side.

Even if spouses are able to agree before going to court, a judge is not obliged to accept this, though normally he will. The following are examples of the sort of issues that may arise while trying to reach agreement.

Firstly, it may be proposed to concede custody in return for extensive visiting rights ('access') or vice versa. Gay fathers might choose to bargain for extended access when they are fairly certain that the court is unlikely to decide in favour of their application for custody. Secondly, financial maintenance or property might be bargained in exchange for custody. Even if this alternative is chosen a judge can still change a custody order at a later stage. Thirdly, a decision by one spouse to tell the former partner about their sexual orientation is complicated. Amongst the relevant concerns will be the ages of the children. Fourthly, the changing needs of children and the attitudes of others have to be taken into account because of the possibility of altering the custody decision. To get custody it is always helpful to have the support of school, medical and other institutional people. If regular contact with them is maintained it is more likely that they will be willing to come to court. It also helps in court to have friendships with 'normal' heterosexual couples and families or with members of the opposite sex. Fifthly, a spouse who is determined to retain custody should always keep their child with them. If the child is voluntarily given to the other spouse there is always a great danger of never getting him or her back. Finally it clearly assists a parent to have the support of their family and to be on good terms with their former partners where possible.

When to make an agreement

The stages of court proceedings in relation to custody disputes between parents are set out in the diagram on page 136.

An agreement can be made before or after a temporary custody hearing (before the divorce is made final) or before or after a permanent custody hearing (after the divorce is made final). An agreement can be made even if the parties have already been to court. Some people are able to reach agreement even before legal papers are exchanged. This is the least destructive for the child, least expensive and usually the most desirable way to end a marriage. It is also the fastest way to get through the courts. Once divorce papers have been filed and exchanged, the legal system becomes very competitive. The two lawyers involved will often try to be overly protective of their clients at the expense of a simple or direct solution.

Some planning is necessary; for example an agreement will have to be reached before certain legal events take place, such as the day of the temporary custody or permanent custody hearing. Nothing may happen until the very day of the hearing. In other cases, the negotiation might occur informally between the spouses and lawyers. An agreement may be reached over the telephone or in a prearranged meeting. The exact timing of an agreement is not too crucial. The agreement can be and often is prepared in writing by one of the two lawyers and then presented to the judge.

In *Scotland* it is usual to deal with custody at an interim stage, on the application of either spouse, before the granting of the decree of divorce. Interim custody can be overruled when the divorce is granted. The courts are reluctant to remove custody where it is well established with one parent over a long period, or to grant custody to a father unless he already has it or the mother has shown herself to be manifestly incapable. It is also possible for spouses to come to an agreement. The court will still intervene, though, if the judge thinks that the agreement is not in the best interests of the child.

Types of custody and visiting arrangements

There are three general types of *custody* arrangements. These are not legal requirements and can be altered to suit particular needs. The definitions given here are flexible: (a) *sole custody*: one parent

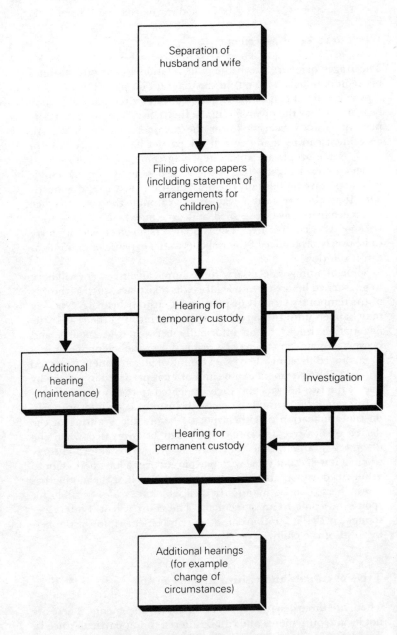

DIAGRAM A. STAGES OF COURT PROCEEDINGS IN CUSTODY DISPUTES
FOLLOWING MARITAL BREAKDOWN.

has custody of at least one child and the other has only visiting rights; (b) *split custody*: each parent has custody of at least one child; (c) *joint custody*: each parent has equal responsibility for each child. The child can either live with each parent part of the time or with one parent most of the time. In each case, both parents have equal decision-making power over major issues concerning the child. However, the parent with physical custody probably has greater decision-making power even if s/he has joint custody.

A note of caution about joint custody. To many people joint custody sounds like the best option available. In reality, joint custody rarely works. This stems in part from the competitive nature of the legal system, in which each spouse is encouraged to win rather than to work together to find the solution that is best for everyone involved. As a result, it is often hard to separate the anger and frustration which came out during the separation process from the need to work together for the best interests of the child. Joint custody involves constant contact between ex-spouses so they must be able to make mutually acceptable decisions concerning the child. This is not the best solution unless both spouses are confident about their present relationship and their ability to continue to share responsibility for the child.

Judges will rarely order joint custody in a custody hearing. In part this is due to the feeling that if spouses could work together, they would not be in court fighting about custody. The refusal to award joint custody also reflects most judges' fears of continuous court appearances whenever former spouses disagree. Joint custody will only be awarded if this is the agreement the spouses have reached. Most judges would throw out joint custody and award sole or split custody if the parties returned to court because of disagreements.

The law states that the parent who does not have custody of his/her child will be given reasonable access, unless these visits would be detrimental to the child. The spouse who is denied custody should be given the right to spend time with the child. Usually this will take place at weekends, or on certain days of the month, and part of some or all holidays. A common access order is one weekend a fortnight or a month, plus a week at Christmas and Easter, some half-terms and two weeks in the summer holidays. Extensive access is as important to fight for as custody itself. Not everyone wants the responsibility and commitment of full-time custody of their child.

It is important for gay fathers to assess realistically the options that are open. Gay fathers face a difficult double bind. Judges refuse to acknowledge that men are able to provide adequate home environments in the absence of women. This is in addition to judges' prejudices against male homosexuality. While it is vital to work towards changing such attitudes in the long term, it is likely to be a mammoth task. It may also be argued that even visits by a gay parent may be detrimental to a child.

Women worried about the strategy to adopt in the early stages of a dispute should contact Action for Lesbian Parents (ALP) (see Appendix V) who can advise not only about custody but also related questions such as getting re-housed. Currently there is no independent organisation for gay fathers, but counselling may be obtained through ALP.

Chapter Eight
Housing and living together

The Thin End of the Wedge

The so-called 'Gay Rights Movement' which is the main organisation acting on behalf of homosexuals in Northern Ireland has made it clear that it regards the proposed changes in the law regarding homosexuality as only the first step. Their spokesman, Kevin Merrett, announced during a televised debate with DUP leader Dr Ian Paisley MP that homosexuals would regard the proposed legalising of homosexuality as a starting point to further and higher demands. Homosexual marriages, homosexuality for Ulster's youth, tax concessions for homosexuals, recognition of homosexuals on the same basis as married couples, these are what Ulster's people will have foisted upon them if the 'Gay Rights Movement' have their wishes granted. ULSTER MUST NOT EMBARK UPON THIS ROAD, IT IS THE ROAD TO MORAL DESTRUCTION AND THOSE WHO WALK THEREON WILL SUFFER GOD'S WRATH

Advertisement issued by the Democratic Unionist Party during their 'Save Ulster from Sodomy' Campaign[1]

Housing problems raise many questions about the nature of lesbian and gay oppression. A great number of gay people have to take unsatisfactory and exploitative jobs, either tied work with bad wages and conditions which at least provide accommodation, or jobs with higher wages for long and unsocial hours which people with family commitments are unwilling to take. Although some landlords will evict gay tenants and gay refuges have their problems (see page 73 above), the main issue in relation to housing is not specifically anti-gay discrimination. The overriding difficulty is that housing policies are geared to the needs of married people and being single is considered merely a brief stage between living at home with parents and getting married. Consequently the long term needs of unmarried and childless people – including gays and lesbians – are usually ignored.

This issue goes beyond housing provision. There is little justification for the differences in legal treatment of married couples, unmarried cohabitees and single people. Gays and lesbians as well as single heterosexuals have an interest in reducing the present legal discrimination against the unmarried.

Housing[2]

Gay people do not conform to the stereotype of the 'average single person', not least because the need for 'single person' housing is likely to be permanent. The extent to which the housing needs and aspirations of lesbians and gays are different from those of other single people and the extent to which gay people suffer from prejudice and discrimination is difficult to assess. A survey conducted by the Gays and Housing Group over 1980 and 1981 showed that one person in five who called Gay Switchboard about housing regarded their homelessness or housing problem as related to their gayness. In practice the housing problems of lesbian women are particularly acute. They have the double disadvantage of being single and female and may well experience particular difficulties, for example, in obtaining a mortgage or loan to buy property.

Although English, Scottish and Northern Irish property laws are very different, much of the statutory law covering tenants' rights is similar. This section points only to the main legal issues. Legal advice should be sought on any particular problem.

Private tenancies

While there remains a substantial supply of rented housing specifically catering for gay people, it is still subject to the problems of the private market in general. Demand always exceeds supply, rents are high and insecurity of tenure – often through loopholes in the Rent Acts – is widespread. Much of the accommodation available at reasonable rents is for flat-sharers. Because of this scarcity single people are particularly vulnerable to schemes designed to evade the protection given to tenants by the Rent Acts. Arrangements such as 'holiday lets' or flat-sharing under a licence to occupy are common. (See page 141 below.) The introduction of shorthold fixed term tenancies (see below) perpetuates the insecurity of single people, who, unprotected by the law, move from one temporary place to another. Despite all this, many private tenants do in fact have Rent Act protection. If in doubt and at the first sign of trouble, legal advice should be sought at a citizens' advice bureau, law centre or housing aid centre.

Landlords have considerable freedom to evict where the letting is not a 'protected tenancy',[3] provided the correct procedures are followed (mainly serving a proper notice to quit). The most common circumstances in which tenants are especially vulnerable are as follows: (a) where the landlord lives on the premises: if the landlord lives in the same house as his/her tenant and has been there since the tenancy began, the tenant may not be 'protected'; (b) where there is a tenancy for a fixed period – a 'protected shorthold tenancy': if a landlord rents accommodation for a fixed period of time between one and five years, tenants will be protected during that time; however when the time runs out, they may have to leave;[4] (c) where the arrangement is a licence, holiday let or food is provided: common schemes to evade Rent Act protection include getting tenants to sign an agreement stating that they have a licence or a holiday let, or where the landlord provides regular food and drink; (d) flat-shares: anyone who has not signed a tenancy agreement with the landlord or does not have their name on the rent book may not have full Rent Act protection.

Owner occupation

For an individual single person on or below the average wage, it is virtually impossible to buy a house or flat because of the savings necessary to meet the deposit and the substantial mortgage repayments and interest rates. A survey by the Gays and Housing Group found that policies on granting mortgages to couples of the same sex varied considerably from one building society to another, and even from one branch to another.

   The types of arrangements for property ownership vary between the different legal systems in the United Kingdom. Some of these arrangements enable more than one or two people to own property. Since the arrangement chosen will affect, for example, what happens to a person's share should s/he die or wish to move, it is essential to get good legal advice.

Public housing

Local authorities are legally obliged to provide housing for homeless families with children under 16 and for single old age pensioners.[5] In the design of public housing, priority has been given to family housing and most accommodation offered to single people has been in flats originally designed for small families. This has meant that in London, for example, the provision of single person housing is usually in units for three or more sharers.

The lack of recognition of gay people's housing needs was high-lighted when the right of succession to a local authority tenancy was provided for under the Housing Act 1980 only in the case of married or cohabiting couples of the opposite sex. An attempt to extend this right to gay couples was rejected during the committee stage of the Bill. On the death of a tenant, the right of succession to the tenancy for members of the family should include not just the surviving member of a 'common law marriage' but also cohabitees of the same sex. The law now recognises the case of men and women who live together without being married, despite the fact that it is always open to them to get married and obtain the rights of spouses. It would not have created difficult problems therefore if gay and lesbian couples were to enjoy the same rights as couples of the opposite sex.

As is often the case with married couples, cohabitees of the same or opposite sex should be given the option of a joint rather than an individual tenancy. The advantage of a joint tenancy is that it extends the rights of each partner to the occupation of the home and leaves responsibility for paying the rent in both their hands.

Alternatives in public housing

Housing co-operatives are organisations run by tenants for their own benefit. A list of co-ops is kept by the Co-operative Housing Agency.[6] Unfortunately most co-ops are small, and not often in a position to take on new members. Some co-ops own their houses outright, others have licence agreements with local authorities to use 'short-life' property. Many housing co-operatives have constitutions which preclude giving security of tenure to their tenants. This is most commonly the case with 'short-life' housing co-ops where the local authority makes this a condition of the licence granted to the co-operative.

Housing associations are another possibility. These are private housing trusts run with government or local authority money. Of those housing associations which provide housing for single people, few are directly approachable by the public, and those that are approachable usually have long waiting lists. Many association lettings to single people are in shared flats. Whether a tenancy is held jointly or is in the name of only one of the sharers will depend on the policy of the particular association.

Housing Advice Switchboard is a useful source of information about housing alternatives for single people (see page 221).

Homelessness

One area in which the law patently discriminates against single people is in housing those who have become homeless. The Housing (Homeless Persons) Act 1977 obliges local authorities to help families with children under 16 who have become homeless through no fault of their own. The councils are only obliged to house single people in similar circumstances if they are pregnant, disabled, suffering from severe mental handicap or illness, are over retirement age, or have become homeless through fire, flood or other natural disaster. Gay people who do not fall within these categories would be entitled to advice and assistance from the homeless families unit at their local town hall, but in practice would have to find their own emergency accommodation.

Many emergency hostels have inmates and perhaps staff who are openly hostile to gays and the few private hotels catering for gays are geared to the needs of tourists. Clearly a remedy must be found to the legal difficulties surrounding proposals to establish a refuge for young gays, already discussed above.

Some homeless people may in the end have little option but to find an abandoned house to squat. Opening a squat is not a criminal offence. It is criminal, however, to trespass with a 'weapon of offence' or enter premises violently if there is someone present opposed to the squatters' entry.[7] A 'weapon of offence' covers something made as a weapon or something which was intended for use as a weapon – this might include household tools if, for example, they were waved at the police. Legal and practical information is given by the Advisory Service for Squatters. (See page 221.)

Living together

One of the important legal consequences of marriage is that only married couples have the right to go to the courts to settle financial and other problems (such as custody and housing) which arise when their relationship breaks down. In some areas, the law has progressed to recognising that financially dependent women in 'common law marriage' relationships have a right to 'proper financial provision' from the 'husband'. There are few obvious solutions to the similar problems which arise in long-standing gay and lesbian relationships. In effect, gay people who live together for a long time are in a legal limbo and must rely on mutual trust and foresightedness to deal with any difficulties that may occur.

Bereavement

One important example affecting long term partners is the problem of inheriting property. If a husband or wife dies without leaving a will there are rules to ensure that all property will be inherited by the surviving spouse and children. Lesbians and gay men can only ensure that their partners inherit if they leave a will, otherwise surviving next of kin will inherit any property.

Since 1975 it has been possible for anyone who was partly or entirely maintained by a deceased person to claim for proper financial provision from the estate. In practice, this provision has helped 'common law wives' who were not provided for by their 'husband's' wills.[8] As yet, this law does not appear to have been used by lesbians or gay men in similar circumstances. In some instances, of course, there may be a direct conflict between a gay lover provided for in the deceased's will and the deceased's ex-wife or ex-husband who has received no provision. In practice, a court might very well override the dead person's wishes and give the major share to, say, a former wife, particularly if she has children. The position of an ex-wife reflects real disadvantage, so that in some instances it may be fair to override the wishes of a deceased person who has provided only for his/her gay partner. In all other situations, a will that makes financial provision for a lesbian or gay partner cannot be contested by the dead person's next of kin unless there are highly unusual circumstances, for example, that it was drawn up with undue influence or whilst the person was incapable of understanding what s/he was doing.

A deceased person's next of kin (including a surviving spouse) are the only ones entitled to sue for compensation if the death occurred in an accident that was somebody's fault. Under the Fatal Accidents Act 1976, lesbian and gay partners have no right to make such claims even if they suffered financial loss as a result of the death.

A 'testamentary guardian' can be appointed in a will to take custody of a child on the death of a parent with sole custody. Where children are living with a lesbian couple this is important. The inviolability of such a provision has not yet been tested in the courts so its validity is not absolutely certain.

Children

Another implication of the lack of recognition for gay relationships is that it is extremely difficult for gay couples to adopt a child. The Adoption Act 1976 provides for adoption by married couples or a single person. In practice, most adoption agencies will not accept single people as adoptive parents. Although private adoptions can still be arranged lawfully, these must be notified to the local authority who will 'investigate the suitability of the applicant'. Fostering is possible where there is a sympathetic local authority social services department. Unlike adoption, fostering is solely at the discretion of the local authority.

Officially, artificial insemination by donor (AID) will not be given to an unmarried woman. Reports that AID was given to lesbians in a London clinic created a media furore in 1978, but apparently there were no legal repercussions for the women or the doctor involved.

Children conceived by AID are, in law, illegitimate. The Law Commission in England and Wales has proposed the abolition of all legal distinctions between legitimate and illegitimate children.[9] At present it seems that existing distinctions operate so as to lessen the opportunity for intervention by the courts, as the father of an AID child is not a 'parent' or a 'guardian' for the purposes of the Guardianship of Minors Act. No issues of custody will therefore arise. The exception to this might be if the social services department of a local authority decided to intervene in extreme circumstances (as described on pages 128-129 above).

Break up of relationships

Lesbian and gay couples are particularly vulnerable if their relationship breaks down. People who live together have few automatic rights: there is no right to remain in a home that has been regarded as the joint house. In England and Wales, for example, a wife who gets a divorce has a very strong claim to the ownership of the property, even though her name is not on the title deeds. Additionally, she has certain rights to stay in the home until the divorce is completed.[10] Unless gay people buy or rent property jointly, the non-owner or non-tenant has no protection or rights if the relationship breaks down. However if the non-owner has contributed either to the purchase price or the expenses generally, it is often possible in English law to establish legal rights over the property through the notion called a 'resulting trust'.

Financial matters

The last major financial and legal repercussion of living together is tax liability and state benefit entitlement. The tax position is undoubtedly more favourable to married couples. A husband can claim a married man's tax allowance, and if a wife is working, can get earned-income relief which amounts to a single person's tax allowance. So between them, a husband and wife can earn several hundred pounds extra before tax. A wife can claim a pension on her husband's national insurance. Lesbian and gay partners only have pension entitlement in their own right and do not have the rights that spouses have in relation to private pension schemes and other trade union negotiated benefits. Of course, there is another side to this matrimonial coin. A dependent wife or woman living with a man cannot claim supplementary benefit in her own right: the so-called 'co-habitation rule'. The husband has to claim the married couples' rate while the wife's personal allowance is less than that of a single person. Same sex couples, regardless of their financial dependency, can both claim supplementary benefit in their own right, without being questioned about whether they are being 'kept' by their partner. A minister at the Department of Social Security, Patrick Jenkin, when in opposition, thought that this was the only example of discrimination in respect of gay people and that it was positive.[11]

As with married couples, it is probably only middle-income bracket gay people with long-term relationships who would benefit financially from joint tax assessments. For rich gay men and lesbians, like rich heterosexual couples, it is usually better to be separately assessed.[12] Changes such as joint tax assessments would run the risk for most gays of introducing some form of cohabitation rule so that the government would be seen to be even-handed.

The Cohabitation Handbook,[13] written by members of Rights of Women, makes proposals directly relevant to lesbian and gay couples. One approach would be the piecemeal reform of statutes that discriminate against partners who live together; another would be to press for the legal recognition of 'cohabitation contracts'.

Piecemeal reform of the statutes suggests that the existing rights of surviving spouses and next of kin be extended to members of the deceased's 'household'. Although such a proposal would widen the number of people who could make claims on the death of a member of their household, the courts would retain their usual discretion to assess claims on the basis of financial loss actually suffered. The two main statutes affected would be the Inheritance (Provisions for Family and Dependents) Act 1975 and the Fatal Accidents Act 1976. Under the former, any person who was a member of the deceased's household immediately before the death could make a claim. The test for financial provision should be the assessment of what is reasonable for the applicant to receive for his or her maintenance. Awards would reflect the financial circumstances of the applicant: they would be based on need and not on the status of marriage. Also at present, the personal goods owned strictly by a cohabitant who dies without leaving a will pass to his/her next of kin. The Act would be amended to allow for separate claims by cohabitants in respect of goods in joint use or of particular personal value. Members of the deceased's household would be added to the existing class of persons who can make claims under the Fatal Accidents Act. This would extend rights to unmarried couples of the opposite sex and gay and lesbian cohabitants. Claims would continue to be assessed on the present basis, that is, the actual financial loss suffered as a result of death. These reforms would have the advantage of providing for situations where partners had neglected to leave a will.

The alternative approach is to develop the idea of a 'cohabitation contract'. Such an agreement, drawn up with legal advice, would set out the partners' mutual obligations. Both partners would have to accept it as legally binding, so that if either person were to break the agreement, it would be possible for the other to go to court. The contract would deal with such matters as mutual financial support, sharing money and property and responsibility for any children. It could also set out what should happen to the children, property and so on if the relationship ended.[14]

In 1976 the California courts upheld such a contract in an action brought against the film actor Lee Marvin. *The Cohabitation Handbook* argues that English courts are likely to follow the example set by this persuasive ruling, at least if cohabitants of the opposite sex are involved. This may not happen in cases concerning lesbian and gay couples. In the current climate, it may be that recognition would be refused on the general grounds that gay cohabitation contracts may encourage homosexual relationships and would therefore be contrary to public policy.[15]

Chapter Nine
Immigration

'You have got to allay people's fears on numbers . . . we must hold out the prospect of a clear end to immigration.

People are really rather afraid that this country might be rather swamped by people with a different culture, and you know the British character has done so much for democracy, for law, and so much throughout the world that if there is any fear that it might be swamped, people are going to react and be rather hostile to those coming in'.

Margaret Thatcher[1]

The Immigration Rules[2] for the United Kingdom recognise and accommodate emotional relationships between individuals of the opposite sex, usually, but not always, formalised in marriage. The Rules make provision for heterosexual relationships outside marriage albeit in limited conditions. They state that 'a woman who has been living in permanent association with a man . . . has no claim to enter but may be admitted . . . as if she were his (the immigrant's) wife'.[3]

By comparison a lesbian or a gay man admitted to the United Kingdom for temporary stay, who develops a strong relationship with a UK resident, is not allowed to remain on the basis of that relationship. Neither does a gay person's emotional commitment provide any claim for admission to the UK. As a result some gay people have been refused entry or have had to leave Britain despite close emotional ties here.

The Home Office have claimed that they cannot devise criteria to assess the strength and stability of long term relationships in the case of gay people. Even if it were possible to construct some alternative test, the Home Office say that they would not want gays to 'queue jump' ahead of legitimate fiancés.

In 1980, the Home Office stated:

'Where a homosexual relationship was the only claim an applicant had for entry [the Minister] foresaw some difficulties. Admission would not simply provide equality with heterosexual relationships, it would mean that partners in such liaisons would be able to avoid the queues and the initial period of limited leave to enter to which, for example, male fiancés were subject. [The Minister] remains of the view that it would be difficult to use the stability of relationships for the purpose of immigration policies.'[4]

It is hard to understand why the assessment of gay relationships should be more difficult than the checking of marriages which are subjected to official investigation to assess their genuineness. (Marriage documents are never sufficient in themselves.) Nor can one understand why acknowledgement of gay relationships as a basis for entry to stay here should necessarily advantage such relationships over heterosexual ones.

What options are open to gays and lesbians wanting to settle in the UK? The majority of the categories which lead to settlement under the Immigration Rules require that an application be made to an Entry Certificate Officer (a UK government official) outside the UK. Therefore if the individual is in the UK s/he will have to leave in order to secure eventual return to Britain under one of the permitted categories. The main categories are: employees with a work permit, self-employed people, sole representatives of an overseas business, people with independent means.

At present it is extremely difficult for immigrants wishing to settle here to do so. Doubtless some gay and lesbian immigrants will have independent means (currently defined as a minimum of £100,000 or £10,000 unearned income a year) or will satisfy the work permit regulations. There are also gay EEC nationals who wish to come to this country to join their lovers. Such nationals are free to work here. But there are also many would-be immigrants who do not have these advantages. There are also a significant number who face severe problems in their own countries because of their sexual orientation and therefore wish to emigrate and settle in western countries such as Britain.

Asylum

An individual may be entitled to claim asylum or refugee status.[5] The UK is a party to the Convention and Protocol Relating to the Status of Refugees. In general terms, a refugee is a person having a well-founded fear of being persecuted (for certain reasons which include membership of a particular social group) if compelled to return to a particular country. The fear must relate to the only country to which the person can be removed. If an applicant has lived in a second country where s/he has not been persecuted and then comes to the UK, asylum is unlikely to be granted.

Asylum is provided for in the Immigration Rules and may be granted with or without refugee status. If refugee status is granted the immigrant will have the full protection of the United Nations High Commissioner for Refugees and will be eligible for a United Nations Convention travel document. There are other advantages, but broadly speaking asylum without refugee status allows the immigrant to remain in the UK on similar terms to asylum with refugee status. In one case, asylum without refugee status was given to a gay man from Iran, where there had been many executions under the Khomeini regime of men convicted of homosexual 'offences'.

Even where the Home Office is not prepared to give political asylum the minister might still allow an individual to enter or remain. Ministerial discretion is not governed by the Immigration Rules. It may be exercised at any time by the Home Secretary (or more usually the minister having special responsibility for immigration).

At one stage the Home Office[6] gave an assurance that the minister would consider using his discretion to admit homosexuals to the UK, particularly those from countries where there was a well-founded fear of persecution.

There is often a considerable problem over evidence with regard to claims for an exercise of ministerial discretion and asylum. This is true of all asylum cases and is especially true of cases involving sexual harassment, since these are likely to be less well documented.

X's case was decided by the minister in 1980. X was born in Venezuela. For many years he had been abused, physically assaulted and ostracised because of his gayness. He was subjected to aversion therapy to alter his sexual orientation, which failed. X's mother then committed suicide. X suffered a nervous breakdown. Soon afterwards he left for Britain where he settled down and also formed a stable relationship, the first he had been able to enjoy. Having out-stayed his time in the UK, X was threatened with the break up of that relationship. The minister was presented with medical evidence pointing to the extreme likelihood that X would commit suicide if returned to Venezuela. Permission to remain was refused, largely it appears because it was impossible to get firm and convincing evidence about the persecution of gay people there. When X left, his UK-born boyfriend left with him. The minister's decision in this case underlines the importance of obtaining such evidence.

By contrast, in the case of an Argentinian applicant who was granted asylum in 1981, the Argentine Gay Liberation Organisation in exile in Spain produced a great deal of material on the situation of male homosexuals. The significant considerations in this man's case were: (1) he had been active in the Argentine gay rights movement before he left; (2) his family's home had been raided and searched by the police; (3) the fact that he was homosexual was recorded on his Argentine Identification Document; (4) there was convincing evidence from the Argentine gay movement of beatings, imprisonment and disappearance of gay people. At one period an estimated two hundred men were being arrested every day. Cases such as this one highlight the tangible value of gay organisations collecting as much information as possible about the position of gays and lesbians.

Marriage

Unfortunately there are many lesbians and gay men who do not fall within any of the foregoing categories. For them marriage may seem to be the only possibility. In the words of one lawyer experienced in this field, 'there is an obvious and unpleasant irony in gay men and women reaching for salvation in a marriage of convenience'.[7]

An immigrant husband is allowed to enter or remain with his wife only if she is a UK citizen born in the UK or is a UK citizen and one of her parents was born here. But even in these circumstances, the marriage will be examined to see if it is really one of convenience. Initially the husband will be given only 12 months' leave to enter. The position will then be reviewed at the end of that period. The husband will not be allowed to remain if it is decided, for example, that one of the parties to the marriage no longer has any intention of living with the other or that the marriage was entered into primarily to obtain settlement in this country. Parties to the marriage may be committing a crime by making false statements relating to the marriage.[8] Furthermore if the man is proved to be an illegal entrant (entry secured by fraud, false representation or concealment of any material facts) the Secretary of State can order his removal from the UK without great formality or judicial safeguard.

An immigrant wife has less difficulty in settling; for example there is no 12-month probationary period. The reasoning behind this is the assumption that the man is the head of the household and the primary source of immigration. Fulfilling the formal requirements of the Rules is not conclusive. A lesbian immigrant still runs the risk of being prosecuted for a criminal offence, deported or treated as an illegal entrant as explained above.[9] However given the scheme of the Rules it is rare for women immigrants to have difficulty in being allowed to settle on the basis of their marriages. Marriage to a man settled here (that is, without UK citizenship) would be sufficient to secure a woman immigrant's settlement.

A woman commonwealth immigrant marrying a UK citizen (who is, for example, a citizen by birth or registration in the UK) will become 'patrial'. This means that she will have the 'right of abode' which means an unchallengeable right to remain in this country.[10]

A spouse of an EEC national working in the UK will be allowed to enter or remain in the UK provided that s/he is living with that spouse.[11]

A possibility which so far seems to have been scarcely explored relates to using the machinery of the European Convention of Human Rights (see Appendix IV). Article 8 paragraph 2 of the Convention states that everyone has the right to respect for his/her private and family life, home and correspondence. Paragraph 2 goes on to specify the circumstances in which this right may be interfered with by a public authority. The European Commission has accepted that extra-marital relationships may constitute 'family life' within the meaning of Article 8. It would seem arguable that homosexual immigrants who have relationships with UK citizens or individuals settled in the UK should be able to claim the protection of this Article.

However in *X and Y v Switzerland* (1977)[12] the Commission decided that the Convention does not as such guarantee an alien's right to be admitted to, or reside in, a particular country where in this case there was no common household of the applicants (German and Austrian nationals of opposite sexes) who did not permanently live together. In effect the Commission decided that a law prohibiting entry can only be considered as interfering with a person's private or family life where the private and family life of that person is firmly established in the territory concerned.

In different circumstances – for instance where a common household had been established – it might be possible to obtain a new ruling. However there are a number of practical problems that would need to be overcome. Until an immigrant asks the Home Office for permission to stay on the basis of his or her relationship it would not be possible to complain of the break up of that relationship by the state. The immigrant would have no right to remain in the UK while his or her application was being vetted by the European Commission. Moreover the immigrant needs to have exhausted all domestic legal remedies relating to the refusal.

The absence of any existing legal recognition for gay and lesbian relationships cannot be accepted as an argument against recognising such relationships as a basis for immigration. Heterosexual relationships are already examined to weed out marriages of convenience. As has been pointed out earlier, the Immigration Rules do take into account relationships outside marriage, albeit in limited conditions. Ministerial discretion is not being exercised effectively so as to permit deserving cases involving homosexual immigrants to remain in this country.

Chapter Ten

The gay response

'The association of homosexuals as a group and the adoption of the
word "gay" are in themselves an indication of the squint from the
norm and I regard it as unhealthy to associate together as a group on
the sole basis of squint sexual activity as being a common interest.'

Solicitor General for Scotland 1979[1]

'I've never been part of the organised gay movement. I suppose I am
a loner by temperament, but this is important to me and I can see
how important it is for everyone who is gay and therefore at risk. It's
like they always say – you never believe it's going to happen to you.
When it does, you have to make up your mind whether to take it
meekly or fight. And I'm going to fight.'

John Saunders, after his dismissal from work.[2]

The gay movement

The limitations of the law described in this book have been exposed
largely through the impact and work of the gay movement. The
fight against an ideology, and the system which supports it, is very
difficult. Action is not easy, either on a personal or organisational
level, and even gay counselling and help services are not entirely
secure. However people need not be alone. As individuals it is possible to draw on the solidarity of the gay movement. On a wider
scale the gay movement has broadened its impact far beyond those
people and groups interested in sexual politics.

During the 1950s and 1960s most of the political work around
gay rights went on behind the scenes through the lobbying of MPs
and other 'opinion makers', educational work and so on. As part of
the general process of coming out in the 1970s, many gay people
have become more public about their politics adding, for example,
the important channels of public meetings, demonstrations and
marches, leafleting, flyposting and so on. Many significant campaigns – national and local – have been fought.[3]

Though British citizens have no rights guaranteed in a written constitution, it is clear that all citizens have a number of 'constitutional'
rights which include the legal right to join and be identified with

other people for common goals. It is not a genuine right unless members of the group are able to meet and communicate with one another and the general public.

Gay groups have faced many obstructions. The press has sometimes refused to print advertisements placed by gay organisations or gay groups.[4] A number of local authority library committees have banned *Gay News*.[5] Veiled threats of legal action have been aimed at various groups distributing stickers and leaflets. It is lawful for owners to refuse to allow groups to use meeting places because of their homosexuality. By comparison, refusal because of sex or race would be illegal. A number of English local authorities have, for example, refused venues to CHE conferences.[6] It took a four-year struggle before Rotherham Council gave permission for the local CHE group to hire the town hall assembly rooms. The authority admitted its fault following a complaint to the Local Commissioner for Administration (the 'ombudsman') who decided that the council was guilty of 'injustice by maladministration'.[7]

The exercise of the right to join together is also inhibited by the very real fear that the police have a practice of keeping records on homosexuals, particularly those who are members of organisations. In Gloucester and Rotherham, there have been documented instances of police surveillance of CHE members. The deputy chief constable of South Yorkshire admitted in October 1978 that his officers had compiled an 'unofficial list' of members of Rotherham CHE by tracing names and addresses from car registration numbers noted by officers watching a branch meeting.[8] A complaint made by Gloucester and Cheltenham CHE about the presence of two plain-clothes detectives at a public meeting was met by a riposte from the deputy chief constable that 'there was nothing sinister about the presence of the officers . . .'.

People who work within the gay movement and who warn of the possibility of police action against gay organisations are thought by some to be alarmist and paranoid. The police action against the Northern Ireland Gay Rights Association (NIGRA) provides a sobering case history.

In a part of the UK where 'God demands righteousness not gay rights' (the slogan of the Paisleyites) it was almost inevitable that the police would attempt to break up a gay rights organisation in its formative period. Gay people in Belfast started organising in 1974. From January 1976 until February 1977 gay activists were interrogated, had their homes searched, documents seized and were threatened with prosecution. Eventually the Attorney

General in London overruled a recommendation by the Director of Public Prosecutions for Northern Ireland to bring charges against members of the Belfast Gay Liberation Society. The charges were based on statements they had made about their relationships – all of which would then have been lawful in England or Wales.

The wave of police activity began after a complaint from an Armagh woman who discovered that her 18-year-old son had a gay relationship. The Belfast home of his friend was searched and diaries and correspondence were removed. The friend was held for two days of questioning. Information obtained enabled the police to widen their net. During the subsequent raids on various homes, a large quantity of private papers as well as correspondence with public figures on gay rights, gay male pin-up books and conventional political literature were removed in what the officer in charge of the enquiry, one Detective Superintendent Cunningham, called 'investigations into homosexuality'.

The secretary of the Homosexual Law Reform Committee, Jeff Dudgeon, was held for six hours and asked to sign a statement about his gay relationships. The committee's files were taken away. The president of the Northern Ireland Gay Rights Association, Richard Kennedy, whose files were also removed, was held for 16 hours of questioning. The police visited his home on six occasions, usually early in the morning. He said that during his interrogation, the police 'kept reading out pieces from my personal diaries which contained rather frank information and making asides to one another to the effect that I was mentally ill'.[9]

Between January and June 1976, some twenty people were interrogated by the police. They all came from the Belfast area and were mostly gay rights campaigners or their friends. None was charged with homosexual offences. Two of the men interrogated were not gay; the police expressed amazement that they could be friendly with men who were. The raids and questioning came in a sequence determined by the names and addresses contained in private correspondence, address books and diaries impounded by the police.

Thirteen months after the first raid, the Attorney General in London decided to veto a recommendation from the Northern Ireland DPP to charge four NIGRA campaigners (all over 21) with homosexual offences. In 1981 the decision by the European Court of Human Rights in the *Dudgeon* case vindicated the stand taken by the gay rights campaigners.

As a movement gay people have responded to society's pressures by developing self-help groups, rejecting the idea that professionals are required to help homosexuals 'adjust to society'. However, gay organisations of this kind are faced with several legal dilemmas, the most serious being concerned with working with gay teenagers (see pages 72-75 above) and access to charitable finance. Some judges think that the encouragement of homosexuality corrupts public morals. Following this opinion, the Charity Commission refuses charitable status to openly gay services and groups who provide help, advice or support to gay people of any age.

The Charity Commission has a legal duty not to accept on to the Register of Charities any institution which might operate contrary to 'public policy or morality'. In applying this principle to gay organisations, the Commission has relied heavily on the distinction drawn by Lord Reid (and other judges) between merely exempting certain conduct from criminal penalties and making it lawful in the full sense. The Commission follows the general line that:

> 'minorities are not to be accorded special rights and privileges, that the moral code is not to be disregarded, and that the fact that material benefits may accrue to homosexuals is not a relevant consideration and cannot prevail over considerations of morality.'[10]

Whether or not a gay institution is 'involved in procuring', has 'proclivities tending towards the promotion of homosexual acts' or 'advocates that way of life as desirable in itself', and its 'general conduct', are all factors that the Commission has stated are relevant to registration as a charity.

Individual cases

The experience of going through the courts (whether because of the police, an employer, a spouse, a landlord or any other person) can be dehumanising. It can also be exhausting, intimidating and frightening. The process of defending a lifestyle, beliefs or sexual orientation to a prejudiced court or tribunal is, to say the least, frustrating. It will also involve some degree of publicity. The best defence to this kind of attack is an active support network of people who can assist in the struggle to keep going.

Such support can be found among friends, family, gay, feminist or community groups, but not only does it need to be congenial and reliable, it also needs to reflect the strategy of the case. For example, if it has been decided to keep homosexuality from being an issue at the trial, it would be better to limit support to friends or family.

Peter Bradley[11] has explained the wider significance of campaigns that concern individuals in trouble.

'The modern gay movement wants to redefine what it means to be gay. Starting from the premise that gay is good we assert that for gays our happiness, well-being and sanity depend on coming out: integrating our gayness into all areas of our lives. The whole movement and groups within it are important in this process but we often also advance through the achievements of individuals. Like the black woman in Alabama who refused to go to the back of the bus, sparking off a civil rights struggle, when John Warburton refuses to promise not to discuss gayness in class and Geoff Brighton refuses to go to the psychiatrist* they extend the range of possible ways of being gay, and reduce the number of ways we can be oppressed, for all gay people. Individual cases can strengthen the whole gay community. As in Geoff's case, such challenges become a testing ground for society's attitudes, and the fight to make that gay person's challenge successful can turn into a campaign with widespread ramifications – with the establishment closing ranks to defend the status quo – and calling on great efforts from the gay community.'

There are not, however, masses of people on call, just itching to confront the authorities. To obtain any support it is necessary to think ahead and organise. For someone who has never had a fight with authority before and has no previous experience of working with gay groups, pressure or community groups, the prospect may be bewildering. This section may provide a few ideas.

When someone has been prosecuted for a so-called homosexual offence, it is likely that the best way to fight back is not individually but in a political campaign on the issue – particularly within one of the national gay rights organisations. The people in the campaigns may think that to organise around a particular case could be a good tactic for getting publicity on the issue.

---

*Geoff Brighton was a university student whose admission to a department of education was partly dependent on passing a routine medical examination. After confirming that he was homosexual the university's doctor refused to issue a medical certificate until Mr Brighton had been examined by a psychiatrist.

The problem is bigger if the issue is the treatment meted out by the legal system as such. Generally there are not active campaigns on issues such as the indifference of lawyers, or the prejudices of tribunals and courts. If an individual comes to see that the legal system is part and parcel of the way society is run in general, it may be more constructive to put energy into wider political struggles rather than into something specifically linked to their particular case. That, however, is really outside the scope of this book. The rest of this section deals with how to go on fighting around a particular case.

Defence groups and getting support

There are two main reasons for forming a defence group: either to provide or obtain moral support and help or as a means of getting publicity and wider interest in the case. In particular it is worth setting up a group where several cases arise from the same incident. The group may be able to assist with preparing the cases, for example by finding witnesses. It could help carry out the work of contacting the media and may be able to organise imaginative publicity on the day of the trial, such as a demonstration outside court or street theatre. This can often be a positive influence and also helps those going into court feel less isolated and more confident.

Pressure groups

The strength and organisation of gay pressure groups* varies from town to town, year to year. The headquarters of the main groups are in London (CHE), Edinburgh (SHRG) and Belfast (NIGRA). There are also a small number of national organisations that are usually willing to talk about cases and to give advice on which issues should be raised and how to go about it. The National Council for Civil Liberties has a Gay Rights Officer, and may take up individual injustices. The NCCL argues for legal reforms through its parliamentary civil liberties group. There is a network of NCCL contacts around the country. Because of their parliamentary lobbying experience, the NCCL should be able to help in contacting

* For addresses see Appendix VI.

local MPs or councillors, or others who might take special interest in the case. The Joint Council for the Welfare of Immigrants will help with immigration cases. Rights of Women will advise lesbians. Gay Legal Advice (GLAD) is an evening telephone advice service. GLAD does not take up individual cases but will refer callers to appropriate lawyers where necessary.

The media

Although the media reports a great many stories about law and law enforcement, it is predominantly disposed in favour of law and order and the status quo. It is very difficult to get sympathetic coverage for a case involving homosexuality. In addition, journalists may feel the case is not important or newsworthy enough to merit attention. Alternatively, it may concern an issue they do not want to publicise. *The Guardian, Observer, Sunday Times, Morning Star, New Statesman, Time Out* and *City Limits* have carried better articles on gay issues than other papers. However, it may be more effective to approach them through an established group or organisation, expressing concern about the injustice of a particular situation, rather than an individual case.

In terms of the gay and feminist press, *Gay News* (national fortnightly) *Capital Gay* (London weekly) and *Spare Rib* (national monthly, women only) will give a sympathetic hearing. The alternative gay press, run voluntarily and in some cases irregularly, includes the *Mancunian Gay, Broadsheet* (CHE), *Gay Scotland* (SHRG) and *Gay Star* (NIGRA).

If a publicity event is being organised it is worth contacting the various radio and television networks, especially the producers of radio phone-ins, current affairs and news-type programmes.[12]

Criminal cases

The major problem for a person being taken to court is the danger of being so overcome by isolation and panic that one will do anything — including pleading guilty when one has a defence — in order to get the ordeal over as swiftly as possible. Legal etiquette and court procedures have the effect of intimidating and isolating accused people. Rather than deal with a large number of technical procedural questions, which in any event may be very specific to a particular case and would therefore need individual advice from a lawyer, this section considers first of all the ways of coping with the pressures and difficulties involved in establishing innocence when faced with false or mistaken accusations. Secondly and as an aid to that process it will outline the positive decisions that can be made while being dealt with by the courts.

Coping with pressures

Probably the easiest way of understanding how to cope with the pressures of being prosecuted by the police is to read the story of someone who did. While in many respects the author of the following, Bob Cant, is untypical, most people can probably identify with his feelings:[13]

'I entered the cottage at about 3.25 a.m. I stood next to a man who was already there. There was neither physical contact nor eye contact between us. I may well have been fantasising but I was so drunk that I cannot remember if I was. Two or three minutes later three policemen entered from both ends of the toilet. We were charged with gross indecency. Eleven months later, after a four day trial in a crown court, the judge instructed the jury to acquit us on the grounds that the police evidence was 'unsafe and unsatisfactory'. The following is an account of some of the things I experienced and learned in that eleven month period.

My immediate responses were very contradictory. As soon as the police came into the cottage I went along with them quietly and obediently almost like a lamb. It would have been stupid to try to escape but I never even thought of it. I made no sound of protest. I knew perfectly well what was happening and showed neither surprise nor anger. The police evidence later said that I looked 'sheepish' and that was certainly how I felt. I was in complete awe of the forces of the state.

But within two minutes, by the time I was in the police van, I was determined to plead not guilty. I had no idea of what that would entail but I wasn't giving in. As a trade unionist activist, I'm fairly used to standing up to authority and that trade union consciousness made me determined to fight. In the police station I made it clear that I would defend my innocence. I tried, as I was legally entitled to do, to stop them taking my fingerprints. I only agreed when they made it clear they would keep me inside until a court gave them permission to take them. When I realised they were searching me for what they called 'traces of homo-sexuality' I told them I was gay because I felt I would have to argue that my sexuality was irrelevant to their case. I asked a police officer to stop using the word 'queer' in my presence.

These contradictions continued throughout the whole period before the trial. On the one hand I was prepared to conform with certain demands made on me by society because I did not want its disapproval; on the other hand, I was going to fight every inch of the way over the case itself, and for my job, if convicted. That tension, between my need for acceptance and my sense of militancy, nearly tore me apart.

One of the most predominant feelings I had was one of fear. I was terrified to go out, at first. I wouldn't, of course, go near a public toilet. I wouldn't even stay on the same side of the street as a policeman. I also found it difficult in supermarkets because I felt that I looked so guilty that store detectives would be bound to watch me. I met no one else who had fought and won such a case and that simply intensified the feeling that my whole view of the world was becoming incomprehensible to everyone else. I felt more and more isolated and in danger of losing contact with everyone around me. My sense of panic increased along with the isolation and a lot of the time I felt I was clutching at fog. One morning at 4 or 5 o'clock after drinking a bottle of whisky, smashing some crockery, playing Billie Holliday to the whole street and screaming hysterically, I was eventually able to tell the friend who was with me that I was terrified of being alone. It seems banal to say that, but as the world I knew slipped away from me I thought I would never be able to return to it. I saw myself as always alone and rejected.

It was to compensate for this fear of being alone that made me adhere to most of my old routines (e.g. work) in a very rigid way. I found their familiarity very comforting. It also helped me to tell people about my arrest and I talked over the whole thing again and again with anyone who would listen. But my other great fear was not helped by talking for I could not express it even to myself. In the event of being found guilty, the case would probably be reported in the local papers. Because I'm a teacher the local paper near my college might well have published the story. And if my trial took place in a thin week for news, it might even be reported in the national press. (The *Daily Mirror* recently published the name and address of a head teacher convicted on a similar charge.) How would I deal with being known as a man who allegedly went cottaging? How would I deal with remarks on the street in the working-class community where I live? How would I face students, many of whom are unsure of their own sexuality but are nonetheless very conventional? How would I face my colleagues at work and in the trade union movement? If I hadn't come out already it is just inconceivable as to how I might have dealt with it. Even so, I was absolutely terrified of a situation where my alleged sexual behaviour and fantasies would be a subject of public discussion.

After the torment of waiting the trial itself was almost a relief when it came. I had a barrister who appreciated the importance of sexual politics and we had prepared the case carefully over the previous months. I had contacted Gay Switchboard as soon as the police released me, five or six hours after my arrest. They had been very helpful and had put me in touch with a solicitor that very morning. After speaking to him I realised that I should opt for a crown court trial. I decided to make notes of every detail of what I had been doing on the night of my arrest and also of the police's treatment of me. I found these very useful in refreshing my memory before I went into the witness box. Despite all my preparations, I still felt that my role was a highly contradictory one. A part of my case depended on the fact that I was a nice, articulate, middle class, white man with a well paid job. My witnesses were also nice articulate middle class white people; as indeed were the group of people who came to court with me every day to give me moral support. People like us are far more likely to be believed by judges than many other members of the community. My gayness, instead of coming over positively, might in fact appear to be a blemish on an otherwise impeccable character. If I did want to be positive about my gayness perhaps I should be prepared to say that I thought cottaging was all right. Perhaps I should say that, in my opinion, cottaging charges were one way in which the gay community was oppressed in Britain today. There would be little point in winning the case if it was by suggesting that my form of gayness was socially more acceptable than that of men who do go cottaging. For many men, and this is particularly true of married men, and men in working class communities, it is their only gay outlet. It is also the case that many men go cottaging simply because they enjoy it. How could I possibly express disapproval of that?

To a great extent the dilemma did not arise in court because of the highly specific nature of the questioning. There was no general discussion at all. I only had to talk about what had happened on that particular Saturday morning. I said what was required in my most authoritative teacher's voice. My shirts were pressed, I wore my tie, the henna had grown out of my hair, my appearance and bearing certainly did not go against me.

The one factor which, undoubtedly, won the case for me, however, was the evidence of an expert medical witness. The police had alleged that when they arrested me my penis was erect and remained so for some minutes (despite the fact that I was looking "sheepish"). They also said that I was not circumcised. In fact, if I had an erection it would have been impossible for them to tell whether or not I was circumcised. Because I was "out" at work, I was able to discuss the evidence there. A friend on the union branch committee suggested that I should get a medical witness to discredit that evidence. With his assistance, I found a consultant with experience in medical jurisprudence who was prepared to testify to this in court. But it was also necessary for him to have a photograph of my erection to show the jury. They were rather more embarrassed than I was by this badly-coloured instamatic representation of a penis trying to remain erect. The picture would have aroused no interest in a porn magazine, but it led to the judge dismissing the police case against me as "unsafe and unsatisfactory". The prosecuting counsel, however, argued for a further hour that my co-defendant could still be guilty. It is a strange idea of justice that one person could be innocent of mutual masturbation and the other guilty. Finally we were both acquitted.

Now it was over. I had expected a fantastic sense of elation but that only lasted an hour or two. It was really all very anti-climactic. Then I had to try to get back to some kind of ordinary life. But while I live in the same house, read the same papers, work in the same job (I got promoted after the acquittal!) and am politically active in the same circles there could be no return anywhere. Long after the main cause of the anger and anxiety had gone, the anger and anxiety remained. There was also a long struggle to regain control of my own language and expression; I seemed to imagine that there was a court of law in judgment on everything I said and thought. Gradually I began to feel more together. I also appreciate much more any real struggles – however small they seem. And so I have more respect for my own small struggles. Yet again, the message seems to be – the personal is political. It can't be bad to re-learn that.'

Making decisions in the courts

England, Wales and Northern Ireland. *The courts*. Less serious cases (for example a plea of guilty to a charge of importuning) are dealt with by magistrates' court where either two or more lay Justices of the Peace preside or there is a legally qualified stipendiary magistrate. More serious cases (for example a defended case of gross indecency) may first be enquired into by a magistrates' court to see if there is sufficient evidence for the case to go further. Often this process is a mere formality and if the defendant's lawyer accepts that there is sufficient evidence, the case goes to the crown court where it is heard by a judge sitting with a jury. (See also Appendix IV.)

First appearance in court. It is very important to keep as many options open as possible. In routine cases, the police want defendants to plead guilty, not to seek legal aid or legal representation and to be dealt with by the magistrates, then and there, or at a later date at their convenience. Given this pressure, it is vital for anyone accused of an offence not to make hasty decisions at the first hearing. Ask the magistrates to adjourn (postpone) the hearing so that there will be time to get legal advice, make an application for legal aid and during this postponement be free to go home (be 'released on bail'). Many courts in Britain have 'duty solicitors' on hand who will assist defendants held in custody either to get bail or, after advice, put in a plea of guilty.

At this stage, the police will decide whether they intend to ask the magistrates to keep the accused person in prison until the next hearing. They are unlikely to object to bail unless the charge is particularly serious, or the person has no permanent home, or they think s/he will commit other offences or interfere with witnesses. The court can ignore these objections if they are thought not to be 'substantial' or take them into account by attaching special conditions under which the defendant is released on bail, for example in serious cases reporting to the police station every day.

Getting reliable advice. The next step is to get advice about whether to plead guilty or not guilty. If someone is advised to plead guilty they will need to know what sort of mitigating evidence should be brought to court. If they are pleading not guilty, they will need to know whether the trial will take place before the magistrates or a judge and jury, and how the defence should be prepared. Legal assistance in criminal cases paid for by the Legal Aid Scheme is available, sometimes subject to financial contributions, both for initial advice and in connection with the court case itself. Legal aid application forms can be obtained from the Clerk's Office before leaving the court building. A local citizens' advice bureau would help anyone to complete the forms.

Rather than pick the nearest firm of solicitors to home, it is best to contact Gay Switchboard or the NCCL for recommendations.

Advice given by police officers should be ignored. In cottaging cases, they may say that publicity can be avoided by pleading guilty and having the case dealt with by the magistrates. They may claim that there will be more publicity over a crown court trial.

In fact the local papers regularly report cases where men have pleaded guilty and nearly all the cases will be reported from the magistrates' court.

The press is just as merciless to those who plead guilty. In London, a person has a far greater chance of being reported in the local press if they are convicted in a magistrates' court. This happens through the network that operates among journalists working in different areas. A journalist from the local paper will cover the magistrates' court every day, and if s/he notices a potentially interesting case from a remote part of the country the local papers in that area will be informed. In this way cases in London can be reported anywhere in the provinces. Reporting from the crown courts is far more haphazard, partly because journalists cannot cover as many cases as they can in the swifter magistrates' courts. In London, very few cottaging trials are reported from the crown courts.

Outside London, the chance of being reported from either of the courts is very high. But the publicity argument should not be decisive. It is an unpleasant ploy designed to play on possible feelings of shame and fears of discovery. The police may say that a guilty plea, or going to a magistrates' court, will get the whole dreadful business over and out of the way as quickly as possible. For many this can be a compelling argument. Some people find the arrest and questioning such a nightmare that they are persuaded by it, because the strain of waiting for a jury trial would be too great. The crown court may mean delay, but chances of acquittal are far greater.

Pleading guilty. Legal aid is not usually granted for a lawyer to represent someone who intends to plead guilty on a 'minor' criminal charge, such as importuning, where the normal sentence for a first conviction is a fine. In these circumstances one would generally expect to have to pay privately for a lawyer or represent oneself, perhaps with the help of a friend.

Anyone who has been correctly advised that there is no defence to the charge must then work out how a fine can be paid and whether there is anything that will minimise it. An alternative strategy would be to make a short defiant statement to the court. On a first offence some people may think it is worthwhile to risk a heavier fine to maintain self-respect.

At court the officer in charge of the case will tell the magistrates the details of the incident and the circumstances of the arrest. The facts are not thoroughly examined. Although a defendant is permitted to challenge details, the police story will be taken as a basically true account. The officer will, in addition, tell the court about the defendant's personal circumstances and criminal record (if any) – information obtained from police records and particulars given at the police station.

The magistrates will then permit the defendant to ask the officer relevant questions. This will be the opportunity to point out any inaccuracies and to remind the officer of anything favourable that has been omitted, for example being co-operative.

After questioning the officer, the defendant is then requested to tell the magistrates about anything that should be taken into account in deciding the appropriate sentence ('mitigating circumstances'). Assuming that the aim is to get the least possible fine, as opposed to risking a heavier sentence through making an uncompromising speech, arguments should be tailored to the type of person on the bench. The 'I had a difficult childhood' approach rarely appeals to magistrates, many of whom are, for example, self-made businessmen. It would repay any defendant who is on bail to sit in the public gallery a few days or weeks beforehand to see how the magistrates react in other cases.

Generally speaking, the magistrates should at least be told that the offence will not be repeated. If the experience of being arrested and held in custody for the first time was devastating, they should be told that too. They should also be told anything about current individual, personal circumstances that will incline them to be more lenient. It helps to call as a witness someone who is a 'respectable and upright citizen' who can give evidence about the defendant from personal knowledge.

Pleading not guilty. In England, Wales and Northern Ireland a defendant may often be able to choose whether a case which involves a sexual offence, such as soliciting or gross indecency, is tried in the magistrates' court or in the crown court.

In serious cases, for example where one of the partners is under

14, the police will ask the magistrates to commit the case for trial in the crown court where judges have power to impose heavier sentences.

Legal aid is almost always granted in defended cases. Someone in these circumstances would expect to be advised by their lawyer about the choice of court, but here are a few points to consider.

Before a trial takes place in the crown court the prosecution must show the defence copies of the police statements given by the witnesses who will be called to give evidence. This means that the defence has time properly to prepare the case rather than being taken unfairly by surprise. By the same token the police must be given prior notification of the general nature of any alibi the defence have and the particulars of alibi witnesses. The police are entitled to interview those witnesses before the trial in order to take statements. By comparison, there is no procedure for advance notification of evidence in trials which take place in the magistrates' courts.

In the experience of most defence lawyers, accused people have a greater chance of establishing their innocence in a jury trial than before magistrates. On the whole magistrates are more likely than juries to be cynical about defendants and are more likely to accept the police version of events.

Although a crown court judge can impose a heavier sentence than a magistrate can, this does not happen invariably. However judges do sometimes award heavy prosecution costs against a convicted defendant and a stiff contribution to the costs of the legal aid defence. A defence lawyer should be able to give advice about the practice of the local courts. The most severe sentence that a magistrate can impose in a case involving several charges is an overall maximum of a year's imprisonment and a fine of £1000 on each charge. (There are charges where the statutory maximum is lower than this.) In serious cases, however, where the power is provided and more severe punishment is thought to be necessary, the magistrates may send the case to the crown court for sentencing.

In order to convict someone of an offence, the prosecution must bring evidence to satisfy the court that the person is guilty beyond all reasonable doubt. The rules determining the kinds of evidence that may be brought into a trial are complex. David Barnard's *The Criminal Court in Action* provides a clear introduction to this very technical subject.[14]

One of the rules of general importance in gay sex trials – corroboration by 'similar fact' evidence – has already been discussed (see pages 81-85 above). There are five other rules which are especially relevant in gay cases.

In charges involving buggery and gross indecency, where sex takes place with mutual consent each man is an *accomplice* in the other's crime. In such cases the jury need not be told by the judge that it is dangerous to convict without corroborating evidence. However the judge must tell them to consider carefully whether there is independent evidence which in some material way points to the defendant being the guilty person.[15]

A child may give evidence in a criminal case if the judge decides that the child can understand the duty of telling the truth. However, the judge must warn the jury about the risk of convicting the defendant on the basis of the child's evidence alone where this has not been corroborated on some material points which implicate the defendant.[16]

In most cases the court will not be told if a defendant has previous criminal convictions because this would prejudice the hearing. However a defendant can lose this protection in some instances. The two main ones are where a defendant falsely claims to have a good character or attacks the character of prosecution witnesses. In *R* v *Bishop* (1974)[17] the defendant's previous convictions were admitted in evidence after he had accused the man he was alleged to have robbed of being homosexual. The defence had claimed that the accused's fingerprints had been found in the victim's room because they were having a sexual relationship. This had been denied by the victim.

During the trial, the prosecution may be permitted to ask the defendant if he is homosexual. It is normal practice for the prosecutor to request the judge's permission while the jury is absent from the court. Often judges will not allow questions about a defendant's sexual orientation because the answers are likely to prejudice the jury rather than actually prove anything. However if the judge does allow such questions, the jury must be warned that admissions of homosexuality in no way show that the defendant committed any offence.[18]

A man accused of importuning will not be allowed to give detailed evidence of his heterosexual relationships in order to rebut the inference from his alleged conduct that he was making homosexual approaches. In *R* v *Redgrave* (1981)[19] the English Court of Appeal ruled that a defendant should be permitted to call only evidence that 'by way of general reputation' he was not the kind of young man who would have behaved in the way alleged.

Scotland. In Scotland, there are three levels of courts: the district court, the sheriff court and the high court (see Appendix IV Diagram 1). The district court is the lowest criminal court dealing with matters like breach of the peace and other minor offences. Cases are tried by a magistrate. At the sheriff court, cases may be heard either under 'solemn' procedure (that is, with a jury) or 'summary' procedure (without a jury). The high court hears the most serious charges (for example, sodomy with a boy) which are tried by a judge and jury.

Lewd and libidinous behaviour is, for example, generally prosecuted at the sheriff's court, by way of either 'solemn' or 'summary' procedure. In a very serious case (where longer than two years' imprisonment is thought appropriate) the sheriff, if with a jury, may send the case to the high court for sentencing.

All criminal prosecutions are conducted by public officials, known as Procurator Fiscals, under the control of the Lord Advocate's department. It is these officials who decide whether or not to prosecute, what charges to bring, and what court a case will go to (unless this is already fixed in law). The police do not prosecute in Scotland and a defendant has no say in whether his/her case will be heard by a jury or not. There is a right to legal advice and representation in criminal trials under a scheme which is similar to the ones administered elsewhere in the United Kingdom.

Anyone who is to be tried under 'solemn' procedure can be compelled to appear at a 'judicial examination' before the trial takes place. Such an examination is at the discretion of the Procurator Fiscal; its purpose is to question an accused person about the charges and any defence. Failure to answer questions, or any inconsistencies between answers given then and evidence given later in the trial can be brought to the attention of the jury at the subsequent trial.

In Scotland, the jury consists of 15 people (as compared with 12 elsewhere in the UK) and only three challenges without any reason may be made. No opening speeches are made by either side and the case opens with witnesses for the prosecution being examined by counsel for the prosecution and cross-examined by the defence and perhaps re-examined by the prosecution. Unlike the system in England, the defence will not have been given the statements of the prosecution witnesses, but they may be interviewed by the defence lawyers. As in England, the defendant is entitled to remain silent, but if s/he does give evidence (which happens in nearly all cases) then that will be heard before other witnesses for the defence. A defendant is also entitled to make or read out a statement from the witness box without being cross-examined. This is an alternative to giving evidence under oath. Although it does not carry much weight as evidence it is often useful and prudent for those defending themselves when such a statement has greater value as evidence.

A conviction is not allowed unless there are two sources of evidence leading to one single conclusion to the exclusion of any others. This is called 'corroboration'. For example, the verbal evidence of one witness plus evidence of the victim would be 'corroborated' evidence. Forensic medical evidence can provide corroboration but it obviously cannot affect the issues of intention to commit an offence or consent which are also relevant to the decision of guilt or innocence. Hearsay evidence is not corroboration. If a confession has been made, very little in the way of corroboration is usually needed. However, a confession on its own is never enough to convict if the accused pleads 'not guilty'.

These rules are subject to the decision in the *Moorov* case (also discussed on page 84 above). Where a defendant is charged with two or more identical offences and where only one source of evidence exists in relation to each charge, but the circumstances of each charge show a course of criminal conduct with similarities, then the evidence on each charge will be held to corroborate the other. This doctrine was designed specifically to meet problems of evidence in rape cases, but it has been extended to sex cases in general and latterly to any criminal offences. It can only be applied in multiple charges of an identical nature.

At the end of the prosecution case, as in England, the defence can make a submission that there is 'no case to answer'. This can be done if the prosecution's evidence is insufficient by itself to support a conviction; then the judge may return a verdict of 'not guilty'. If the judge finds that there is a *prima facie* case, then the defence case proceeds as usual.

Following final speeches for the prosecution and defence, the judge will sum up and direct the jury on the law. As in England, juries must be satisfied beyond reasonable doubt of the defendant's guilt before convicting.

If the verdict is 'not guilty' or 'not proved', the defendant is discharged and cannot be tried again for the same offence. However, the prosecution has the right to appeal against an acquittal and a defendant could be retried if that appeal is successful. If the verdict is 'guilty' the prosecution will ask the court to sentence and will inform the court of any previous convictions. The defence will address the court about any mitigating circumstances (see page 168 above).

Civil cases

For cases going to civil courts or tribunals (see Appendix IV Diagram 1) issues discussed above, such as getting support, are equally relevant. However, in civil cases, in contrast to criminal cases, there may be a *choice* to play down the question of sexuality. It is on this that the following section concentrates.

Expressing sexual feelings toward someone of your own sex goes against common behaviour in this society. Therefore, the way in which people bring this difference to the attention of others is more than a private decision. Talking with a spouse, one's children, fellow workers, an employer, lawyers, witnesses or a judge about homosexuality is a significant action. Because the decision to come out or not to come out is so significant it is also a political decision. The question of sexual orientation is political because at this time in history, in this society, openly gay people are taking a position against what is generally accepted behaviour. However someone has not given up their politics if they choose to tone down or give up their social connections with the gay scene so that, for example, they are more likely to obtain custody of their child. They are still gay: they are taking an important decision for their child so that they can be brought up in their own way.

Personal decisions are also political decisions. For example: how do you deal with the evident anti-gay prejudices of judges and tribunal officials? Is it better to come out and say, run the risk of losing one's child, or is it better to avoid the issue of sexuality so as to ensure retaining custody?

Deciding to come out in the court or tribunal is not a decision to be made in a vacuum. The decision to come out is part of being able to come out in other aspects of life. The decision to come out is part of a very long struggle to overcome prejudice. Each person is ready for different steps at different times in their lives.

The decisions that are made regarding relationships with lovers and the kind of political activities engaged in are decisions that deeply affect life. Increased activity – either sexual or political – can for example, give a spouse grounds to challenge custody or an employer grounds to consider continued employment. The ways in which people are able or willing to live and change their lives will not be the same.

Some may choose to play down the issue of homosexuality at the trial and to concentrate on, say, their fitness as a parent or employee. This alternative may be possible if recognition can be obtained from the other side that the person has been a good parent or employee. It could also be played down by arguing, where there has been a direct attack on a person's sexual orientation, that this question is irrelevant to anyone's fitness as a parent or employee.

It is essential to get reliable legal advice. Varying degrees of assistance are available under the Legal Aid Schemes administered by the Law Societies in England and Wales, Northern Ireland and Scotland. Contact Gay Switchboard, GLAD and the NCCL (see Appendix VI for addresses) for the names of suitable firms of solicitors.

Chapter Eleven
Conclusion:
Towards gay rights?

'You can't legislate for what people think. That requires a change in attitude. But you can say "whatever you *think*, there are things you will not do".'

> *Peter Newsam*, chairman, Commission for Racial Equality[1]

Limits of the law

Although discrimination and prejudice cannot be combated by legislation alone, it can be used as part of a strategy to achieve this end. The aims of gay rights are long term. There is no immediate prospect of action in parliament. This is not therefore an appropriate time to spell out detailed proposals. Instead the following are broad principles, generally accepted in the gay movement, that could be shaped and particularised in the future. Appendix III, however, does show the kind of specific reforms that have been devised.

The overall aim of legislation would be to stop activity that discriminates against homosexuality. Gays and lesbians are entitled to protection against such activity and to a right to respect for a distinctive social and sexual culture. This implies that the law would play a diminishing role in promoting marriage as a central aim of public policy. To curtail interference in the lives of gay people it would be necessary to ensure that:

1. Any law specifying a minimum age for sexual relationships (the so-called age of consent) should be the same for everyone, regardless of sexual orientation. Apart from abolishing the criminal status of gay male teenagers, this would help reduce the legal obstructions in the path of those engaged in social work or counselling with young gays. The Law Commission's recommendation to abolish conspiracy to corrupt public morals should be implemented.[2]

2. The laws protecting the public from sexual nuisance should be the same for everyone. No special provision, such as the law of soliciting, is needed against gay men. Gays are at present harassed, watched and hauled through the courts when there are no victims,

only police officers who appear as if on behalf of a hypothetically shocked general public. Any person who is aggrieved by a nuisance should be called upon to give evidence in court.

3. Discrimination on the grounds of sexual orientation by employers, owners of public facilities, businesses and housing should be unlawful. Such a proposal needs to be linked to the strengthening of employment protection law generally and more positive action on race relations and women's rights.

4. The law on domestic relations should be reformed to achieve equality of treatment for those who live in ways alternative to the heterosexual nuclear family. Custody rights and rights arising from the death of a partner are two areas where the law actively discriminates against non-heterosexual arrangements.

5. The law on privacy should be reformed positively to take account of the distinctive nature of gay men's sexual culture. The law at present reflects irritation with or revulsion against specific forms of homosexual behaviour. It indicates the high level of intolerance in heterosexual standards. For example, the law aims to suppress casual sex between men in private places such as parties and clubs. Many countries in Western Europe, and some states in both North America and Australia have long since abandoned this Victorian attitude towards law enforcement.

6. The question of man/boy love should be urgently considered. The treatment of many convicted paedophiles verges on the barbaric. Long terms of imprisonment are abhorrent in cases where men are not guilty of violence.

7. An effective law against incitement to hatred of gays and lesbians should be devised. There are those who disingenuously argue that parliament should not legislate on gay rights for fear of a backlash against gay people. Even if this were likely, the better response is to deal with those who whip up hatred or ridicule.

Law reform proposals will be difficult and an anti-discrimination statute protecting gays and lesbians would not be straightforward, if only because of the flaws in the present anti-discrimination laws for women and blacks. The Commission for Racial Equality, for example, in its annual report for 1980, lamented that 'discrimination in employment so far from being eliminated was actually increasing in some areas'.[3]

The main criticisms of the legislation are threefold. First, that at present too much depends on the personal character, tenacity and qualifications of the individuals who bring complaints. There is no procedure for group actions, whereby someone whose claim is typical of many others could represent their interests in court or at the tribunal. Second, that neither the Commission for Racial Equality nor the Equal Opportunities Commission has developed into an aggressive law enforcement body, even though both have powers to investigate all forms of discrimination without the necessity of individual complaint. This may be due to a combination of factors – particularly the inherent conflict of bodies with a dual role of conciliator and prosecutor, severe financial constraints and judicial hostility. Third, that employers and educational institutions are not required to remedy past discrimination by positive action. On the contrary, 'positive discrimination' is prohibited except for industrial training, where it is permissible but not compulsory.[4]

The Race Relations and Sex Discrimination Acts can also be faulted for using the same wording in their main provisions[5] with 'insufficient account being given to whether different social reality requires different legal treatment'.[6]

Despite all these difficulties an amendment of the Sex Discrimination Act to include discrimination on the grounds of sexual orientation would be one way forward for gay people. It would require only minor amendments to existing legislation; it would be easier to 'sell' politically to the general public. But, it is unlikely to be very effective on its own. Given the social reality of discrimination against homosexuality and the highly diverse composition of lesbians and gay men as a minority group, legislation designed for other purposes could scarcely provide what is required. But such a measure would at least have the great value of being a positive statement of approval for gay people.

The present economic crisis is having a profound impact on the general usefulness of reforms in the law. Mass unemployment undermines the practical value of civil rights which are closely connected with having a job and money to spend. For example, legislation on equal pay, non-discrimination, maternity rights or access to mortgage facilities is useless to the millions of women workers who are now permanently unemployed. The lack of prospects for vast numbers of people in Britain affects the kind of civil rights demands that must be made.

The likelihood of law reform

None of the major political parties in the UK has produced a convincing commitment to legislate on gay rights. At its constitutional convention, the Social Democratic Party voted to delete a written commitment in the party constitution to fight for equal social rights for homosexuals. The Liberal Party has gone furthest, while the Labour Party has produced a well argued discussion document which it is hoped will form the basis of party policy.[7] Positive speeches about gay rights made by the Labour leader of the Greater London Council have been followed by practical action. Despite political opposition in County Hall, the council gave a small number of grants in 1982 to groups providing important voluntary services for gay men and lesbians in the London area.

Parties in government respond to domestic and international pressures for change. Improvement in the status of women and racial minorities has become a major international as well as domestic question. International treaty obligations under the European Convention of Human Rights[8] and the European Economic Community have obliged governments to introduce specific legislative protection. Though gay rights is far from being generally accepted in the same way as the rights of women and blacks, the first steps have been taken towards comprehensive prohibition of discrimination against gays under the European Convention of Human Rights. In 1981 the European Court of Justice and the Parliamentary Assembly of the Council of Europe made two historic decisions. They may contribute to the long term pressures for positive reform.

The two articles in the European Convention that have been invoked by European gays against discrimination are:

'Everyone has the right to respect for his private and family life, his home and his correspondence.' Article 8(i)

and:

'The enjoyment of the rights and freedoms set forth in this convention shall be secured without discrimination on any ground such as sex, race, colour, language, religious, political or other opinion, national or social origin, association with a national minority, property, birth or other status.' Article 14

In relation to Article 8, defending states have relied on the exception clause which permits restrictions on those rights if made,

'in accordance with the law and is necessary in a democratic society in the interests of national security, public safety or the economic well-being of the country for the prevention of

disorder or crime, or for the protection of health or morals, or for the protection of the rights and freedoms of others.'
Article 8 (ii)

The European Commission (see Appendix IV) has decided that legislation which fixes the age of consent for male homosexuals higher than that for heterosexuals has been needed for reasons of 'social protection'. In *X v Federal Republic of Germany* (1975) the Commission stated that 'masculine homosexuals often constitute a distinct socio-cultural group with a clear tendency to proselytise adolescents and the social isolation in which it involves the latter is particularly marked'. These remarks were not based on reliable evidence and went far beyond what was justified by the facts of the particular case. Similar fallacious observations were made by the Commission in *X v United Kingdom* (1978): '. . . young men in the 18 to 21 age bracket who are involved in homosexual relationships would be subject to substantial social pressures which could be harmful to their psychological development'.

As shown on page 14 above, the judgment of the European Court of Human Rights – the ultimate legal body that interprets the Convention – was progressive in *Dudgeon v United Kingdom* (1981). The government were found to have violated the right to respect for private life by retaining criminal penalties against homosexual sexual acts between consenting adults in private. This was the first international judicial ruling to condemn the use of law as a means of repressing homosexuality. The court specifically left open the question of whether it was lawful under Article 14 for member states to discriminate between the ages of consent for heterosexuals and male homosexuals. An application related to this provision of the Convention has been made subsequently by an English gay teenager.

Also in 1981 the Parliamentary Assembly* 'reaffirming its vocation to fight against all forms of discrimination and oppression' voted to recommend that the Committee of Ministers:

(i) urge those member states, where homosexual sexual acts

---

* The Parliamentary Assembly is one of the institutions of the Council of Europe. Its members, nominated by all major European political parties (including those in the UK) meet in Strasbourg. One of the Assembly's functions is to monitor the development of human rights in Europe. It does this by debating issues and passing resolutions to the Committee of Ministers, who report back on action that has been taken. Such resolutions have been the main source of progressive changes.

between consenting adults are liable to criminal prosecution, to abolish those laws and practices;

(ii) urge member states to apply the same minimum age of consent for homosexual and heterosexual acts;

(iii) call on the governments of the member states:

(a) to order the destruction of existing special records on homosexuals and to abolish the practice of keeping records on homosexuals by the police or any other authority;[9]

(b) to assure equality of treatment, no more no less, for homosexuals with regard to employment, pay and job security, particularly in the public sector;

(c) to ask for the cessation of all compulsory medical action or research designed to alter the sexual orientation of adults;

(d) to ensure that custody, visiting rights and accommodation of children by their parents should not be restricted on the sole grounds of the homosexual tendencies of one of them;

(e) to ask prison and other public authorities to be vigilant against the risk of rape, violence and sexual offences in prisons.

This is a significant political step and can be seen in the context of action already taken by individual European states to remove discrimination. Holland, Denmark, Norway, Sweden and most recently France have made the age of consent equal for everyone. Legislation has been introduced in Norway[10] and proposed by the government in Holland to make incitement to hatred or ridicule of homosexuals unlawful. In addition many European police forces have drastically reduced the amount of time spent watching and harassing gay men.

In response to pressure on this question in the UK, a report was eventually produced by a Home Office Committee in 1979.[11] Although it recommended a reduction in the age of consent to 18 (for England and Wales only) it maintained that discrimination between homosexuals and heterosexuals was justified. Nor have any positive reforms been suggested on the law in relation to soliciting or sex in private places. In any event a Conservative government is unlikely to take the initiative since the Conservative Party usually regards this question as a 'Private Members' matter. This means that no reform is likely unless: either the government gives a Private Member's Bill on the subject its fullest support; or as in the case of the law reform for Scotland in 1981, MPs are able to tack on a reform to a major government Bill that is going through parliament;

or, as in the case of the law reform for Northern Ireland in 1982, a successful case before the European Court of Human Rights compels the government to legislate.

European liberalism creates positive pressure for change. In Britain, however, backward attitudes, particularly in parliament and the law, diminish the likelihood of spontaneous law reform. So, too, does the fact that many humanising concessions made in the sixties and early seventies are being whittled away under the excuse of combating the recession.

Action needed to achieve reform

The experience of the women's movement shows clearly the difficulties of overturning legal connivance at social discrimination. Only sixty or so years ago, judges and lawyers consistently denied even that women were 'persons'. In case after case, the male monopoly of power was upheld by decisions that statutes referring to 'persons' meant only men. Women were described by judges as alternatively fickle, a bad influence on young male students, physically defective, or so honourable and decorous that to permit them a part in public affairs would be degrading. The resoluteness with which women pursued their aims was seen not as proof of consistency but as evidence of hysteria. Similarly the process of self-realisation by homosexuals is seen not as proof of validity but as evidence of proselytisation. No victories comparable to those of the suffragettes and today's feminists will be achieved without a militant and collective struggle.

The law is sometimes the cutting edge of social attitudes and sometimes the tail-end. What one does in relation to the law is only part of a general approach. And to challenge social attitudes is a very fundamental, long term task. On the question of gay rights, clearly deep inroads will have to be made into public apathy or hostility before there is sufficient general support to outlaw discriminatory behaviour and promote equality. Support in the labour movement, traditionally the principal motor for civil rights reform in Britain, is essential. Without this, any parliamentary support is likely to evaporate at the first dawning of a reactionary campaign to block change.

A proposed strategy for change is likely to depend on one's view of the nature of obstructive social attitudes and practices.

Three main reasons for homosexual oppression emerge from the literature:[12] first, that homosexuality poses some kind of threat to social stability; second, that homosexuality is a threat to the dominant view of gender and to generally accepted views on morality; and third, that homosexuality threatens sexuality, lifestyle or status.

Gay lifestyles are only a threat to social stability in that they are living proof that there are other viable alternatives to traditional sexuality regulated through family life. Many regard the family as a key social institution, regulating sex drive, training and socialising children, providing core identities and relationships. Undermine the family and you undermine stability in society generally. In its written evidence to the European Commission of Human Rights in the *Dudgeon* case, the British government stated:

'. . . the law is also designed to uphold the moral standards supported by significant elements of the Northern Ireland community. These standards tend to protect the family as a fundamental social unit and the threat to the position of that unit as a basic constituent of society comes more from homosexual than from heterosexual relationships'.

Some would argue that anti-gay discrimination is essentially an unintentional result of organising society in a particular way. Discrimination may be a by-product of people's defensiveness towards their families in an uncertain economic order.

Such an argument implies that to accept homosexuality would require a major upheaval in traditional ideas about the way personal life should be ordered in the 'interests of society'.

The second line of reasoning stems from the fact that homosexuality blurs the clear cut division between the sexes and their roles. Feminists argue that gay and lesbian oppression is intimately linked to the wider oppression of women. Feminism challenges assumptions about the 'natural' capacities and behaviour that is appropriate for women and thereby challenges the traditional preserves and power of men. Linked to this is the idea that any sexual behaviour outside certain forms within a marital relationship is immoral and sinful. Homosexual sex thereby upsets moral sensibilities that are supposed to form an existing moral consensus.

The implication of this reasoning is that to achieve acceptance of homosexuality, the traditional roles and behaviour of men and women would have to change fundamentally.

The third line of reasoning looks at the individual's response to homosexuality. A popular view is simply that gays are hated because homosexuality exposes the raw nerve of latent bisexuality in everyone; and the greater that repression, the greater the hostility. Another view argues that people, particularly the 'lower middle class', experience homosexuality with a kind of disgusted envy. For a group that views itself as having made the greatest sacrifices, working hard, saving up and leading responsible lives, it is thought to come as a shock that there are happy, socially and occupationally mobile gay men and lesbian women. Finally, attacks on gays and lesbians are sometimes seen not as action against homosexuality itself but instead as an indirect way of enhancing the status of those who have hostile views. Groups at the bottom of the social heap – the poor, working class, blacks, inner city youth – have at least 'queers' and 'dykes' to attack as the 'scum of the earth'.

What these arguments show is the absolute necessity of overcoming widespread personal repression, neurosis and anxiety and of liberating human sensual and emotional potential. Throughout history divisions within groups and the exploitation of folk devils have been powerful weapons in maintaining the status quo. Legitimate anger and frustration must be vented on real culprits, not scapegoats.

Liberation for gays and lesbians is not linked to changes in the law alone, but in the way everyone lives their lives. The issues that have been briefly raised here are complex, and the explanations given are not mutually exclusive. If one accepts some or all of them then action cannot be reduced to a single, simple formula.

It is necessary to keep an open mind on the sort of action to be pursued, to remain flexible and adaptable organisationally, and to ally with other forces for positive change. The challenge from gay people needs to continue to be as diverse as the facets of homosexual oppression.

Appendix I
The armed forces and merchant navy

In Britain, homosexual activity is prohibited in the merchant navy and armed forces.[1] It is a crime for a man who is a member of a crew to commit 'buggery' or 'gross indecency' with another merchant seaman on board a UK merchant ship.[2] This is so, even if they are both over 21 and make love in private. This special exclusion from the 1967 and 1980 reform Acts does not apply to men working on deep-sea oil rigs.

Special statutes for the armed forces provide that any man or woman who is guilty of 'disgraceful conduct of an indecent kind' can be imprisoned, if convicted by court martial, for a maximum of two years.[3] 'Disgraceful conduct of an indecent kind' includes not only all sexual contact between gay men or lesbian women, but also any conversation which 'does not amount to an attempt in law but only to a preparation to commit an offence'.[4] Offences relating to service discipline apply to activity and relationships which take place both on and off duty. The military police can use evidence of sex with civilians. Normally the civilian police will inform their counterparts if they discover a gay serviceman.

Most people subjected to action because of their homosexuality are discharged administratively without any court martial proceedings being taken. This is useful for gays who want to get out of the forces but punitive for those who do not. It is official policy neither to recruit nor to retain any person who admits to being homosexual.[5]

It is also official policy[6] normally to prosecute in cases where (1) the alleged homosexual act involved coercion or the commission of a civil offence (for example, when one or more of the people involved is under 21); (2) there is a difference in rank, or (3) the conduct had been harmful to service discipline or brings the service into disrepute. This last category gives any commanding officer an almost unfettered discretion to prosecute.

Between 1976 and 1980, nearly two-thirds of those convicted for 'homosexual misconduct' were sentenced to prison.[7] Sentences of up to six or nine months have been given by courts martial, though apparently these are often overruled by the military confirming authority who would substitute a sentence of immediate dishonourable discharge.

As a result, few people are willing to talk freely unless they have themselves been dismissed. This relative secrecy makes it helpful to include a full account of how a lesbian was discharged from the Women's Royal Navy Service (WRNS).[8]

'I enlisted in the WRNS in June 1973, intending to make a career of it.

I completed my training in October and went on my first draft. I was discharged in the first week of January 1974, after only six months' service, which included two weeks' Christmas leave and one week terminal leave, both taken after I had been told I would be discharged.

I had only been in my first draft for a little over a month when I had to report to the office of the WRNS officer-in-charge, where I was told I had been seen in a "compromising position with a member of the WRAF" in the Naafi bar the previous Friday night, and did I have any comments? I admitted I was a lesbian and incredibly we discussed the situation.

The case of a certain homosexual spy, whose blackmail by the Soviets formed the basis of a security film I had seen in training, and which was the only official mention of homosexuality I can remember, was foremost in my mind – his "sin" being not that he was homosexual, but that because he was a covert homosexual he had allowed himself to be blackmailed. I reasoned with First Officer that, surely, if I was an overt lesbian there was no possibility of my being approached. This she conceded but explained that, in addition, my presence was undesirable and a disruptive influence. I rejoined that I would have considered adultery within the service was a more disruptive element, and also more common, which again she conceded. But, nonetheless, even before I had said anything, my fate had been fixed. I was told to carry on working as normal unless ordered to the contrary.

At this point I should explain that I was a watch-keeper, that is, I worked shifts. These were, in chronological order, the afternoon watch 12.30 p.m. to 7.30 p.m; the forenoon watch 7.30 a.m. to 12.30 p.m; and the night watch 7.30 p.m. to 7.30 a.m; all worked consecutively over a period of three days. I had my interview during a forenoon watch.

After my initial interview I went back to work, finishing at 12.30 p.m. I went to the Naafi bar for a couple of drinks at lunchtime to help me sleep before I went on the night watch at 7.30 that same evening. I was unable to contact my friend as she was off camp somewhere playing hockey. I had cried at work that morning and pretty soon the whole camp was aware of the situation. I had been asleep only a little while when I became aware vaguely of my name being hailed over the tannoy system telling me to contact the Quarters Office. I phoned through and was told to report to First Officer, in full uniform, as soon as possible. I was also berated for not reporting in sooner to which I replied that I had been sleeping in between forenoon and night watches. I received a poor apology.

I reported to First Officer and was told that two corporals from the RAF military police (MPs) wanted to interview me and search my belongings. Due to some technicality they had to have my permission to do all this, though I was advised that if I refused it would make things worse for my friend. I didn't have very much choice – it was obvious we would both be discharged and that this was merely a formality. But I was loathe to make their job any easier. I would only co-operate on my own terms, so I refused to answer any questions etc. until I had seen my Divisional Officer (DO) (the only representative I had), and would only co-operate in her presence. This lamb was determined to run the shepherd ragged and breathless before she went to the slaughterhouse.

My DO was unavailable immediately, so off I went to try and find my friend to warn her to get rid of any damaging evidence to make her situation worse, and also to get something to eat as I was still expected to work that night. I couldn't find my friend. About 5 p.m. I was eventually interviewed and had my room searched, both of which were thoroughly unpleasant experiences. I was only passably co-operative, I wanted to be as awkward as possible. At 7.30 p.m. I went to work and received a phone call from my friend. She had had a similar experience except the RAF MPs had had no cause to be polite to her. She had been interrogated (rather than interviewed) for almost four hours without a break, threatened with a court martial (which is publicly announced and all details are released), she had broken down completely and then between the four of them (she was also accompanied by the WRAF officer-in-charge) they had produced a statement. It was a wonder she lasted four hours.

The line of questioning adopted is always the same and common to all three services. Again due to a technicality, my answers were allowed to be evasive and were recorded as such, but if you are a WRAF or a WRAC you are asked the same question repeatedly until you give the answer the interrogator wants, whether or not it is the truth or the whole truth. Examples of these questions are as follows (presuming you have already admitted to being gay and having a relationship):

1. Who was the initiator? (place, date, time) and where on the body did she touch you/you touch her?
2. Did you/she respond? If so, where on the body? (place, date, time)
3. What clothes were you wearing (if any) – civilian clothes, uniform?
4. If none, did you undress yourselves or each other? Who undressed who first? Were you both undressed? (place, date, time)
5. Did you use any sex devices or other similar foreign objects, and if yes, did you both use them, only you on her, only she on you? (place, date, time)
6. If no to question 5, how did you 'make love' (their quote marks) – i.e. did you use hands, mouths, both, another part of the body (if yes, which part?), and did she do this to you, or you to her, or both? (place, date, time)
7. How many times have you slept together, made love together etc? (place, date, time)
8. How long has your relationship lasted?
9. How many relationships have you had? How long have these lasted, give all details as above, place, date, time etc. etc.

10. Who else is gay?
11. Who else *knows* you are gay? (It is a chargeable offence to withhold this type of information.)

The search of your belongings is for incriminating or corroboratory evidence (love letters, apparati, club memberships, diary entries, addresses, anything and everything).

Your statement is typed, you both have to sign it. For the first time you see your lovemaking in black and white, in loveless technical terms. You feel dirty and shocked initially, then downright angry, then finally impotent because there is absolutely nothing you can do. You are "Undesirable", your services are no longer required, you lose your career, your new "home", your friends and very frequently your lover.

You have a lot of explaining to do to friends and family, as once the wheels are in motion your discharge takes very little time at all. The grapevine buzzes, everyone else is in constant fear of similar treatment. You are made an example. You have had virtually no representation, no one to give you advice because either you incriminate yourself or else the people who know and help you become accessories before, during and after the "act".

Even if you don't confess, you cannot disprove the allegations, and though they in turn cannot prove them either, once they have decided you are gay, they will not change their minds. More often than not, the person interrogating/discharging you is also gay and possibly an ex-lover or a potential lover. The higher your seniority the smaller the possibility of being discharged; you are usually warned, given a separating draft, and of course, remonstrated. Thereafter, you are observed and of course likely to be charged with the same offence again if you seem to be getting too attached to another woman. It is a hypocritical, double-standard business.'

The Ministry of Defence have given three reasons for maintaining a draconian attitude towards homosexuality in the forces: the potentially disruptive influence of 'homosexual practices' in a closed community; the necessity to ensure that there is no abuse of authority by those in charge of younger or junior personnel; those who engage in homosexual activity may be liable to blackmail and are therefore likely to be a security risk.

Even if these arguments were sound they do not appear to apply to many particular cases of discharged military personnel. An ex-serviceman, John Bruce, has made an application under Article 8 of the European Convention on Human Rights arguing that his discharge because of homosexual relationships whilst off-duty contravenes the right to respect for private life guaranteed by the Convention.

Appendix II
Transsexuals and transvestites

'Having regard to the essentially heterosexual character of the relationship which is called marriage, the criteria must, in my judgment, be biological, for even the most extreme degree of transsexualism in a male or the most severe hormonal imbalance which can exist in a person with male chromosomes, male gonads and male genitalia cannot reproduce a person who is naturally capable of performing the essential role of a woman in marriage.'

Mr Justice Ormrod[1]

One of the main points of this book has been to show that certain legal definitions run against the course of human behaviour. The law is intolerant of the variety and fluidity of sexual definition and peaceful sexual activity. Homosexuality seen as a sexual orientation is sometimes crudely described as a problem of 'child-love'; and it is in this sense that in this book paedophiles are described as the exposed nerve of male homosexuality. Lesbianism and male homosexuality are also sometimes seen as problems about gender: a failure to be a 'real' woman or man. Transsexuals (and to a lesser extent) transvestites raise the question of gender in its most acute form. In this sense they are the exposed nerve of the 'gender problem' and in respect of which the law has failed to give a positive and tolerant response.

Transsexual[2] is the term used to describe men and women who have two incompatible sexes. They are torn between a physical sex recognised by the legal and administrative authorities at birth, and a different psychical sex to which they believe they belong. The specific object of 'sexual conversion' or 'sex change' surgery is to reduce these contradictions as far as possible.[3]

As a result of the development of hormone treatment and plastic surgery, people now have the possibility of transforming their bodies. During the last twenty years, men and women have taken advantage of these medical advances and so transsexuals have appeared in significant numbers. Throughout the world governments have been slow to respond to the new situation. This section indicates the areas where legal adjustments must be made to give those who have undergone medical treatment their new rights.

Transsexuals are not transvestites. For transsexuals it is vital to their psychological needs that they dress in the clothes of the sex to which they have decided to belong. In the course of pre-operative therapy, transsexual patients are required to live in the conventional role of their chosen sex — often according to stereotyped ambitions, desires and so on.

Transvestites are men and women of heterosexual or homosexual orientation who enjoy expressing themselves by regularly wearing clothes of the opposite sex. It is important for a transvestite that s/he wishes to dress in clothes *opposite* to the sex which s/he defines his or her sex to be. 'Cross-dressing' does not mean that someone wishes to identify with the opposite sex in the sense of wanting to assume permanently all the characteristics of that sex, including the different sexual organs. The largest established transvestite organisation in Britain, the Beaumont Society, has an overwhelmingly heterosexual membership.

Unlike some US states, there is no law in Britain forbidding men to wear women's clothes in public, or women to wear men's. However, some police officers and magistrates have taken the view that it is insulting behaviour likely to cause a breach of the peace, contrary to the Public Order Act 1936 section 5 (or under local Acts of parliament or common law).

Exactly what is 'insulting' behaviour or conduct is a question of fact decided by the magistrates. The charge cannot be heard in the crown court before a judge and jury. There has to be some evidence of the likely reaction of members of the public nearby to justify a conviction, but 'reasonable apprehension' by a police officer that adverse reaction might occur would justify an arrest. As usual, it is not those likely to create the disturbance who are arrested. It is difficult to say how often transvestites are prosecuted for such public order offences. Minor cases are not often reported and details of such charges are not published in the official criminal statistics.

Transsexuals

For all sorts of administrative, economic and social reasons the state lays down the criteria of sexual identity and the procedure for identification of sex. This identification is traditionally based on the physical form recorded at birth – simply the presence or absence of male or female external or internal sexual organs. The development of medical science has cast doubts on the absolute validity of these criteria.

It is incompatible with respect for people's private lives that a transsexual, who has taken on the appearance and social behaviour of an ordinary member of their chosen sex, should not be defined as a member of the sex opposite to that on their birth certificate. Birth certificates are required in an increasing number of circumstances; for example, employers ask to see them, particularly the civil service, and they are required as proof of pensionable age. In such instances a transsexual must reveal information relating to his or her private life to third parties. They may subsequently be excluded from certain jobs, rights, activities and relationships on account of the explanations given. It is very important if the operation and therapy are to be successful that a transsexual can pass as a member of their chosen sex. So being required to reveal the sex change is not only embarrassing but psychologically distressing and socially demeaning.

Birth certificates and civil status

Many authorities are 'discreet and tactful' in changing documentation. It is therefore usually possible to obtain: (1) a new medical card by writing to the local family practitioner committee with a note from your doctor or psychiatrist; (2) income tax form change by personal application to the local tax office with proof of new identity, that is, a new medical card or note from a doctor or psychiatrist; (3) a new driving licence by re-applying in a new name; (4) a new British Visitor's Passport may be obtained or changed at the Post Office with a new medical card. A full passport may only be changed after completed surgery with a letter from a doctor or psychiatrist. If the surgery has not been completed, the patient's doctor can request that the case be considered on its merits; (5) a change of name. First names can be changed without any formal legal process, a full name can be changed either by way of Deed Poll or Statutory Declaration. In Scotland names can be changed without any formal registration. There is no arrangement for Deed Polls. To be effective any change of name must be notified to all friends, family and work contacts.

Obtaining such new documentation clearly saves day-to-day embarrassment and administrative inconvenience. However, although it seems to be administrative practice that transsexuals should be treated as their chosen sex for National Insurance purposes, they will not be so treated in any question of benefit or pension entitlement.[4] Transsexuals have no legal right to these arrangements.

The major legal problem for the civil status of transsexuals is amending the entry of sex on the birth certificate. If this were done, transsexuals would have the rights of their chosen sex. It is a difficult problem because although the Registrar General of Births has power to order a complete entry to be altered, this can be done only if there has been an error of fact (for example about the place of birth) or of substance (for example about sex because of uncertain physical formation) in relation to the birth. The official view is that the entry is a record of the facts at the time of the birth, and has nothing to do with any future events. Another argument to be dealt with is that the decision about a child's sex at birth must be based on biological criteria if only because the child's psychological perception of his or her sexuality does not develop until later. So if there is no error, the Registrar has no power under the present law to alter the birth certificate.

In a House of Commons written reply in 1977 the Under Secretary at the Department of Health and Social Security stated that medical experts believed that a true change of sex could not occur. It might be possible to change some documents after the operation 'but a birth certificate is a record of the facts at the time of birth. To alter the birth register in such cases would be to falsify it and could assist in the perpetration of a deception'.[5] The position appears to be the same in Scotland. Scots birth certificates can be changed only where there was a genuine mistake on registering the birth. The Lord Advocate has stated that 'subsequent surgical treatment which purports to effect a change of sex is not necessarily evidence that the sex was wrongly stated when the birth was registered'.[6]

In order to alter the birth certificate a new procedure would have to be devised whereby a transsexual could apply to a court for a declaration of change of apparent sex and, if granted, the change of sex could be recorded and an altered certificate obtained. In West Germany the law provides that a transsexual may apply for judicial declaration that s/he belongs to the other sex. To obtain the declaration a transsexual must (a) be over 21, (b) usually have had successful sex conversion surgery (but if for medical reasons this is not possible, it is enough if the treatment has been sufficient to render it impossible for the applicant to revert to his or her biological sex), (c) the applicant is no longer capable of procreation. There is no definition of transsexual as it was felt that there was no difficulty in distinguishing transsexualism from transvestism or homosexuality. Nor need the applicant be unmarried but, once the declaration is made, any existing marriage is void. However, a transsexual retains his or her original sex in relation to any children, so that maintenance obligations remain unaltered.

In 1979 the European Commission of Human Rights ruled that the failure of the Belgian government to authorise a rectification of the applicant's sex in the birth certificate constituted an unjustified interference with the right to respect for private life guaranteed by Article 8 of the European Convention on Human Rights. The finding, which concerned a female-to-male transsexual, was overturned by the European Court of Human Rights in the following year on the technical ground that the applicant had not exhausted all the domestic remedies available under Belgian law.[7] The issue therefore still remains open for transsexuals.

A valid marriage can be contracted only by two people of the opposite sex. Whether someone is 'male' or 'female' is determined in law by the description on their birth certificate.

The issue of a transsexual's marriage went to the English courts in 1970. In *Corbett* v *Corbett*[8] Mr Justice Ormrod had to decide whether or not the respondent wife, a male-to-female transsexual who had undergone sex conversion surgery, was a woman for the purpose of marriage. He ruled that biological criteria should determine the issue, as they do for the determination of sex registered on the birth certificate. Since it was accepted that the biological sexual constitution of a person is fixed at birth and cannot be changed, it followed that the respondent remained male and was therefore not a woman for the purpose of marriage even though psychologically she regarded herself as a woman, physically resembled a woman (including having an artificial vagina), and was socially accepted as a woman. The court based its decision on the reproductive biological characteristics of the sexes, that is: chromosomal factors (the presence or absence of the XY (male) or XX (female) chromosomes); gonadal factors (the presence or absence of testicles or ovaries); and genital factors (the presence or absence of male or female genitals).

Corbett v *Corbett* is the leading case so far as transsexuals are concerned and its reasoning has been followed in cases not connected with matrimonial law. Reference has been made to the case by the Registrar of Births when refusing to change birth certificates. *Corbett* has also been used to define gender for the purposes of the Sex Discrimination Act 1975 (*White* v *British Sugar Corporation* – see below). Judges and magistrates refer to *Corbett* when insisting that transsexuals in the dock should be addressed by their original biological gender.

Employment

At industrial tribunal level, it has been decided that a female-to-male transsexual (who had not undergone sex conversion surgery) is not a 'man' for the purposes of the Sex Discrimination Act 1975. The tribunal thought that the Act only prevented employers from discriminating against 'women' who are biologically female and 'men' who are biologically male.

In *White* v *British Sugar Corporation* (1977)[9] the employee, Edwyn White, was biologically a woman but for many years had regarded himself as a man, dressed as a man, was socially accepted as a man and treated for national insurance purposes as a man. The corporation when employing him was under the impression that he was a man. He worked Sunday shifts which in this particular factory would have been unlawful for a woman (there being no exemption order granted to the employer under the Factory Acts). Eventually, fellow employees reported their suspicions to management and when the story came out Edwyn White was sacked. The tribunal decided that the employee had been fairly dismissed *not* on account of sex but because he lied to the company about being a man: as a result there had not been discrimination on the grounds of sex. The decision was not appealed to the employment appeal tribunal.

There are serious legal implications for transsexuals if this ruling is generally applied. For example, if a male-to-female transsexual has had sexual surgery and appears to be a woman and is discriminated against on the grounds that she is a woman, the Sex Discrimination Act cannot apply because she is not biologically female and therefore not a 'woman' for the purposes of the Act. On the other hand, if it is discovered that she is male-to-female transsexual then, since any discrimination by the employer is likely to be on the ground that the employee is a transsexual rather than because she is biologically a male, the Sex Discrimination Act will not apply because it only outlaws discrimination on the grounds of a person's sex, not his or her sexual orientation. As seen in Chapter 6, industrial tribunals have generally found that employers have dismissed reasonably when an employee's sexuality differs from the norm. In the case of transsexuals it is likely that tribunals would follow the *White* case and decide that the employee had been dismissed for deceit and the employer had acted reasonably in treating the deception as sufficient reason for the dismissal.

However it may be that a properly argued case taken to an employment appeal tribunal might produce a positive result since the purpose of the Sex Discrimination Act 1975 (and the Equal Pay Act 1970) is to prevent discrimination on the ground of sex in employment and other *social* spheres. So the sex people live out socially should be regarded as relevant, not their biological sex.[10]

Custody and Access

In 1981 the English Court of Appeal heard the first case in which a pre-operative transsexual's right to visit her child was disputed by her former spouse.[11] C was a male-to-female transsexual. As a married man, C had had a daughter with his wife. Later on, as a transsexual, C lived with her boyfriend and sought access to her daughter aged four. The daughter had always known C as 'Daddy', but had seen her dressed in female clothes regularly and knew she was also called C. Reports were obtained from the Court Welfare Officer, C's consultant psychiatrist at the gender identity clinic, and a US authority on transsexualism, Professor Richard Green. The welfare report covered such matters as C's role with her daughter, the feasibility of being in a sexually ambiguous role with the daughter, and the impact of the change of sexual identity on C's daughter, spouse and her family. The report recommended continuing access on a regular basis in a female role because 'the child could be more confused by half-truths than knowing for certain what is happening'. Both psychiatric reports stated that the relationship between C and her daughter was a close and deep one, and that her daughter knew and understood quite a lot about the situation and displayed no signs of any disturbance or gender-role confusion. Professor Green believed that a child should have a continuing relationship and knowledge of the genetic parent.

A High Court Judge granted C access once every three weeks, on condition that she was not accompanied by her boyfriend and that she should be in a 'male-orientated' role with no make-up, jewellery, or female clothing. The judge apparently described C as having conducted a 'one track crusade on behalf of transsexualism'. C appealed against the judge's conditions. In the Court of Appeal the dress restriction was removed with the warning that C should not dress in a 'bizarre or aggressively feminine way'. The rest of the appeal was dismissed. Lord Justice Ormrod commented: 'It is very finely balanced whether it is in the interests of the child to keep contact with the father in these confusing circumstances.'

Prisoners

The unusual issue of the rights of pre-operative transsexual prisoners to the continuation of hormone therapy has arisen in the course of the NCCL's work. Withholding female hormones from someone well advanced in taking them can be both physically painful and psychologically stressful, involving someone in deep mental suffering. In one case, following representations on her behalf a pre-operative male-to-female transsexual prisoner (whom the authorities insisted must be detained in a male prison) was seen by a visiting psychiatrist for assessment and prescribed hormone treatment in the period before release.

There is a cruel but central contradiction in the law relating to transsexuals. It is lawful to prescribe hormone treatment and to have surgery to change genital sex; these are available on the National Health Service and indeed some men and women are encouraged to take this medical option. Yet, the government and the courts refuse to acknowledge the full legal consequences that follow.

Appendix III
Legal status of homosexuality

European laws regarding minimum age for lawful homosexual relationships between men

	legal status of homosexuality
Austria	legal at the age of 18
Belgium	legal at the age of 18 (sexual conduct between two men, both between 18 and 21 is legal, but if one is under 21 and the other over, it is a criminal offence)
Bulgaria	legal at 21
Cyprus	completely illegal for males
Czechoslovakia	legal at 18
Denmark	legal at 15
Eire	completely illegal for males
Finland	legal at 18
France	legal at 15
German Democratic Republic	legal at 18
Federal German Republic	legal at 18
United Kingdom	
England & Wales	legal at 21
Northern Ireland	legal at 21
Scotland	legal at 21
Greece	legal at 17
Holland	legal at 16
Hungary	legal at 10
Iceland	legal at 18
Italy	no special legal restrictions applicable
Luxembourg	legal at 18
Malta	legal at 18
Norway	no special legal restrictions
Portugal	no special legal restrictions
Romania	completely illegal for males
USSR	completely illegal for males
Poland	legal at 15
Spain	homosexuality is punishable by the law either as a case of 'public scandal' or 'corruption of minors', defined as persons under 23

Sweden	legal at 18
Switzerland	legal at 16
Yugoslavia	legal at 18

Note: It appears that only in Ireland, Cyprus, Romania and the USSR is male homosexuality subject to complete prohibition by law. No states appear to have any specific legislation restricting lesbianism.

Sources: UK government conspectus prepared in connection with proceedings before the European Commission of Human Rights in the *Dudgeon* case (1979 unpublished).

The Committee on Social and Health Questions of the Parliamentary Assembly of the Council of Europe, *Report on Discrimination Against Homosexuals*, Strasbourg 1981.

Model sexual offences reform law

proposed by the Campaign for Homosexual Equality

Amend the law relating to certain forms of sexual conduct, to make better provision for the display, advertisement or distribution of matter concerned with homosexuality and for the protection of public decency; and for the purposes connected therewith.

BE IT ENACTED by the Queen's most Excellent Majesty, by and with the advice and consent of the Lords Spiritual and Temporal, and Commons, in this present Parliament assembled, and by the authority of the same as follows:-

Lawfulness of certain sexual conduct between male persons
1. (1) Except as otherwise provided in this Act, it shall not be unlawful for male persons to engage in or be a party to sexual intercourse or any other form of sexual conduct with or between other male persons.
   (2) In this Act 'sexual intercourse' includes sexual intercourse per anum, and otherwise has the meaning ascribed to it in section 44 of the Act of 1956.

Equality of treatment in law of homosexual and heterosexual behaviour
2. It shall not be alleged in any proceedings that any conduct or thing is unlawful, contra bonos mores, obscene, lewd, indecent, likely to cause offence or likely to lead to a breach of the peace by reason only of its being or relating to sexual conduct between persons of the same sex; and in deciding whether any conduct or thing amounts to conduct or thing described as aforesaid or by words of similar purport in any enactment (including this Act) or any byelaw or rule of common law such conduct or thing shall be

deemed to have taken place or relate to conduct taking place between members of opposite sexes.

Redefinition of Rape to include sexual intercourse per anum
3.　　For the purposes of this Act and of the Act of 1956 the offence of rape is committed when there is an act of sexual intercourse per anum committed in circumstances where sexual intercourse per vaginam would amount to rape and section 1 subsection 1 of the Act of 1956 is to be interpreted as though the reference to a woman included reference to a man.

Procurement by threats, false pretences or the administration of drugs
4.　　Sections 2, 3 and 4 of the Act of 1956 are to be interpreted in all respects as if the references therein to women included references to men.

Meaning of 'Consent'
5.　　In this Act consent means free and voluntary consent and any consent obtained by means of any threat, inducement, trick or any form of undue or improper pressure or influence shall not be regarded as consent affording a defence to any charge under any section of this Act nor shall it be presumed that consent given on one occasion continues to be operative on any subsequent occasion.

Intercourse with boys under the age of 16
6.　　It is an offence for a man to have sexual intercourse with a boy under the age of thirteen.
7. (1)　It is an offence, subject to the exception mentioned in this section, for a man to have sexual intercourse with a boy not under the age of thirteen but under the age of sixteen.
　 (2)　A man is not guilty of an offence under this section because he has sexual intercourse with a boy under the age of sixteen if he proves that he believed the boy to be of or over the age of sixteen and had reasonable grounds for that belief.
　 (3)　A boy under the age of sixteen is not capable in law of giving any consent that would provide any defence to a charge under this section or under section 6.

Intercourse with mentally subnormal persons
8. (1)　A man who is suffering from severe subnormality within the meaning of the Mental Health Act 1959 cannot in law give any consent which by virtue of any section of this Act would prevent an act from being an offence, but a person shall not be convicted, on account of the incapacity of such a man to consent, of an offence consisting of such an act if he proves that he did not know

and had no reason to suspect that man to be suffering from severe subnormality.

(2) Section 128 of the Mental Health Act 1959 (prohibition of men on the staff of a hospital, or otherwise having responsibility for mental patients, having sexual intercourse with women patients) shall have effect as if any reference therein to having unlawful sexual intercourse with a woman included a reference to sexual intercourse with another man.

Sexual conduct other than sexual intercourse with persons under the age of sixteen

9. (1) It is an offence for a person to engage in or be a party to conduct of a sexual nature with, between or towards a person under the age of sixteen which does not amount to sexual intercourse, is not an offence by virtue of any other section of this Act and does not amount to an assault.

(2) It shall not be a defence to a charge under this section that the other person involved consented to the conduct.

(3) A person shall not be guilty of an offence under this section if he proves that he believed the other person or persons to be of or over the age of sixteen and had reasonable cause for this belief.

Homosexual conduct in the Armed Forces

10. (1) Nothing in this Act shall prevent an act or conduct from being an offence (other than a civil offence) under any provision of the Army Act, the Air Force Act or the Naval Discipline Act for the time being in force where the act or conduct

(a) is prejudicial to good order and discipline, and

(b) takes place in any naval, army or air force ship, vehicle, aircraft, barracks, camp, station or other service premises, or in any other circumstances where any body of naval, military or air force personnel is under naval, military or air force orders.

(2) No act or conduct of a homosexual nature shall be considered to be prejudicial to good order and discipline so as to be an offence under this section unless heterosexual acts or conduct of like nature and in like circumstances would be so regarded.

Procuration of others for the commission of offences under this Act

11. (1) It is an offence for a person to procure a boy under the age of thirteen to become, in any part of the world, a prostitute.

(2) It is an offence for a person to procure a man to have sexual intercourse or to engage in any other conduct of a sexual nature which would if committed be an offence under any section of this Act.

(3) A person shall not be convicted of an offence under this section on the evidence of one person only, unless the witness is corroborated

in some material particular by evidence implicating the accused.

(4) The Act of 1952 shall have effect as if offences under this section were included among those specified in paragraphs 1 to 18 of Schedule 1 to that Act (indictable triable summarily with the consent of the accused).

Living on earnings of male prostitution.

12. (1) It is an offence for a man or woman knowlingly to live wholly or in part on the earnings of prostitution of a man.

(2) A person accused of an offence under this section may claim to be tried on indictment under section 25 of the Act of 1952 (right of accused to trial by jury for summary offences punishable with more than three months imprisonment).

Premises resorted to for homosexual practices

13. Premises shall be treated for purposes of sections 33 to 35 of the Act of 1956 as a brothel if people resort to it for the purposes of homosexual practices in circumstances in which resort thereto for heterosexual practices would have led to its being treated as a brothel for the purposes of those sections.

Protection of public order and decency

14. (1) It is an offence for any person to commit an act of indecency in any place where he knows or has reasonable cause to believe that he is likely to be visible to any other person who is

(a) in a public place, or

(b) lawfully present on any private premises or place and who does not condone, consent to, or acquiesce in the commission of the Act.

(2) An act of indecency means an act which is seriously offensive to the public at large and which seriously affronts contemporary standards.

(3) An act or conduct involving persons of the same sex shall not be considered to be indecent so as to amount to the commission of an offence under this section unless like conduct in like circumstances involving persons of opposite sexes would be so regarded.

(4) In any proceedings for an offence under this section a person shall not be convicted unless it is proved that at least one member of the public (other than a police officer) was offended by his conduct; and it shall be a defence that such member of the public incited, encouraged or consented to the commission of the act.

Soliciting

15. (1) It is an offence for any person in any public place persistently to solicit any other person for the purpose of engaging in any

conduct of a sexual nature whether or not such conduct would be an offence if committed.

(2)   Solicitation is persistent if it is directed at the same person repeatedly or over a period of time.

(3)   In any proceedings under this section there shall be no conviction in the absence of evidence from the person alleged to have been the object of the solicitation and the evidence of a police officer shall not be sufficient for this purpose. It shall be a defence to prove that the person alleged to have been the object of the solicitation incited or encouraged it.

(4)   Conduct involving persons of the same sex shall not be regarded as an offence under this section where like conduct in like circumstances involving persons of opposite sexes would not be so regarded.

Time limit on prosecutions

16. (1)   Subject to the exceptions mentioned in subsection (2) of this section, no proceedings for an offence under any section of this Act shall be commenced after the expiration of twelve months from the date on which the offence is alleged to have been committed.

(2)   This section does not apply to an offence under section 3 (rape), sections 6 and 7 (sexual intercourse with a boy under the age of sixteen), section 11 subsection (1) (procuring a boy under the age of eighteen for prostitution), section 12 (living on the earnings of prostitution), and section 13 (keeping a brothel).

Restrictions on prosecutions

17.   No proceedings shall be instituted except by or with the consent of the Director of Public Prosecutions against any man for the offence of sexual intercourse with another man, for attempting to commit such an offence or for aiding, abetting, counselling, procuring or commanding its commission where either of the men concerned was at the time of the offence under the age of sixteen PROVIDED THAT this section shall not prevent the arrest, or the issue of a warrant for the arrest, of a person for any such offence, or the remand in custody or on bail of a person charged with any such offence.

Past offences

18. (1)   Except as provided by the following provisions of this section, the provisions of this Act shall have effect in relation to acts done before the passing of the Act as they apply to acts done after its passing.

(2)   Except as provided by the next following subsection, this Act shall not have effect in relation to any act which is, or apart from this Act would be, an offence, where the defendant to an indictment for

that offence has been committed for the trial of that offence before the passing of the Act or, as the case may be, a court martial has been ordered or convened for the trial of that offence before the passing of this Act.

(3)   The foregoing provisions of this section shall not operate so as to permit the award of any punishment for offence committed before the passing of this Act greater than the punishment for the corresponding offence in this Act do not disclose any corresponding or equivalent offence under this Act the proceedings shall be discontinued.

Prohibition on revival of offences

19. (1)   Except as provided by the next following subsection of this section, no prosecution shall be commenced and no offence shall be alleged under the provisions of any other Act or rule of common law where the particulars of the offence are covered by the terms of any section of this Act.

(2)   This section shall not have effect to prevent the prosecution of any offence under sections 14 or 15 of the Act of 1956 nor of the attempt, incitement or conspiracy to commit any offence under this Act.

Modification of existing law

20. (1)   The enactments specified in the third schedule to this Act are repealed to the extent shown in the schedule.

(2)   It is hereby expressly declared, but without prejudice to the generality of Section 2 of this Act, that it shall be lawful for a person or for two or more persons acting in concert to possess, publish, sell or distribute whether by post or otherwise any book, pamphlet, handbill, newspaper, magazine or periodical or any film, gramophone record or tape recording which contains advertisements of a homosexual nature, or which depicts or describes homosexual conduct where like advertisements of a heterosexual nature, or the depiction or description of like heterosexual conduct would not be unlawful.

(3)   The expression 'advertisements of a homosexual nature' in subsection (2) of this section includes advertisements for homosexual clubs or societies and invitations to homosexual men and women to meet other homosexual men and women whether such invitations might be construed as invitations to take part in sexual conduct or not; but does not include any invitation to take part in sexual conduct that would, after the passing of this Act, be an offence under this Act or otherwise, or any advertisement for premises that would constitute a brothel as defined in section 13 of this Act.

Punishments for offences

21. (1) The Fourth Schedule of this Act shall have the effect, subject to and in accordance with the following provisions of this section, with respect to the prosecution and punishment of the offences listed in the first column of the Schedule, being offences under this Act or under the Act of 1956 as amended by this Act and attempts to commit certain of those offences.

   (2) The Second Schedule to the Act of 1956 is amended to the extent necessary to give effect to the revised maximum punishments for certain offences under the Act of 1956 listed in the Fourth Schedule to this Act.

   (3) The second column in the Schedule shows, for any offence, if it may be prosecuted on indictment or summarily, or either, if the indictment is not triable by any court and what special restrictions (if any) there are on the commencement of a prosecution.

   (4) The third column in the Schedule shows, for any offence, the punishments which may be imposed on conviction on indictment or on summary conviction, a reference to a period giving the maximum term of imprisonment and a reference to a sum of money the maximum fine.

   (5) The fourth column in the Schedule contains provisions which are either supplementary to those in the second or third column or enable a person charged on indictment with the offence specified in the first column to be found guilty of another offence if the jury are not satisfied that he is guilty of the offence charged or of an attempt to commit it, but are satisfied that he is guilty of the other offence.

   (6) Where in the Schedule there is used a phrase descriptive of an offence or a group of offences followed by a reference to a section by its number only, the reference is to a section of this Act, and the phrase shall be taken as referring to any offence under the section mentioned.

   (7) Nothing in this section or in the Fourth Schedule to this Act shall exclude the application to any of the offences referred to in the first column of the Schedule –

   (a) of section 20 or 21 of the Magistrates' Courts Act 1952 (which relates to the summary trial of young offenders for indictable offences); or

   (b) of subsection 5 of section 98 of that Act (which limits the punishment which may be imposed by a magistrates' court sitting in an occasional court-house); or

   (c) of any enactment or rule of law restricting a court's power to imprison; or

   (d) of any enactment or rule of law authorising an offender to be dealt with in a way not authorised by the enactments specially relating to his offences; or

(e) of any enactment or rule of law authorising a jury to find a person guilty of an offence other than that with which he is charged.

Short title, citation, interpretations and extent

22. (1) This Act may be cited as the Sexual Offences Act, 19.

(2) In this Act 'the Act of 1952' means the Magistrates' Courts Act 1952, and 'the Act of 1956' means the Sexual Offences Act 1956.

(3) In this Act, Section 46 of the Act of 1956 (interpretation of 'man' 'boy' and other expressions) shall apply for the purposes of this Act as it applies for the purposes of that Act; 'public place' has the meaning assigned to it by Section 9 of the Public Order Act 1936 and, without prejudice to the generality of the foregoing, includes any lavatory to which the public has access whether on payment or otherwise.

(4) References in this Act to any enactment shall, except in so far as the context otherwise requires, be construed as references to that enactment as amended or applied by or under any subsequent enactment including this Act.

(5) It is hereby declared that where in any proceedings it is charged that an act involving conduct between persons of the same sex is an offence, the prosecutor shall have the burden of proving where relevant that any of the parties had not reached the appropriate age or was a defective.

(6) Subject to the modifications mentioned in the First and Second Schedules respectively to this Act, this Act shall apply to Scotland and to Northern Ireland.

FIRST SCHEDULE
Adaptions necessary to apply the Act in Scotland.

SECOND SCHEDULE
Adaptions necessary to apply the Act in Northern Ireland.

THIRD SCHEDULE
Enactments repealed   Extent of repeal

Magistrates' Courts Act 1952

Section 25: for the words 'section 30 or 31 of the Sexual Offences Act 1956 or any offence under section 32 of that Act where the immoral purpose is other than the commission of a homosexual act' there shall be substituted the words 'section 30 or 31 of the Sexual Offences Act 1956'.

Sexual Offences Act 1956

Section 12: in subsection (1) for the words 'It is a felony for a person to commit buggery with another person or with an animal' there shall be substituted the words 'it is a felony for a person to commit buggery with an animal'.

Section 12: subsection (2) shall have effect as if the words 'except on a charge of an offence with a person under the age of seventeen' were omitted.

Section 12: subsection (3) is wholly repealed.

Section 13 is wholly repealed.

Section 16: subsection (1) shall have effect as if the word 'buggery' were replaced by the word 'rape'.

Second schedule:

paragraph 13 is wholly repealed

paragraph 16 is wholly repealed

paragraph 18, for the words 'ten years' in column 3 there shall be substituted the words 'two years'.

paragraph 19, for the word 'buggery' in column 1 there shall be substituted the word 'rape'.

paragraph 32 is wholly repealed.

Sexual Offences Act 1967

The whole Act.

FOURTH SCHEDULE
Table of Offences, with Mode of Prosecution, Punishments etc.

offence	mode of prosecution	punishment
1. sexual intercourse with boy under 13 (s. 6)	indictment	life
2. sexual intercourse with boy under 16 (s. 7)	indictment	2 years
3. sexual intercourse with defective (s. 8)	indictment	2 years
4. sexual conduct with person under 16 (s. 9)	indictment	2 years
5. procuring boy under 18 for prostitution (s. 11(1))	indictment summarily	2 years 6 months
6. procuring offence under the Act (s. 11(2))	indictment summarily	2 years 6 months
7. living on earnings of male prostitute (s. 12)	indictment summarily	2 years 6 months
8. public indecency (s. 14)	summarily (but subject to right to claim trial on indictment)	6 months
9. soliciting (s. 15)	summarily (but subject to right to claim trial on indictment)	6 months

Model gay civil rights law
devised by Matt Coles, Attorney for Gay Rights Advocates, San Francisco, California

Section 1.

Policy and Intent. It is the policy of the (enacting policy) to insure that no individual within the ...... is subject to discrimination (as that term is defined in this ordinance) as a result of her or his sexual orientation.

Section 2.

Findings. After public hearings and consideration of testimony and documentary evidence, the ...... finds that discrimination based on sexual orientation exists in ...... The ...... finds further that such discrimination poses a substantial threat to the health, safety and general welfare of this community. Such discrimination foments strife and unrest, and it deprives ...... of the fullest utilization of its capacities for development and advancement. The ...... finds further that existing State and Federal restraints on arbitrary discrimination are not adequate to meet the particular problems of discrimination based on sexual orientation in this community, so that it is necessary and proper to enact local regulations adapted to the special circumstances which exist in this ....

Section 3. Definitions.

(a) *Business Establishments.* As used in this ordinance, the term 'business establishment' shall mean any entity, however organised, which furnishes goods or services to the general public. An otherwise qualifying establishment which has membership requirements is considered to furnish services to the general public if its membership requirements: (1) consist only of payment of fees; (2) consist of requirements under which a substantial portion of the residents of this ...... could qualify; or (3) consist of an otherwise unlawful business practice.

(b) *Discrimination.* As used in this ordinance, the term 'discrimination' shall mean any act, policy or practice which, regardless of intent, has the effect of subjecting any person to differential treatment as a result of that person's sexual orientation. The phrase 'differential treatment' includes any limitation on a person's full unsegregated and equal access to or enjoyment of, employment, real estate transactions, business establishments, (*municipal or county*) services and educational services.

(c) *Person.* As used in this ordinance, the term 'person' shall mean any natural person, firm, corporation, partnership or other organisation, association or group of persons however organised.

(d) *Real Estate Transactions*. As used in this ordinance, the term 'real estate transactions' shall include the sale, repair, improvement, lease, rental, or occupancy of any interest or portion of any interest in real property and shall also include the extension of credit, financing insurance or services in connection with the sale, repair, improvement, lease, rental, or occupancy of any such interest in real property.

(e) *Sexual Orientation*. As used in this ordinance, the term 'sexual orientation' shall mean an individual's actual or supposed sexual or affectional preference (including homosexuality, heterosexuality or bisexuality by preference or practice) including but not limited to a preference that may be imputed on the basis of personal mannerisms, physical characteristics or manner of dress.

Section 4. Unlawful Practices.

(a) *In General*. It shall be unlawful for any person to do anything which has the effect of discriminating against any person as a result of that person's sexual orientation, with respect to any of the following activities:
(1) *Employment*: any aspect of employment, opportunities for employment, or union membership;
(2) *Real Estate*: any real estate transaction;
(3) *Business Establishments*: the availability or purchase or goods or services from any business establishment;
(4) *City Services and Facilities*: the use or availability of any (*municipal or county*) service or facility;
(5) *City Supported Services and Facilities*: the use or availability of any service or facility wholly or partially funded or otherwise supported by the (*city or county*);
(6) *Educational Institutions*: admission to any educational institution, or the use or availability of the facilities and services of any educational institution.

(b) *Exceptions*:
(1) *Employment*.
(A) *Bona Fide Occupational Qualifications*.
(i) *Bona Fide Occupational Qualification*. Nothing contained in Section 4 (a) (1) shall be deemed to prohibit selection or rejection based upon a *bona fide* occupational qualification.
(ii) *Burden of Proof*. In any action brought under Section . . . . . . of this Ordinance (*Enforcement*), if a party asserts that an otherwise unlawful discriminatory practice is justified as a *bona fide* occupational qualification, that party shall have the burden of proving: 1) that the discrimination is in fact a necessary result of a *bona fide* occupational qualification; and 2) that there exists no less discriminatory means of satisfying the occupational qualification.
(B) *Seniority Systems*. It shall not be unlawful discriminatory practice

under Section 4 (a) (1) for an employer to observe the conditions of a *bona fide* seniority system or a *bona fide* employee benefit system, provided such systems or plans are not a subterfuge to evade the purposes of this Ordinance; provided further that no such system shall provide an excuse for failure to hire any individual.

(2) *Real Estate Transactions:*

(A) *Owner Occupied Dwellings.* Nothing in Section 4 (a) (2) shall be construed to apply to the rental or leasing of any housing unit in which the owner or lessor or any member of his or her family occupies one of the living units and it is necessary for the owner, lessor, or family member to use either a bathroom facility or a kitchen facility in common with the prospective tenant.

(B) *Effect on Other Laws.* Nothing in Section 4 (a) (2) shall be deemed to permit any rental or occupancy of any dwelling unit or commercial space otherwise prohibited by law.

(3) *City Supported Services and Facilities.* Subsection 4(a)(5) of this ordinance shall not apply to any facility or service which does not receive any assistance from the city which is not provided to the public generally.

(4) *Educational Institutions.* Subsection 4(a)(6) of this ordinance shall not prohibit a religious or denominational institution from limiting admission to, or giving preference to, applicants of the same religion.

(c) *Notices.*

(1) *Requirements.* Every employer with fifteen or more employees, every labour organisation with fifteen or more members, and every employment agency shall post and keep posted in conspicuous places upon its premises where notices to employees, applicants for employment and members are customarily posted, the following notice:
Discrimination on the basis of sexual orientation is prohibited by law.
. . . . . . Code, sections . . . .

(2) *Alternate Compliance.* Notwithstanding the above, the provisions of this subsection may be complied with by adding the words 'sexual orientation' to all notices required by federal or state law, and indicating on the notice that discrimination on the basis of sexual orientation is prohibited by . . . . . . Code, sections . . . . . .

(3) *Penalty for Noncompliance.* Wilful violations of this subsection shall be punishable by a fine of not more than $50 for each offense. This is the exclusive remedy for violations of these notice provisions.

(d) *Advertising.* It shall be unlawful for any person to make, publish or disseminate any notice or statement which indicates that such person engages in or will engage in any practice prohibited by this ordinance.

Section 5. Civil Liability.

(a) *Mandatory Liability.* Any person who violates or aids in the violation of any provision of this ordinance shall be liable for:

(1) in any civil action brought to enforce this ordinance, costs and attorneys' fees;

(2) in any civil action brought to enforce this ordinance by the person whose rights were violated, actual damages and, in addition thereto, a civil penalty of five hundred dollars ($500).

(b) *Discretionary Liability*. In a proper case, a court may award punitive damages to the person whose rights were violated.

Section 6. Civil Enforcement.

(a) *Human Rights Commission*. The provisions of this ordinance may be enforced by the . . . . . . Human Rights Commission, by mediation or in a civil action.

(b) *Civil Action*. Any aggrieved person may enforce this ordinance in a civil action in any court of competent jurisdiction.

(c) *Injunctions*. Any person may bring a civil action in any court of competent jurisdiction to enjoin any person who commits or proposes to commit any act in violation of this ordinance.

Section 7. Criminal Liability.
Violation of any provision of this ordinance is a misdemeanor.

Section 8. Limitation on Action.
Judicial actions or requests to the Human Rights Commission under this ordinance must be filed within two years of the alleged discriminatory acts. Filing a complaint with the Commission tolls the running of this time period for the purpose of filing any civil action.

Section 9. Severability.
If any part or provision of this ordinance or the application thereof to any person or circumstance, is held invalid, the remainder of the ordinance, including the application of such part or provision to other persons or circumstances, shall not be affected thereby and shall continue in full force and effect. To this end, provisions of this ordinance are severable.

Machinery of the law in the United Kingdom

Laws in the United Kingdom come from two main sources: legislation made in parliament in London (statutes, or Acts of Parliament, and orders-in-council); and the legal decisions of courts and tribunals (that is, case law). Statutes are often separately enacted for the three legal systems. Since the suspension of the Stormont parliament in Belfast, legislation for Northern Ireland has been made at Westminster through orders-in-council. The system of case law or 'common law' is important throughout the United Kingdom. Although English and Scottish common law are based on different principles, the two systems share the fundamental idea that in similar cases, courts and tribunals are bound to follow the decisions of judges in higher courts. As a general rule, where the facts differ in kind from previously decided cases, a new legal principle may be developed by the court. The courts also create law by the way they interpret and apply statute law. And generally speaking, where the law is uncertain or unclear it can be clarified only by bringing an individual case. Hypothetical cases or questions cannot be brought to court. The structure of the different legal systems is shown in Diagram 1 on pages 210-212.

The laws of other nations have no direct effect in the UK. However the United Kingdom has signed a number of international agreements which are not legally enforceable but which the government does regard as binding. In the field of civil liberties, the 1950 European Convention of Human Rights is the most important international agreement for the protection of the rights of UK citizens. Decisions made by the European Commission or Court of Human Rights exert strong pressure on the government. When the Court has decided that the terms of the Convention have been broken, the government has taken some sort of corrective action. Diagram 2 on page 213 outlines the progress of a case brought under the Convention; the entire process can take five or six years.

Finding a suitable lawyer to help fight or use the law can be difficult. Legal expertise is more readily available to the rich, traditionally in fields connected with property, business and finance. However, Legal Aid, either free or with a means-tested contribution towards the costs, should be available from private solicitors for work and advice in respect of most of the problems discussed in this book. In some areas Legal Aid is very limited. It will not be paid, for example, for a lawyer to represent a client at an industrial tribunal. General advice and referrals to appropriate lawyers can be obtained from agencies such as Gay Switchboard or the National Council for Civil Liberties (NCCL) or Gay Legal Advice (GLAD). Legal services are available from local organisations such as citizen's advice bureaux or neighbourhood law centres who would refer people to appropriate specialist agencies or lawyers where necessary.

DIAGRAM 1. LEGAL SYSTEMS IN THE U.K.

A. England & Wales / Criminal

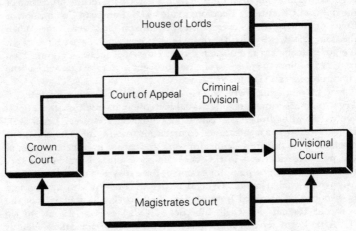

B. England & Wales / Civil

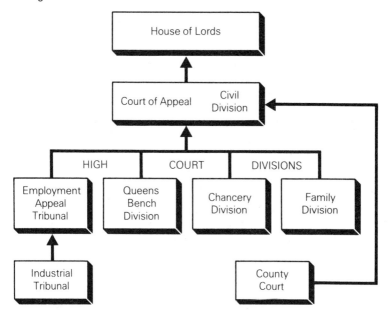

C. Scotland / Civil

/ Criminal

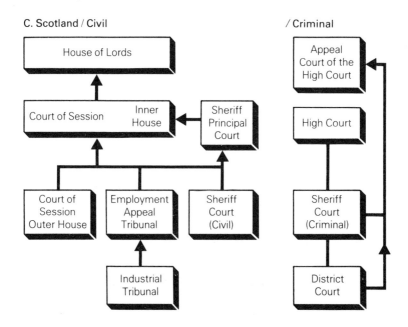

D. Northern Ireland / Civil and Criminal

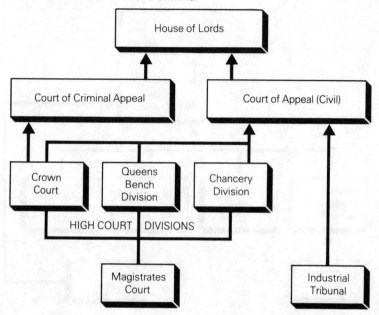

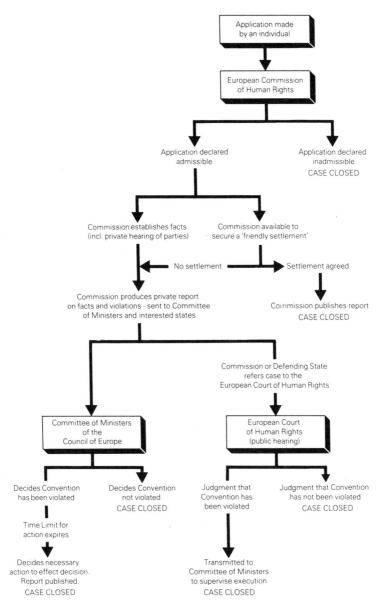

DIAGRAM 2. TAKING LEGAL ACTION UNDER THE EUROPEAN
CONVENTION OF HUMAN RIGHTS

Appendix V
The gay movement

The gay movement is fragmented and diverse. For convenience it can be separated into three strands.

Political pressure groups

At present the main autonomous gay political organisations in the UK are: The Campaign for Homosexual Equality (CHE, active in England and Wales), the Scottish Homosexual Rights Group (SHRG) and the Northern Ireland Gay Rights Association (NIGRA). These are pan-political groups. Their activity covers an enormous range from parliamentary work (lobbying and so on) to demonstrations and leafleting, organising talks and meetings, social and cultural events. It is to these groups that the media and government bodies conventionally turn for comment on proposals concerning gay people. The smaller Gay Activists Alliance formed in 1977 is a loose national federation of groups, now active only in northern England and Scotland. Groups like GAA have taken positions on such issues as Northern Ireland and made sure that there was a gay presence within other political movements such as black and women's struggles. There are local groups, whose activities are not nationally co-ordinated, such as East London GLF and Norwich Radical Gays. Lesbians are involved in all the groups to varying degrees as well as having a very strong presence within the women's movement. There are several exclusively lesbian groups (see listings on page 217 below) including Sappho which also organises meetings. It has a political presence, making governmental submissions, lobbying, arranging briefings etc. There are small sectional groups working within the main stream political parties – the Conservative Party (the Conservative Group for Homosexuality Equality), the Liberal Party, the Social Democratic Party the Labour Party (the Labour Campaign for Gay Rights), the Communist Party and the Socialist Workers Party (the SWP Gay group).

Counselling and befriending

For many, these groups provide the first contact with gay people and gay organisations. They do not play a traditional political role (for example Gemma, for disabled lesbians, operates as a pressure group within the gay movement). Friend provides formal counselling and self-help groups;

Icebreakers provides less formal counselling of a more personal kind and organises well attended social gatherings. As well as the national Gay Switchboard, there are many local gay switchboards which although oriented to giving information, usually also provide some sort of basic counselling over the phone. They often play a vital supportive role within the local gay community.

Special interest groups

There are a very large number of special interest groups that also provide a source of friendship and sometimes act as pressure groups, for example London Motor Sports Club. (For further details see the regular listings in *Gay News*.)

In Britain, unlike the USA, gay commercial concerns – clubs, bars, travel agencies, 'beefcake' publishers and retailers – have not played a political role. American gay businesses have supported gay demonstrations and provided money for campaigning and other resources. As yet this has not happened on any scale in Britain. There has also been strong resistance from the politicised gay community to the involvement of commercial enterprises.

International Gay Association (IGA)

The IGA is an international association of gay groups whose main aim is coordinating information and political pressure. The IGA is working in the world arena, for example taking up the World Health Organisation's definition of homosexuality as a disease – which is important in some areas in shaping opinion, particularly in the third world; seeking consultative status in the United Nations; seeking to get Amnesty International to take up the plight of homosexual prisoners. The IGA has organised three major demonstrations – two in Moscow and one in Teheran. There are two active groups within the IGA working on issues connected with education and trade unions with a view to establishing a lobby in the international teaching and labour organisations.

The IGA is a new organisation. Understandably it has problems in organising the large number of groups that come from all parts of the political spectrum. The skills and expertise required for campaigning at an international level are particular skills that few individuals have; people are having to learn. There is no independent group within the women's movement which has established a permanent international pressure group that could show the way. The membership of the IGA is predominantly from Europe, also from Australia, New Zealand, Canada and the United States. Representatives from South American gay organisations in exile attend conferences. Firm contact has been made with third world gay groups. Relations between gay men and lesbians are proving as problematic on the international level as on the national scene. At the Turin

Conference in 1981 the lesbian representatives voted to disaffiliate from the IGA.

Because this type of work has not been attempted by groups (nor has it been government sponsored) and because there is no obvious international interest, as for example in the women's or black people's issue, it is not clear in what way the IGA could be most effective. One of the activities it has been fulfilling most thoroughly is establishing the systematic collation of information about the condition of gay people from all countries.

Appendix VI
National gay rights organisations
(as at 1 May 1982)

International Gay Association (IGA)
Secretariat
c/o CHLR
P.O. Box 931
Dublin, Ireland

Treasury
c/o COC
Rozenstraat 8
Amsterdam 1016NX
Netherlands

Campaign for Homosexual Equality (CHE)
274 Upper Street
London N1 2UA
Telephone 01-359 3973

Northern Ireland Gay Rights Association (NIGRA)
P.O. Box No 44
Belfast BT1 1SH

Scottish Homosexual Rights Group (SHRG)
60 Broughton Street
Edinburgh EH1 2SA
Telephone 031-556 4040

National Council for Civil Liberties (NCCL)
Gay Rights Officer
21 Tabard Street
London SE1
Telephone 01-403 3888

Gay Rights at Work
7 Pickwick Court
London SE9 4SA
Telephone 01-857 3793

Lesbian groups
Action for Lesbian Parents
c/o Peace Works
58 Wakefield Road
Huddersfield, Yorkshire

Gemma
  BM Box 5700
  London WC1N 3XX

Kenric
  BM Kenric
  London WC1N 3XX

Sappho
  BCM Petrel
  London WC1N 3XX

Sequel
  BM Sequel
  London WC1N 3XX

Wages due Lesbians
  PO Box 287
  London NW6 5QU

Youth groups
Gay Youth Movement
  BM GYM
  London W1N 3XX

Joint Council for Gay Teenagers
  BM JCGT
  London WC1 3XX

London Gay Teenage Group
  Telephone 01-263 5932
  (Sunday 3 p.m. to 6.30 p.m.; Wednesday 7 p.m. to 10 p.m.)

National Union of Students Gay Liberation Campaign
  3 Endsleigh Street
  London WC1 0DU

Trade union groups
Gay ASTMS
  100 Adelaide Grove
  London W12

Civil & Public Services Gay Group
  271 Kensal Rise
  London W10 5DB

NALGO Gay Group
7 Pickwick Court
London SE9 4SA

NATFHE Gay Group
99 Tollington Way
London N7 6RE

Gay Post and Telecom Workers
BM GPTW
London WC1 3XX

Gay Social Workers Group
21 Devonshire Parade
Lenton
Nottingham

Gay Teachers Group
112 Broxholm Road
London SE27

Gay Workers in Print
PO Box 82
London E2 9DS

Party political groups
Conservative Group for Homosexual Equality
BM/CGHE
London WC1N 3XX

Communist Party Gay Rights Committee
16 St John Street
London EC1
Telephone 01-251 4406

Gay Social Democrats
c/o 30 Mildmay Park
London N1

Labour Campaign for Gay Rights
c/o 61A Bloom Street
Manchester M1 3LY

Liberal Gay Action Group
PO Box 86
Bath, Avon BA1 7YQ

Socialist Workers Party Gay Group
  PO Box 82
  London E2

Advice/information/counselling
Gay Switchboard
  Telephone 01-837 7324
  (Always open for national and international gay information, advice
  and help)

London Lesbian Line
  Telephone 01-837 8602
  (Monday and Friday 2 p.m. to 10 p.m; Tuesday, Wednesday and
  Thursday 7 p.m. to 10 p.m)

Friend
  274 Upper Street
  London N1 2UA
  Telephone 01-359 7371

Gay Legal Advice (GLAD)
  Telephone 01-821 7672
  (7 p.m. to 10 p.m. every night)

Gay Icebreakers
  Telephone 01-274 9590
  (7.30 p.m. to 10.30 p.m. every night)

Cara Friend
  Telephone Belfast (0232) 22023
  (Monday to Wednesday 7.30 p.m. to 10 p.m; Women: Thursday
  7.30 p.m. to 10 p.m.)

Glasgow Gay Switchboard
  Telephone 041-322 1725
  (7 p.m. to 10 p.m. every night)

Glasgow Lesbian Line
  Telephone 041-248 4596
  (Monday 7 p.m. to 10 p.m.)

There are also a large number of less well-established groups, local
switchboards and special interest groups: for details phone Gay Switchboard or see *Gay News* (available fortnightly direct from 1A Normand
Gardens, Greyhound Road, London W14 9SB, Telephone 01-381 2161).

In London, events and discussion group meetings are held regularly at
Gay's The Word Bookshop, 66 Marchmont Street, London WC1 (Telephone 01-278 7654 for details).

Other organisations

Advisory Service for Squatters
2 St Paul's Road
London N1
Telephone 01-359 8814

Beaumont Society
BM Box 3084
London WC1N 3XX

Housing Advice Switchboard
Telephone 01-434 2522

Joint Council for the Welfare of Immigrants
44 Theobalds Road
London WC1
Telephone 01-405 5527

Law Centres Federation
164 North Gower Street
London NW1
Telephone 01-387 8570

National Association of Citizens Advice Bureaux
110 Drury Lane
London WC2
Telephone 01-836 9231

Rights of Women
374 Gray's Inn Road
London WC1
Telephone 01-278 6349

Scottish Association of Citizens Advice Bureaux
12 Queen Street
Edinburgh EH1 1JE
Telephone 031-225 5323

Scottish Council for Civil Liberties
146 Holland Street
Glasgow G1
Telephone 041-331 5960

SHAFT (Self-Help Association for Transsexuals)
46 Lidell Way
South Ascot
Berkshire SL5 9UX

Notes and references

Introduction pages 1-70

1.   Denis Altman, *Coming Out in the Seventies*, Sydney, Wild & Woolley 1979.
2.   Albie Sachs and Joan Hoff Wilson, *Sexism and the Law*, Oxford, Martin Robertson 1978. See also A. Coote and T. Gill, *Women's Rights: A Practical Guide*, Harmondsworth, Penguin 1978; E. Hunter, *Scottish Women's Place*, Edinburgh, Edinburgh University Students Publications Board 1978.
3.   See for example Ruth Simpson, *From the Closets to the Courts*, Harmondsworth, Penguin 1976; Jane Rule, *Lesbian Images*, London, Peter Davies 1976; Gay Left Collective (eds.), *Homosexuality: Power and Politics*, London, Allison & Busby 1980; E.M. Ettorre, *Lesbians, Women and Society*, London, Routledge & Kegan Paul 1980; Adrienne Rich, *Compulsory Heterosexuality and Lesbian Existence*, London, Only Women Press 1981.
4.   Northern Ireland has substantially the same employment laws but they are enacted by special Northern Ireland Acts and Orders. The only major difference is that the Race Relations Act 1976 prohibits discrimination on grounds of religious or political opinion; it applies only to employment matters.
5.   A Bell and M. Weinberg, *Homosexualities: A Study of Diversity Among Men and Women*, London, Mitchell Beazley 1978; W. Masters and V. Johnson, *Homosexuality in Perspective*, Boston, USA, Little, Brown 1979; K. Plummer (ed.), *The Making of the Modern Homosexual*, London, Hutchinson 1981.
6.   See for example Aubrey Walter (ed.), *Come Together: The Years of Gay Liberation 1970-73*, London, Gay Men's Press 1980.
7.   The first comprehensive book published in England on this subject was S. Cohen and others, *The Law and Sexuality*, Manchester, Grass Roots Books 1978. Also see Bob Sturgess, *No Offence: The Case for Homosexual Equality at Law*, Manchester, CHE 1975; Chris Beer and others, *Gay Workers: Trade Unions and the Law*, London, NCCL 1981; Tony Honore, *Sex Law*, London, Duckworth 1978, chapters 4, 6 and 7; E. Carrington Boggan and others, *The Rights of Gay People: An American Civil Liberties Union Handbook*, New York, Avon Books 1975; D.C. Knutson (ed.), 'Homosexuality and the Law', special issue of *Journal of Homosexuality*, New York, Haworth Press 1980.
8.   Policy Advisory Committee on Sexual Offences, *Working Paper on the Age of Consent in relation to Sexual Offences*, London, HMSO 1979.

The Criminal Law pages 8-39

1.   Phyllis Chessler, *Women and Madness*, New York, Avon Books 1972.
2.   In addition sex with a woman suffering from severe subnormality is unlawful: Sexual Offences Act 1956 section 14. Also a woman who commits an act

of 'gross indecency' with or towards a girl (or boy) under 14, or who incites a child under 14 to commit an act of gross indecency with herself or someone else is liable to a maximum punishment of two years imprisonment: Indecency with Children Act 1960 section 1.

3. Jeffrey Weeks, *Coming Out: Homosexual Politics in Britain*, London Quartet 1977, quoted from the House of Lords debate on the Criminal Law Amendment Bill 1921.

4. Criminal Law Revision Committee, *Working Paper on Sexual Offences*, London, HMSO 1980.

5. Unpublished report.

6. *Daily Mirror*, September 1978.

7. Children and Young Persons Act 1969.

8. Quoted in Geoffrey Robertson, *Obscenity*, London, Weidenfeld & Nicolson 1979.

9. A remark attributed to the monarch when told that someone he knew quite well was homosexual, quoted in Z. Bankowski and G. Mungham, *Images of Law*, London, Routledge & Kegan Paul 1976, p. 46.

10. Louis Crompton, 'Gay Genocide from Leviticus to Hitler' in *The Gay Academic*, Palm Springs, California, Etc Publications 1978.

11. A. D. Harvey, *The Historical Journal*, vol. 21, no. 4, 1978, pp. 939-48.

12. A German doctor, R. Krafft-Ebing (1840-1902), who carried out research on homosexual criminals in prisons came to the conclusion that homosexuality was a congenital degeneration. These men were not therefore 'real' criminals but people who needed medical care. His work, first published in London in 1892 under the title, *Psychopatio-Sexualis*, was highly influential. Although it is now widely viewed as an anachronism, para. 302 of the World Health Organisation's International Classification of Diseases still lists homosexuality as a mental disorder.

13. Jeffrey Weeks, *Coming Out, op.cit*, chapter 1. See also Jeffrey Weeks, *Sex, Politics and Society*, London, Longman 1981, chapter 6.

14. *Report of the Committee on Homosexual Offences and Prostitution* ('Wolfenden'), Cmnd 247, 1957, para. 124.

15. *The Times*, 20 December 1966, 14 July 1967.

16. Home Office, *Sexual Offences, Consent and Sentencing*, London, HMSO 1979.

17. *The Times*, 22 July 1967.

18. Judgment of the European Court of Human Rights in the *Dudgeon* case, 22 October 1981.

19. *Dale v Smith* [1967] 2 All ER 1133.

20. *R v Graham Ford* [1978] 1 All ER 1129.

21. *R v Grey*, Times Law Reports, 27 November 1981.

22. *Horton v Mead* [1913] I KB 154.

23. Sexual Offences Act 1956 section 37 and Schedule II (32).

24. *McLaughlan v Boyle* [1934].

25. 'Any male person who (a) knowingly lives wholly or in part on the earnings of prostitution or (b) in any public place persistently solicits or importunes for immoral purposes, should be deemed a rogue and a vagabond within the meaning of the Vagrancy Act 1824 and may be dealt with accordingly.'

26. *Crook v Edmondson* [1966] 2 QB 81.

27. *R v Dodd* (1978) 66 Cr. App. R. 87.

28. *The Guardian*, 1 October 1980.

29. Street Offences Act 1959 section 1 (1).
30. *Marsh* v *Arscott, Times Law Report*, 3 March 1982.
31. *Brutus* v *Cozens* [1973] AC 854 where the House of Lords refused to interfere with a magistrates' decision that running on to the centre court at Wimbledon and disrupting a match whilst annoying was not 'insulting behaviour' within the meaning of the Public Order Act 1936.
32. *Gay News*, no. 204, p. 3.
33. *Leeds Other Paper*, no. 130, 16-30 May 1980.
34. Police Act 1964 section 51 (3); Police (Scotland) Act 1967; Highways Act 1959 section 121; Burgh Police (Scotland) Act 1892.
35. *R* v *Reakes* [1974] Crim. L.R. 615.
36. *R* v *Preece* [1970] Crim. L.R. 296.
37. *R* v *Pearce* (1951) 35 Cr. App. R. 214.
38. *R* v *Clayton* [1981] Crim. L.R. 425.
39. Home Office, *Sexual Offences, Consent and Sentencing, op.cit.*.
40. Stephen Mitchel (ed.), *Archbold: Pleading, Evidence and Practice in Criminal Cases*, 40th edn., London, Sweet & Maxwell 1979, p. 1467.
41. *R* v *Mayling* [1963] 2 QB 717.
42. *Norman* v *Parkin, Times Law Report*, 13 March 1982.
43. *The Times*, 12 February 1966.
44. Mario Mieli, *Homosexuality and Liberation*, London, Gay Men's Press 1980.
45. Sexual Offences Act 1967 section 1; Criminal Justice (Scotland) Act 1980 section 80.
46. Criminal Justice (Scotland) Act 1980; also see G. H. Gordon, *The Criminal Law of Scotland*, Edinburgh, W. Green & Son 1978, p. 894.
47. In one of the leading textbooks on forensic medicine Home Office pathologist Keith Simpson comments on the investigation of homosexual offences that, '"Homo" and "queer" have become almost playful epithets, and the psychiatrist has done little but excuse or condone such practices. They are rotting the fabric of the arts as well as the more solid principles of family life, and the law properly regards such unnatural sex practices with a stern eye.' K. Simpson, *Forensic Medicine*, London, Edward Arnold 1979, p. 214.
48. Sexual Offences Act 1967 section 3 (amend. Sexual Offences Act 1956) Schedule II para. 3.).
49. Home Office, *Sexual Offences, Consent and Sentencing, op.cit.*
50. Criminal Law Revision Committee, *Working Paper on Sexual Offences*, London, HMSO 1980, para. 150.
51. *South Wales Echo*, 14 January 1982.
52. *Gay News*, no. 197.
53. Criminal Law Revision Committee, *op.cit.*.
54. Sexual Offences Act 1956 section 13; Sexual Offences Act 1967 section 4(1); Sexual Offences (Scotland) Act 1976 section 7.
55. *R* v *Miskell* (1973) 37 Cr. App. R. 214.
56. Sexual Offences Act 1956 sections 22, 23; 2, 3 and 9; Sexual Offences (Scotland) Act 1976 sections 1 and 2.
57 Sexual Offences Act 1967 section 4(1).
58. Sexual Offences Act 1956 section 15(2).
59. Sexual Offences Act 1967 section 1(3); Criminal Justice (Scotland) Act 1980 section 80; Homosexual Offences (Northern Ireland) Order 1982 section 4.
60. Mental Health Act 1959 section 4(2).

61. Sexual Offences Act 1967 section 1(4).
62. Such an offence has been proposed by the Justices' Clerks Society: *Daily Telegraph*, 14 August 1979.
63. John Rechy, *The Sexual Outlaw*, New York, Doe Publishing 1977, p. 153.
64. *The Times*, 19 February 1982; The *Observer*, 21 February 1982.
65. Sections 4, 5 and 6.
66. Section 80.
67. D. J. West, *Homosexuality Re-assessed*, London, Duckworth 1977.
68. *Gay News*, no. 93, p. 16.
69. Gay organisations run disco clubs in Glasgow, Belfast and Chester.
70. Peter Wildeblood, *Against the Law*, Harmondsworth, Penguin 1955.
71. *Gay News*, no. 75, p. 28.
72. *The Guardian*, 11 April 1978.
73. Defence counsel's verbatim note of the trial at the Central Criminal Court.
74. Local Government (Miscellaneous Provisions) Act 1982.
75. *Time Out*, 23 March-3 April 1980.
76. *Gay News*, no. 7 1978.
77. *Northamptonshire Evening Telegraph*, 25 September 1980.
78. *Gay News*, no. 204, p. 7.
79. *Gay News*, no. 97, p. 1, 1978.
80. Brian Deer, 'Trust is a two-way street', *New Statesman*, 27 June 1980.
81. Stephen Mitchell (ed.). *Archbold*, *op.cit.* p. 1815: 'any person who shall at any time hereafter appear or behave him or herself as master or mistress, or as the person having the care, government or management of any bawdy-house, or other disorderly house, shall be deemed taken to be the keeper thereof, and shall be liable to be prosecuted as such, notwithstanding he or she shall not in fact be the real owner or keeper thereof': Disorderly Houses Act 1751 section 8.
82. *Gay News*, no. 204, p. 9.
83. CHE, London 1979.

Police and prisons pages 40-61

1. O. W. S. Fitzgerald, *Prison Medical Journal*, July 1971.
2. As an example of this: twice in Manchester in recent years there have been apparent surges in particular sorts of crime. This evidently had less to do with the extent of the crime than with the priority given by new Chief Constables to tackling it. One was Sir John McKay. Before his arrival in 1959, there was only one prosecution for male importuning in 1955, none at all in 1956 or 1957 and only two in 1958. The figures thereafter were: 30 in 1959, 105 in 1960, 135 in 1961 and 216 in 1962. James Anderton was appointed Chief Constable of Greater Manchester on 1 July 1976. That year 55 search warrants were executed under the Obscene Publications Acts and there were proceedings in 25 cases. The comparable figures in 1977 were 287 warrants and 134 proceedings; and in 1978, 151 warrants and 91 proceedings. *The Times*, 25 March 1982.
3. Grampian Police, *Scottish Criminal Law, Police Duties and Procedures*, Aberdeen University Press 1980, pp. 7, 8.
4. David Powis, *Signs of Crime: A Field Manual for Police*, London, McGraw-Hill 1978.

5. In certain circumstances injured victims of assaults are eligible for special government compensation. The scheme is administered by the Criminal Injuries Compensation Board, 10-12 Russell Square, London WC1, to whom a claim should be made as soon as possible after the incident.

6. CHE Discrimination Commission, *Attacks on Gay People*, London, CHE 1980.

7. *Bell* v *Devon & Cornwall Police* [1978] IRLR 283.

8. See generally Adrian Fulford, 'Defending Homosexuals', *LAG Bulletin*, April 1982.

9. See CHE's Evidence to the Criminal Law Revision Committee to the Royal Commission Criminal Procedure.

10. See *New Law Journal*, vol. 119, 29 May 1969, p. 513: Home Office Circular to the Police on Crime and Kindred Matters, para. 92(1).

11. *R* v *Sang* [1979] 2 WLR 439, 444.

12. *R* v *Birtles* [1969] 1 WLR 1047.

13. NCCL file.

14. Barry Irving and Linden Hilgendorf, *Police Interrogation: The Psychological Approach*, London, HMSO 1980.

15. Judges Rules and Administrative Directions on Interrogation and the Taking of Statements (para. 4) Home Office Circular no. 89, 1978.

16. Roger Moody, *Indecent Assault*, London, Peace News 1980.

17. See generally The Royal Commission on Criminal Procedure, *The Investigation and Prosecution of Criminal Offences in England and Wales: The Law and Procedure*, London, HMSO 1980, chapter 5.

18. See Home Office Circular no. 89, 1978 *op. cit.*

19. *R* v *Lemsatef* [1977] 2 All ER 835.

20. *R* v *Allen* [1977] Crim L.R. 163.

21. *R* v *Lemsatef, op. cit.*

22. Criminal Law Act 1977 section 62.

23. 'Bedfordshire on Sunday', 24 June 1979.

24. See generally Barry Prothero, NCCL Gay Rights Officer, *Gay News*, no. 204.

25. Statement by the Home Secretary, *Computing*, vol. 6, no. 22, 1 June 1978.

26. Magistrates' Courts Act 1980, section 43.

27. See generally Release, *Trouble with the Law*, London, Pluto Press 1978, chapter 7; Scottish Council for Civil Liberties, *Your Rights*, Edinburgh, Polygram Books 1980, chapter 3; D. MacDonald and J. Sim, *Scottish Prisons and the Special Unit*, Glasgow, SCCL 1978.

28. Prison Rules 1964. These are Home Office regulations which govern prison procedures made from time to time under the Prison Act 1952.

29. By virtue of Prison Standing Orders (amended December 1981).

30. Mental Health Act 1959 section 60; Mental Health (Scotland) Act 1960.

31. Mental Health Act 1959 section 72; Mental Health (Scotland) Act 1960.

32. *The Guardian*, 29 March 1980.

Young Gays pages 62-75

1. Joint Council for Gay Teenagers, *I Know What I Am*, Liverpool, JCGT 1980; also, M. Burbridge and J. Walters (eds.), *Breaking the Silence*, London, JCGT 1981.

2. *R* v *Willis (Peter)* I WLR 292.

3. The apparently arbitrary age of 14 comes by an indirect route from Roman law in which 14 was the age of puberty and majority; in English law, children under 10 cannot be prosecuted for criminal offences: Tony Honore, *Sex Law*, London, Duckworth 1978, p. 60.

4. Sexual Offences Act 1956 section 15(2).

5. Children and Young Persons Act 1969 section 28.

6. Sexual Offences Act 1967 section 8.

7. Director of Public Prosecutions, 'Written Evidence to the Royal Commission on Criminal Procedure', December 1978, unpublished.

8. Gay Activists Alliance, *A Submission to the Royal Commission on Criminal Procedure on Paedophilia and Homosexuality*, London, 1979.

9. Notes of the proceedings in the *Dudgeon* case prepared by the Registrar of the European Court of Human Rights.

10. NIGRA *News*, 1976.

11. Policy Advisory Committee on Sexual Offences, *Working Paper on the Age of Consent in relation to Sexual Offences*, London, HMSO 1979.

12. For a helpful critical summary of the inconclusive research into the origins of homosexuality, see John Hart and Diane Richardson, *The Theory and Practice of Homosexuality*, London, Routledge & Kegan Paul 1981.

13. Prepared in connection with the *Dudgeon* case; also see Martin Dannecker, *Theories of Homosexuality*, London, Gay Men's Press 1981.

14. Joint Council for Gay Teenagers, *I Know What I Am*, *op.cit.*

15. For a general discussion see A. C. E. Lynch, 'Counselling and Assisting Homosexuals', *Criminal Law Review*, 1979, p. 630.

16. *Knuller* v *Director of Public Prosecutions* [1973] AC 434.

17. *R* v *Anderson* [1971] 1 WLR 939.

18. Tony Palmer, *The Trials of Oz*, Manchester, Blond & Briggs 1973, p. 263.

19. The Law Commission, *Report on Conspiracy and Criminal Law Reform*, London, HMSO 1976, Part III D, para. 3. 143.

Paedophilia pages 76-86

1. Glanville Williams, *Textbook of Criminal Law*, London, Stevens & Sons 1978, p. 193.

2. See generally Brian Taylor (ed.), *Perspectives on Paedophilia*, London, Batsford 1981; Daniel Tsang (ed.), *The Age Taboo: Gay Male Sexuality, Power and Consent*, London, Gay Men's Press 1981; T. O'Carroll, *Paedophilia: The Radical Case*, London, Peter Owen 1981.

3. Home Office, *Sexual Offences, Consent and Sentencing*, London, HMSO 1979.

4. *R* v *Willis (Peter)* [1975] 1 WLR 292.

5. Glanville Williams, *op.cit.* p. 194.

6. Sexual Offences Act 1956 Schedule II (as amended by Sexual Offences Act 1967 section 3).

7. Home Office, *op.cit.*

8. *R* v *Willis (Peter) op.cit.*

9. D. A Thomas, *Principles of Sentencing*, London, Heinemann 1979.

10. *Thompson* v *DPP* [1918] AC221.

11. *R* v *Sims* [1946] 1 All ER 697.

12. *Boardman* v *DPP* [1974] 3 All ER 887.

13.   *R* v *Novac* (1977) 65 Crim. App. R. 107.

14.   *R* v *Johanssen* (1977) 65 Crim. App. R. 677.

15.   *R* v *Scarrott* (1977) 65 Crim. App. R. 125.

16.   *R* v *Inder* (1977) 65 Crim. App. R. 143.

17.   Lord Hailsham in *Boardman* v *DPP, op.cit.* referring to *Moorov* v *Lord Advocate* [1930] JC 68.

Obscenity pages 87-98

1.   Gregg Blachford, 'Looking at Pornography', in Pam Mitchell (ed.), *Pink Triangles*, Boston, USA, Alyson Publications 1980.

2.   Geoffrey Robertson, *Obscenity*, London, Weidenfeld & Nicolson 1979.

3.   Section 2.

4.   Section 3.

5.   Post Office Act 1953 section 11 makes it an offence to 'procure to be sent' by post an indecent article. The offence is technically committed whether or not the packet is received.

6.   Customs and Excise Act 1952.

7.   Indecent Advertisements Act 1889; Vagrancy Act 1824; Indecent Displays (Control) Act 1981; Local Acts of Parliament.

8.   Obscene Publications Act 1959 section 4(1) (2).

9.   *DPP* v *Whyte* [1972] 3 All ER 12.

10.   *DPP* v *Jordan* [1976] 3 All ER 1023.

11.   *R* v *Stamford* [1972] 2 All ER 427.

12.   Geoffrey Robertson, *op.cit.* p. 82.

13.   A similar provision has been enacted for Northern Ireland. To date the Act has not been extended to Scotland.

14.   Protection of Children Act 1978 section 3.

15.   *Report of the Committee on Obscenity and Film Censorship* (Williams Committee), London, HMSO 1979.

16.   *The Guardian*, 27 June 1981.

17.   *Whitehouse* v *Gay News Ltd. and Lemon* (1979) 68 Crim. App. R. 381.

18.   The traditional teaching of the Anglican Church has been based on an abhorrence of homosexuality. In a statement to the General Synod in February 1981 the Archbishop of Canterbury, Dr Runcie, called on the Church to combat the widespread hatred and denigration of homosexuality; he asked that homosexuality should be viewed no longer as a sin or sickness but as a 'handicap'. He confirmed that he did *not* believe that it was possible for anyone to be 'loyal to the Christian tradition and to see homosexual and heterosexual relations as having equal validity'. This new doctrine does little more than add religious authority to the perpetuation of contemporary discriminatory attitudes and practices.

19.   Law Commission (Working Paper No. 79) *Offences Against Religion and Public Worship*, London, HMSO 1981, para. 9.2.

20.   G. H Gordon, *Criminal Law of Scotland*, Edinburgh, W. Green & Son 1978, p. 998.

21.   Geoffrey Robertson, *op.cit.* p. 248.

22.   *Gay News*, no. 212, p. 9.

23.   *A. G.'s reference (No. 5 of 1980)* [1980] 3 All ER 816.

24. *Attorney General* v *IBA ex p. Mc Whirter* [1973] 1 QB 629.
25. Martin Kettle, 'Anderton's Way', *New Society*, 8 March 1979.
26. Andrea Dworkin, *Pornography: Men Possessing Women*, London, The Women's Press 1981.

Employment pages 99-120

1. CHE, *Queers Need Not Apply*, Manchester, CHE 1978.
2. Rehabilitation of Offenders Act 1974.
3. Having been found guilty of importuning in a public lavatory, H, a practising barrister, was suspended by the disciplinary tribunal of the Senate of the Inns of Court and the Bar for conduct unbecoming a barrister. His appeal against the decision was upheld by the Visitors to Grays Inn who distinguished between professional misconduct and misconduct outside the profession, found that there were no aggravating circumstances and accordingly, since the conviction had already received local publicity, decided that the appropriate sentence was a reprimand without publication. *Re H. (A Barrister)* [1981] 125 S.J. 609.
4. See generally C. Beer, R. Jeffrey and T. Munyard, *Gay Workers: Trade Unions and the Law*, London, NCCL 1981.
5. *Gardiner* v *Newport C. B. C.* [1974] IRLR 262.
6. *Jarrett* v *Governors of the Bishop of Llandaff School*, unreported, Cardiff Industrial Tribunal, 1977.
7. *McNamee* v *St. Monica's R.C. Primary School*, unreported, Liverpool Industrial Tribunal, 1977.
8. *Nottinghamshire C.C.* v *Bowly* [1978] IRLR 252.
9. *Saunders* v *Scottish National Camps Association Ltd.*, [1980] IRLR 174 [1981] IRLR 277.
10. *Wiseman* v *Salford C.C.* [1981] IRLR 202.
11. *Hurley* v *Mustoe* [1981] IRLR 208.
12. *Stancombe* v *Devon A.H.A.*, unreported, Exeter Industrial Tribunal 1979.
13. *Davies* v *L.B. of Tower Hamlets*, unreported, London North Industrial Tribunal, July 1976.
14. *Z.* v *Portsmouth C.C.*, unreported, Southampton Industrial Tribunal, February/March 1980.
15. See generally J. M. Evans, *de Smith's Judicial Review of Administrative Action*, London, Stevens & Son 1980, chapter 5.
16. *Halsbury's Laws of England*, Butterworth, vol. 1, para. 69, p. 84.
17. CHE, *Queers Need Not Apply*, op.cit.
18. *Boychuck* v *H. J. Symons Holdings Ltd.* [1977] IRLR 395.
19. *Burman* v *Trevor Page Ltd.*, unreported, Norwich Industrial Tribunal, April 1977.
20. John Warburton, *Open and Positive*, London, Gay Teachers Group 1978.
21. Councillor Andrew Harris, quoted in *Gay News*, no. 234.
22. See CHE, *What About the Gay Workers*, London, CHE 1981.
23. *Gay News*, no. 236.
24. Gay Rights At Work Committee, *Gays At Work*, London, GRAW 1980.

Lesbian and Gay Parents and Children pages 121-138

1. *Spare Rib*, no. 107, June 1981, p. 33.
2. Case noted in *Spare Rib*, August 1976.
3. *Re D (an infant)* [1977] 2 WLR 79.
4. *W v W*, unreported, Court of Appeal, 3, 4 November 1976.
5. Matrimonial Causes Act 1973; Divorce (Scotland) Act 1976; Matrimonial Causes (Northern Ireland) Order 1978.
6. *C v C* [1979] All ER 556.
7. Guardianship Act 1973 section 1 (1). This statute also applies in Scotland.
8. Guardianship of Minors Act 1971 section 1.
9. *W v W, op. cit.*
10. *M v M*, unreported, Court of Appeal, July 1977.
11. *Re D (an infant), op. cit.*
12. [1977] 2 WLR 79, 87.
13. [1977] 2 WLR 79, 104.
14. Guardianship of Minors Act 1971 section 4 (4). The court may order that a relative is given custody if the parent is found to be 'unfit to have custody of the minor'. See Roger Smith, *Children and the Courts*, London, Sweet & Maxwell 1979, p. 173.
15. See *Re F (a minor)* [1976] 1 WLR 189.
16. See Children and Young Persons Act 1969 section 1, and Roger Smith, *op. cit.*, pp. 126-28 for a list of the various circumstances in which someone under 17 can be put into care.
17. Sadie Robarts, 'Whose Child', a paper delivered at the NCCL Gay Rights Conference, May 1977, unpublished.
18. *M v M, op. cit.*
19. *W v W, op. cit.*
20. M. Rutter and S. Golombok, London, Institute of Psychiatry, 1982, unpublished paper. See also the chapter on psycho-sexual development in M. Rutter (ed.), *Scientific Foundations of Developmental Psychiatry*, London, Heinemann Medical 1980.
21. P. Gebhard, J. Gagnon, W. Pomeroy, C. Christensen, 'Sex Offenders', 1965; De Francis, 'Protecting the Child Victim of Sex Crimes by Adults', 1969, referred to in: E. Carrington Boggan and others, *The Rights of Gay People*: An American Civil Liberties Union Handbook, New York, Avon Books, 1975.
22. Also see Roger Smith, *op. cit.* pp. 64-67.

Housing and Living Together pages 139-148

1. *Belfast Newsletter*, 3 January 1978.
2. The themes in this section are based heavily on material produced by the Gays and Housing Group, c/o London Friend, 274 Upper Street, London N1.
3. See generally Andrew Arden, *Housing, Security and Rent Control*, London, Sweet & Maxwell 1978.
4. 'Shortholds' were introduced under sections 51-55 of the Housing Act 1980 and apply to lettings created after 28 November 1980 in respect of which a fair rent has been registered.

5. Housing (Homeless Persons) Act 1977.
6. 180 Tottenham Court Road, London W1.
7. Criminal Law Act 1977 sections 8 and 6.
8. Applications may be made under the Inheritance (Provision for Family and Dependents) Act 1975. Bromley's *Family Law* comments that a deceased person's 'mistress' must have a claim if he set her up in her own home and paid all her domestic bills but not if he did no more than make her casual payments or gifts. See P.M. Bromley, *Family Law*, London, Butterworth 1981.
9. Law Commission Working Paper No. 74.
10. Matrimonial Houses Act 1967 and see generally P.M. Bromley, *Family Law*, *op. cit.*; E.C. Clive and J.G. Wilson, *The Law of Husband and Wife in Scotland*, Edinburgh, W. Green & Son 1974.
11. Letter to Conservative Group for Homosexual Equality.
12. See B. Pinson, *Revenue Law*, London, Butterworth 1981.
13. Anne Bottomley and others, *Cohabitation Handbook*, London, Pluto Press 1981.
14. See *ibid.* chapter 11.
15. It has been suggested by US legal writers that the logic of the decision on *Marvin* v *Marvin* would apply to a gay relationship: '*Marvin* v *Marvin: Preserving the Options*', California Law Review, vol. 65.

Immigration pages 149-154

1. Margaret Thatcher in an interview, 'World in Action', Thames TV, 30 January 1978.
2. Immigration Rules (H.C. 394). See generally L. Grant and I. Martin, *Immigration Law and Practice*, London, Cobden Trust 1982.
3. Immigration Rule 45.
4. Letter to the Joint Council for the Welfare of Immigrants.
5. Immigration Rules 120, 138 and 150.
6. Following a meeting in August 1978 with the then minister Mr Brynmor John.
7. David Burgess, 'Advising the Homosexual Immigrant', unpublished paper. I am indebted to him for assistance in the preparation of this chapter.
8. Immigration Act 1971 section 26(1).
9. In the case of Astrid Proll (*R* v *Secretary of State for the Home Department ex p. Puttick*, 14 November 1980) the court would not compel the Home Office to register a wife who would thereby have benefited from her crimes – at least in serious cases. Ms Proll had married under a false identity.
10. Immigration Act 1971 section 2 (2).
11. Immigration Rule 131.
12. *X and Y* v *Switzerland*, European Commission of Human Rights *Decisions and Reports*, vol. 9, p. 57.

The Gay Response pages 155-174

1. *Gay News*, no. 178, p. 10.
2. *Gay News*, no. 182.

3. Jeffrey Weeks, *Coming Out*, London, Quartet 1977, parts 4 and 5; also see Aubrey Walter (ed.), *Come Together: The Years of Gay Liberation 1970-73*, London, Gay Men's Press 1980; Stephen Gee, 'Gay Activism' in Gay Left Collective (eds.), *Homosexuality: Power and Politics*, London, Allison & Busby 1980.

4. Refusals by the press to print advertisements placed by gay organisations or groups has been widespread. Groups refused include the Gay Christian Movement, Friend, Switchboards, CHE groups, and Gemma (a group for disabled lesbians). Local or religious papers that have refused advertisements include: *Catholic Herald*, the *Friend and the Universe*, the *London Weekly Advertiser*, the Leicester *Mercury*, the *Eastern Daily Press, Eastern Daily News, Mid-Sussex Times*, Ellesmere Port *Observer, Yorkshire Post, South Wales Echo, Teesside Times, Shields Gazette, Newham Recorder, Brighton Argus, Kent Messenger* and Sunderland *Echo*. National papers include the *Daily Mirror* and the *Sunday Express*. The *British Medical Journal* refused to publish an advertisement announcing the formation of a group of gay medics based in Edinburgh.

5. Library committees that have banned the stocking of *Gay News* include Belfast, Croydon, Rotherham and Walsall.

6. Scarborough, Bradford, Bournemouth and Preston.

7. *Gay News*, no. 129 and no. 180, pp. 15-18.

8. *Rotherham Advertiser*, 13 October 1978.

9. *Community Care*, 30 June 1976.

10. Correspondence from the Charity Commission with reference to Gay Sweatshop Theatre and the Birmingham Gay Community Centre 1978.

11. *Gay Left*, no. 10.

12. Denis MacShane, *Using the Media*, London, Pluto Press 1979.

13. Bob Cant, 'Living with Indecency', *Gay Left*, no. 8.

14. David Barnard, *The Criminal Court in Action*, London, Butterworth 1979.

15. *R v O'Reilly* [1967] 2 QB 722.

16. *R v Cleal* [1942] 1 All ER 203.

17. *R v Bishop* [1974] 2 All ER 1206.

18. *R v King* [1967] 1 All ER 319.

19. *R v Redgrave* [1981] Crim. L.R. 556.

Conclusion: Towards Gay Rights? pages 175-183

1. Peter Newsam, in an interview, *The Observer*, 17 January 1982.

2. The Law Commission, *Report on Conspiracy and Criminal Law Reform*, London, HMSO 1976, Part III D. para. 3. 143.

3. Commission for Racial Equality, *Annual Report for 1980*, London, HMSO 1981.

4. See generally J. Gregory, 'Sex Discrimination, Work and the Law', in *Capitalism and the Rule of Law*, London, Hutchinson 1979; Albie Sachs and Joan Hoff Wilson, *Sexism and the Law*, Oxford, Martin Robertson 1978; First Report from the Home Affairs Committee, 1981-82, London, HMSO 1982.

5. Direct discrimination is defined similarly in both Acts. The Race Relations Act (1976) section 1 provides:
    (1) A person discriminates against another in any circumstances relevant for the purposes of any provision of this Act if-

(a) on racial grounds he treats that other less favourably than he treats or would treat other persons; or

(b) he applies to that other a requirement or condition which he applies or would apply equally to persons not of the same racial group as that other but-

   (i) which is such that the proportion of persons of the same racial group as that other who can comply with it is considerably smaller that the proportion of persons not of that racial group who can comply with it; and

   (ii) which he cannot show to be justifiable irrespective of the colour, race, nationality, or ethnic or national origins of the person to whom it is applied; and

   (iii) which is to the detriment of that other because he cannot comply with it.

6. L. Lustgarten, 'The New Meaning of Discrimination', *Public Law*, 1978.

7. 'The Rights of Gay Men and Women', a Labour Party Discussion Document, London, 1981.

8. For a short general introduction to the Convention, see Lawrence Grant and others, Civil Liberty: *The NCCL Guide to Your Rights*, Harmondsworth, Penguin 1979, chapter 29; also R. Beddard, *Human Rights and Europe*, London, Sweet & Maxwell 1980.

9. This recommendation evokes the memory of the Nazi Party's legal campaign against homosexuals. The object was to remove 'symptoms of racial degeneracy' (together with Jews, gypsies and leftists). Gay men who had come to the attention of the police prior to 1935 were rounded up. Lists of suspected homosexuals were used: the Berlin police alone had 30,000 names. Reasonable estimates of the number of homosexuals from Germany and the occupied countries who died from illness, medical experiments and in the gas chambers vary from 100,000 to more than 400,000. See Heinz Heger, *The Men with the Pink Triangle*, London, Gay Men's Press 1980.

10. In 1981 the Norwegian government extended the law prohibiting discrimination on the grounds of race or religion to grounds of homosexual orientation or lifestyle. The amendment prohibits public statements that threaten or scorn a person or group of persons, or expose anyone to hatred, persecution or contempt because of their homosexual orientation or lifestyle. In addition, it makes it illegal for someone in business to refuse anyone services or goods that are provided to others because of that person's homosexual orientation or lifestyle.

11. Policy Advisory Committee on Sexual Offences, *Working Paper on the Age of Consent in relation to Sexual Offences*, London, HMSO 1979; conclusion adopted by the Criminal Law Revision Committee in its *Working Paper on Sexual Offences*, London HMSO 1980.

12. See for example, D. Altman, *Homosexual: Oppression and Liberation*, London, Allan Lane 1971; G. Weinberg, *Society and the Healthy Homosexual*, New York, Anchor Books 1973; J. Katz, *American Gay History*, New York, Thomas Y. Crowell 1976; J. Weeks, *Coming Out: Homosexual Politics in Britain*, London, Quartet 1977; A. Evans, *Witchcraft and the Gay Counterculture*, Boston, USA, Fag Rag Books 1978; G. Hocquenghem, *Homosexual Desire*, London, Allison & Busby 1978; M. Mieli, *Homosexuality and Liberation*, London, Gay Men's Press 1980; Gay Left Collective (eds.), *Homosexuality: Power and Politics*, London, Allison & Busby 1980;

K. Plummer (ed.), *The Making of the Modern Homosexual*, London, Hutchinson 1981; D. Fernbach, *The Spiral Path*, London, Gay Men's Press 1981; J. Hart and D. Richardson, *The Theory and Practice of Homosexuality*, London, Routledge & Kegan Paul 1981; M. Dannecker, *Theories of Homosexuality*, London, Gay Men's Press 1981; J. Weeks, *Sex, Politics and Society*, London, Longman 1981.

Appendix I: The armed forces and merchant navy pages 184-187

1. Sexual Offences Act 1967 section 1(5).
2. Sexual Offences Act 1967 section 2; Criminal Justice (Scotland) Act 1980 section 80.
3. The Army Act 1955, the Air Force Act 1955, The Naval Discipline Act 1957 (as amended by the Armed Forces Act 1981).
4. Ministry of Defence, *Manual of Military Law*, London, HMSO 1972, p. 347.
5. Minutes of the Select Committee on the Armed Forces Bill, 14 April 1981.
6. Letter from Parliamentary Under Secretary of State for the Armed Forces to Sir Anthony Royle, 14 August 1981.
7. *ibid.*
8. Reported at 'A Fair Deal for Homosexuals', NCCL Conference 14 May 1977, unpublished.

Appendix II: Transsexuals and transvestites pages 188-194

1. *Corbett v Corbett* [1970] 2 All ER 33, 48.
2. For a detailed account of the emergence during the present century of the separate clinical categories of transsexualism and transvestism, see D. King, 'Gender Confusions: Psychological and Psychiatric Conceptions of Transvestism and Transsexualism' in K. Plummer (ed.), *The Making of the Modern Homosexual*, London, Hutchinson, 1981. See also Janice G. Raymond, *The Transsexual Empire*, London, The Women's Press 1980.
3. At the Fourth World Congress of Sexology in Mexico in December 1979, Dr Wolf Eicher of Munich presented a paper concerning the H-Y antigen. This antigen is present in all 'normal' male skin and serum tissue, but is significantly absent in males subject to the 'transsexual syndrome'. (The antigen, however, is present in female-to-male transsexuals.) The implication of Dr Eicher's research is that the H-Y antigen may be the genetic component affecting the future sex of embroyos and that its absence in apparent males and its presence in apparent females may be directly connected to an individual's dissatisfaction with his or her 'biological' sex. This is the first research that points clearly to a genetic origin for transsexualism.
4. Decisions of the national insurance commissioner under the Social Security Act 1975 case nos. R (P) 1/80 and R (P) 2/80.
5. *Daily Telegraph*, 25 November 1977.
6. Letter from the Lord Advocate to M. Bain, MP, 29 April 1977.
7. *Van Oosterwijck v Belgium*, Report of the Commission, 1 March 1979; Judgment of the Court, 6 November 1980.
8. *Corbett v Corbett, op. cit.*

9. *White* v *British Sugar Corporation* [1977] IRLR 121.
10. See generally J.M. Thomson, 'Transsexualism: A Legal Perspective', *Journal of Medical Ethics*, vol. 6, 1980, pp. 92-97 on which much of this chapter has been based.
11. Unreported, Court of Appeal.

Table of cases

Page numbers are given in bold type and footnote numbers follow in square brackets where relevant.

Attorney General v IBA ex p. McWhirter (1973) 1 QB 629 * **96**
Attorney General's reference (No. 5 of 1980) (1980) 3 All ER 816 * **96**

Bell v Devon & Cornwall Police (1978)   IRLR 283 * **45, 111**
Boardman v DPP (1974) 3 All ER 887 * **82**
Boychuck v H. J. Symons Holdings Ltd (1977) IRLR 395 * **112**
Brutus v Cozens (1973) AC 854 * **224** [71]
Burman v Trevor Page Ltd unreported Norwich industrial tribunal April 1977 * **114**

C v C (1979) All ER 556 * **124** [6]
Corbett v Corbett (1970) 2 All ER 33 * **191**
Crook v Edmondson (1966) 2 QB 81 * **17** [26]

Dale v Smith (1967) 2 All ER 1133 * **15**
Davies v London Borough of Tower Hamlets unreported London North industrial tribunal July 1976 * **110**
DPP v Jordan (1976) 3 All ER 1023 * **88**
DPP v Whyte (1972) 3 All ER 12 * **88**

Gardiner v Newport County Borough Council (1974) IRLR 262 * **103**

Horton v Mead (1913) 1 KB 154 * **16** [22]
Hurley v Mustow (1981) IRLR 208 * **107**

Knuller v DPP (1973) AC 434 * **73**

M v M unreported Court of Appeal July 1977 * **126**
Marsh v Arscott Times LR 3 March 1982 * **18** [30]
Moorov v Lord Advocate (1930) JC 68 * **84** [17]

McNamee v St Monica's Roman Catholic Primary School unreported Liverpool industrial tribunal July 1977 * **104**
Norman v Parkin Times LR 13 March 1982 * **22**
Nottinghamshire County Council v Bowly (1978) IRLR 202 * **104**

R v Anderson (1971) 1 WLR 939 * **74**
R v Allen (1977) Crim. LR 163 * **53** [20]
R v Birtles (1969) 1 WLR 1067 * **50** [12]
R v Bishop (1974) 2 All ER 1206 * **170**
R v Clayton (1981) Crim. LR 425 * **22**
R v Cleal (1942) 1 All ER 703 * **170** [16]
R v Dodd (1978) 66 Cr. App. R. 87 * **17** [27]
R v Ford (Graham) (1978) 1 All ER 1129 * **16**
R v Grey Times LR 27 November 1981 * **16**
R v Inder (1977) 65 Cr. App. R. 143 * **84**
R v Johanssen (1977) 65 Cr. App. R. 677 * **84**
R v King (1967) 1 All ER 319 * **170** [18]

R v *Lemsatef* (1977) 2 All ER 835 * **53**

R v *Mayling* (1963) 2 QB 717 * **22**

R v *Miskell* (1973) 37 Cr. App. R. 214 * **26** [55]

R v *Novac* (1977) 65 Cr. App. R. 107 * **83**

R v *O'Reilly* (1967) 2 QB 722 * **170** [15]

R v *Pearce* (1951) 35 Cr. App. R. 214 * **21**

R v *Preece* (1970) Crim. LR 296 * **21**

R v *Reakes* (1974) Crim. LR 615 * **21**

R v *Redgrave* (1981) Crim. LR 556 * **170**

R v *Sang* (1979) 2 WLR 439 * **50** [11]

R v *Scarrott* (1977) 65 Cr. App. R. 125 * **84**

R v *Sims* (1946) 1 All ER 697 * **82**

R v *Stamford* (1972) 2 All ER 427 * **88**

R v *Willis (Peter)* (1975) 1 WLR 292 * **64**

Re D (an infant) (1977) 2 WLR 79 * **126**

Re F (a minor) (1976) 1 WLR 189 * **230** [15]

Re H (a barrister) (1981) 125 SJ 609 * **229** [3]

Saunders v *Scottish National Camps Association Ltd* (1980) IRLR 174 (1981) IRLR 277 * **105**

Stancombe v *Devon Area Health Authority* unreported Exeter

industrial tribunal April 1979 * **108**

Thompson v *DPP* (1918) AC 221 * **82**

W v *W* unreported Court of Appeal 3, 4 November 1976 * **123** [4]

White v *British Sugar Corporation* (1977) IRLR 121 * **192**

Wiseman v *Salford City Council* (1981) IRLR 202 * **106**

Z v *Portsmouth City Council* unreported Southampton industrial tribunal March 1980 * **111**

European Convention of Human Rights cases

Dudgeon v *United Kingdom* Eur. Court of H.R. 1981 * **179**

Van Oosterwijck v *Belgium* Eur. Court of H.R. 1980 * **191**

X v *Federal Republic of Germany* Eur. Commission of H.R. 1975 * **179**

X and Y v *Switzerland* Eur. Commission of H.R. 1977 * **153**

X v *United Kingdom* Eur. Commission of H.R. 1978 * **179**

Table of Statutes

Page numbers are given in bold type and footnote numbers follow in square brackets where relevant.

Adoption Act 1976, **145**
Air Force Act 1955, **184** [3]
Armed Forces Act 1981, **184** [3]
Army Act 1955, **184** [3]

Burgh Police (Scotland) Act 1892, **18,
19** [34]

Children and Young Persons Act 1969
  generally, **11** [7]
  section 4, **129** [16]
  section 28, **65** [5]
Cinematograph Act 1952, **92**
Cinematograph Amendment Act
  1982, **92**
Civic Government (Scotland) Act
  1982, **92**
Criminal Justice (Scotland) Act 1980
  section 80, **20, 24** [45], [46], **27**
  [59], **29** [66], **184** [2]
Criminal Law Act 1977
  section 62, **53** [22], **143** [7]
Criminal Law Amendment Act 1885
  generally, **12**
  section 11, **20**

Disorderly Houses Act 1751
  section 8, **35** [81]
Divorce (Scotland) Act 1976, **123** [5]

Employment Protection
  (Consolidation) Act 1978 (as
  amended), **101**

Fair Employment (Northern Ireland)
  Act 1976, **101**
Fatal Accidents Act 1976, **144, 147**

Guardianship Act 1973
  section 1, **125** [7]
Guardianship of Minors Act 1971

section 1, **125** [8]
section 4(4), **128** [14]

Highways Act 1959
  section 121, **19** [34]
Homosexual Offences (Northern
  Ireland) Order 1982
  generally, **15, 68**
  section 3, **20**
  section 4, **27** [59]
Housing Act 1980
  sections 51-55, **141** [4]
Housing (Homeless Persons) Act 1977,
  143

Immigration Act 1971
  section 2(2), **153** [10]
Indecency with Children Act 1960
  section 1, **8** [2], **65**
Indecent Advertisement Act 1889, **88**
  [7]
Indecent Displays (Control) Act 1981,
  88 [7], **92**
Independent Broadcasting Authority
  Act 1973
  section 4, **94**
Inheritance (Provision for Family and
  Dependents) Act 1975, **147**

Local Government (Miscellaneous
  Provisions) Act 1982, **32** [74], **92**

Matrimonial Causes Act 1973, **123** [5]
Matrimonial Causes (Northern
  Ireland) Order 1978, **123** [5]
Magistrates' Courts Act 1980
  section 43, **55** [26]
Mental Health Act 1959
  section 4(2), **27**
  section 60, **60** [30]
  section 72, **61** [31]

Mental Health (Scotland) Act 1960,
   60 [30], 61 [31]
Metropolitan Police Act 1839
   section 54 (13), 18

Naval Discipline Act 1957, 184 [3]
Northern Ireland (Emergency
   Provisions) Act 1973, 57

Obscene Publications Act 1959
   section 2, 87 [3]
   section 3, 87 [4]
   section 4, 88 [8]
Offences Against the Person Act 1861
   section 61, 24

Police Act 1964
   section 51(3), 19 [34]
Police (Scotland) Act 1967, 19 [34]
Post Office Act 1953
   section 11, 88 [5]
Prison Act 1952, 59 [28]
Prevention of Terrorism Act 1976, 57
Protection of Children Act 1978
   section 1, 90
   section 3, 91 [14]
Public Order Act 1936
   section 5, 18, 22, 189

Race Relations Act 1976
   section 1, 177 [5]
Rehabilitation of Offenders Act 1974,
   100 [2]
Rent Act 1977, 140

Sex Discrimination Act 1975, 177, 193
Sexual Offences Act 1956
   sections 2, 3 and 9, 27 [56]
   section 12, 24
   section 13, 26, 94
   section 14, 8
   section 15, 27 [58], 64 [4]
   sections 22 and 23, 27 [56]
   section 32, 15
   Schedule II, 17 [23], 24 [48], 78 [6]
Sexual Offences Act 1967
   section 1(1), 20, 24 [45], 26
   section 1(2), 21
   section 1(3), 27 [59]
   section 1(4), 28 [61]
   section 1(5), 184 [1]
   section 2, 184 [2]
   section 3, 24 [48]
   section 4(1) 26, 27 [57]
   section 4(3) 26
   section 5, 29 [65]
   section 6, 29 [65]
   section 8, 65 [6]
Sexual Offences (Scotland) Act 1976
   sections 1 and 2, 27 [56]
   section 7, 20, 27 [54], 65
Street Offences Act 1959
   section 1, 17 [29], 28

Theatres Act 1968, 94

Vagrancy Act 1824, 88 [7]
Vagrancy Act 1898, 12, 17

Index

abuse of authority, 80, 81, 187
access (to children), 134, 137, 193
accomplice (*see* sexual offences)
Administrative Directions to Police
    (*see* Judges' Rules)
advice and help (organisations for)
    217—21
adoption, 126, 145
advertisements, 94, 201
age: mistake as to, 65;
    of consent, 8, 175, 179, 180, 195,
    196;
    of criminal responsibility, 227 [3];
    of sexual capacity, 64
agent provocateur, 49
aiding and abetting (*see* sexual
    offences)
alibi, 169
anal intercourse (*see* buggery)
arrest, 55
Archbishop of Canterbury, 228 [18]
Argentina, 152
armed forces, 184—7, 198
Arran, Lord, 14
artificial insemination by donor
    (AID), 145
asylum, 150—2
attempt (*see* sexual offences)
Attorney General, 94
aversion therapy, 151, 180

badges, 112
bail, 166
BBC, 96
birth certificates, 189, 190, 191
blackmail, 20, 185, 187
Blackstone, Sir William, 12
blasphemous libel, 92—3
breach of the peace, 18, 19, 22, 23,
    189
British Board of Film Censors, 95
brothel, 29, 199
buggery, 24, 25, 64, 79, 184 (*see also*
    sentences)

by-laws, 19

care proceedings, 11, 65, 128—9
case law, 209
cautioning, 20, 52—3
change of name, 190
Channel Islands, 15
Charity Commission, 158
chief constables, 225 [2]
children: access to, 126, 137—8;
    arrangements for, 123;
    custody of, 124;
    guardianship of, 128, 144;
    illegitimate, 145;
    welfare as paramount consideration,
    125;
    wishes of, 130—1 (*see also* adoption;
    fostering; AID)
church courts, 11
civil proceedings, 173—4
clubs, 25, 31, 32
co-habitation contracts, 147
co-habitation rule, 146
Coleherne pub, 33
'coming out', 62, 100, 159, 173—4
Commission for Racial Equality, 176
Committee of Ministers of the Council
    of Europe, 179
common law, 209
common law marriage, 142, 143
common prostitute, 28
confessions (to the police), 52
consent: in fact 79; in law, 27, 64,
    197; to divorce, 124
Conservative Party, 180
conspiracy (*see* sexual offences)
conspiracy to corrupt public morals,
    31, 73, 85—6
Convention and Protocol Relating to
    the Status of Refugees, 150
'cottaging', 19, 34
Council of Europe, Parliamentary
    Assembly of, 179
council tenancy, 142

counselling and befriending, 72, 138, 175, 214–15
courts martial, 184
cross-dressing, 189
Criminal Injuries Compensation Board, 60
Criminal Law Revision Committee, 8, 9, 25, 26
criminal proceedings, 166–73
'cruising', 15
custody (of children), agreements, 133–5; definition of, 121; divorce and, 123; transsexual parents and, 193; types of, 135–7 (see also children)

Dannecker, Martin, 69
death penalty, 11, 12
defence groups, 160
Department of Education, 109
Department of Health and Social Security, 190
Director of Public Prosecutions, 64, 65, 66, 68, 73, 91, 96
disgraceful conduct of an indecent kind, 184
dismissal from employment, 101, 102
disorderly house, 31, 35, 225 [81]
district court, 171
divorce, 124, 145
drunk and disorderly, 33, 45

educational curricula, 64
EEC nationals, 150, 153
Employment Appeal Tribunal, 101
entrapment, 49–51
Equal Opportunities Commission, 177
equal opportunities in employment, 119
evidence (criminal): in sex cases, 170, 171; medical, 24; obtained by entrapment, 49, 50; Scottish rules, 172; 'similar fact' rule, 81–5
exceptional depravity, 123
exceptional hardship, 123

family, 182
Festival of Light, 97
films, 95, 96

fingerprinting (by police) 56, 57
flatsharers, 141
forfeiture proceedings, 87
fostering, 145

gay (see sexual orientation)
Gay News, 25, 32, 33, 59, 93, 156
gender, 2, 182, 188
Greater London Council, 118, 178
gross indecency, 14, 20, 21, 184; procuring, 26, 94–5; with or towards a child under 14, 65 (see also sentences)
group sex, 25
guilty plea, 167, 168

holiday let, 141
homelessness, 141, 143
home ownership, 141
homophobia, 41
homosexuality (see sexual orientation)
hormone treatment, 60, 188
Hospital Orders, 60, 61
housing associations, 142
housing co-operatives, 142
Human Rights: European Commission of, 179; European Convention of, 153, 178, 191, 209, 213; European Court of, 14–15, 67, 179
H-Y antigen, 234 [3]

illegal entrant, 152
illegitimate children, 145
Immigration Rules, 149
immoral purposes, 16
importuning (see soliciting)
income tax, 146
incest, 78, 79
incitement (see sexual offences)
indecency with children, 65
indecent assault, 8, 64
indecent publications, 87, 88, 90, 91
Independent Broadcasting Authority, 96
inheritance, 144, 147
injustice by maladministration, 156
Inner London Education Authority, 118
International Gay Association, 215, 216

242 / Gays and the Law

interrogation, by police, 51, 52;
  by military police, 186
insulting words and behaviour, 18
Isle of Man, 15

joint custody, 137
Judges' Rules, 52
judicial examination, 171
judicial separation, 123

'kerb-crawling', 17
Kincora boys home, 29
Kinsey, Dr Alfred, 70
kissing, 8, 18, 19, 64
Krafft-Ebing, R, 223 [12]

Labour Party, 178
Law Commission, 74, 145
law reform, 175−7; criminal,
  196−204; civil, 205−8
legal aid, 166, 174, 209
legal system, 210
legislation, 209
lesbianism: as an issue in custody
  proceedings, 129−30; compared
  with male homosexuality, 2, 4, 6;
  military offence of, 184;
  official attitudes towards, 9, 10,
  121; sexual offences affecting, 8,
  184, 222 [2]; (see also lesbians;
  sexual orientation)
lesbians; assaults on, 43; badges,
  112−14; household, 122−3, 132;
  housing, 140; kissing, 19; marriage
  of convenience, 153; organisations,
  138, 217−18, 220; questioning by
  military police, 185−87;
  questioning by police, 47−9;
  teenagers, 10−11, 73
lewd, indecent and libidinous
  practices and behaviour, 65, 171
licentious dancing, 31
licensing laws, 31
Liberal Party, 178
Lord Advocate, 67
Lord Chamberlain, 94
loitering, 33, 42

maintenance, 134
marriage, 150, 152−3, 191
medical examination, 38, 56, 63

mental illness, 27, 80, 81, 197
mental hospital staff, 27−8, 103
merchant navy, 184
military police, 185, 186
Ministry of Defence, 187
mitigating circumstances, 50, 168
'moral danger', 11, 65
moral authoritarians, 96, 97
mortgages, 140, 141

national insurance benefits, 146, 190
National Viewers and Listeners'
  Association, 97
natural justice, 111
Nazi Party, 233 [9]
newspapers, 10, 92−3, 156, 161, 167
Northern Ireland: differences, 2, 139;
  employment, 101, 222 [4];
  legal system, 209, 212−3;
  obscenity, 228 [13]; organisations,
  160, 161, 217, 220;
  police, 57−8, 156−7;
  property law, 140; reforms, 181;
  sexual offences, 14−15, 17, 20, 21,
  24, 25, 27−8, 29, 65, 67−8
Northern Ireland Gay Rights
  Association, 156
Norway, 233 [10]
Not guilty plea, 168−69

obstruction: of the highway, 19, 33;
  of the police, 19
obscenity: blasphemous libel and,
  92−3; defence to, 88;
  definition of, 87; films, 95;
  paedophile publications, 90−1;
  plays, 94; reform of, 91;
  Scots law of, 88−9
Ombudsman, 156
oppression of homosexuality (theories
  about), 181−3
outraging public decency, 22

Paedophile Information Exchange,
  84−5
paedophilia: definition of, 76;
  hormone treatment and, 60−1;
  judicial attitudes to, 77, 79−80,
  83, 84; pornography and, 90−1
patrial, 153
pensions, 146

photographing (by police), 32, 56, 57
pimps, 29
place of safety order, 65
police: arrest by, 55; assaults by, 44; attitudes, 40−6; detention by, 51, 53, 55, 56, 57; enquiries, 53, 54; powers, 55−8; questioning, 47−8, 51−3, 63; raids, 31−2, 35−9; records, 55, 156, 180
Police Federation, 41
Police Advisory Committee on Sexual Offences, 68
pornography (see obscenity)
positive discrimination, 177
Presidential Commission on Obscenity and Pornography (USA), 88
pressure groups, 160, 161, 214
procurator fiscal, 65
procuring (see sexual offences)
promiscuity, 30, 71−2
prostitution, 17, 28−9
prisoners: accommodation of, 59; assaults on, 60, 180; categories of, 58; correspondence, 59; medical treatment of, 60−1; transsexual, 193−4
private place, 21
psychiatric reports, 131, 193
public place, 15, 16
public good, 88

'queer bashers', 34, 43, 44

rape, 78, 79
refugees, 151
Registrar General of Births, 190
rehabilitation of offenders, 100
resulting trust, 146
Romans in Britain, 26, 94−5
Royal College of Psychiatrists, 69

saunas, 35
Save Ulster from Sodomy, 139
Scotland: birth certificates, 190−1; change of name, 190; criminal trials, 84, 171−3; custody of children, 2, 135; employment, 2, 101, 105−6, 118; legal system, 209, 212−13; obscenity, 88−9, 92, 93, 94, 228 [13]; organisations, 160, 161, 174, 217, 220; police, 50,

56−7; property law, 2, 140; sexual offences, 17, 18, 20, 21, 24, 25 27, 29, 65, 66−7, 68; reforms, 180
security clearance, 112
seduction (myths about), 29, 64, 68−72
sentences: buggery, 24; gross indecency, 21−2; indecent assault, 78; indecency with children, 65; rape, 78; soliciting, 17; unlawful sexual intercourse, 78
sex change surgery, 188
sex cinemas, 92
Sex Discrimination Act, 107, 192
sex shops, 92
sexual offences: accomplices, 170; aiding and abetting, 72; attempt, 21, 24, 27; conspiracy, 29; incitement, 27; procuring, 26, 27, 198
sexual orientation, 4−6, 9, 12, 68−72 77, 131−2
sexual partners (advertisements for), 94
shameless indecency, 17
sheriff court, 171
Shulz Committee (Switzerland), 69
similar fact evidence, 83
silence (right to), 52
Social Democratic Party, 178
social workers, 100, 110
Sodom, 11
sodomy, 11, 12, 24 (see also buggery)
solemn procedure, 171
soliciting, 12, 14, 15, 16, 28, 199
solicitors, 174; access to suspects, 53, 58
Speijer Committee (Netherlands), 69
squatting, 143
stereotypes, 41, 107
summary procedure, 171
suspicion (by police), 46−8

Taxi Zum Klo, 95−6
teachers, 73, 100, 103−4, 106−7, 109, 115−18
television, 161
tenancies, 141−2
testamentary guardian, 144
theatres, 94, 95
toilets, 19, 20, 21, 34, 49−51

trade unions, 118
transsexuals: birth certificates, 188;
   children of, 193; civil status, 188;
   European Convention of Human
   Rights, 191; marriage, 191;
   prisoners, 193–4; sex change
   surgery, 188;
   Sex Discrimination Act, 192–3;
   West German law, 191
transvestites, 189

unfair dismissal, 101
United Nations Commissioner for
   Refugees, 151

Venezuela, 151
video, 25, 92

Warhol, Andy, 96
weapon of offence, 143
welfare officer, 133
West Germany (law relating to
   transsexuals), 191
Whitehouse, Mary, 92, 93, 95
Wolfenden, Sir John, 12
women's movement, 180
Women's Royal Navy Service, 184
wills, 144
Williams, Professor Bernard, 91
witnesses: alibi, 169; prosecution,
   170; questioning by police, 54, 56;
   Scots rules, 171

youth workers, 72–4, 100, 102,
   105–06